The
Presbyterian Church (U.S.A.)
Foundation

The
Presbyterian Church (U.S.A.) Foundation

A Bicentennial History
1799-1999

R. Douglas Brackenridge

GENEVA PRESS
LOUISVILLE, KENTUCKY

Grateful acknowledgment is made for permission to utilize some material from *Presbyterians and Pensions: The Roots and Growth of Pensions in the Presbyterian Church (U.S.A.)*, published by John Knox Press in 1988. Permission granted by Westminster John Knox Press.

Book design by Lois A. Boyd

First Edition
Published by Geneva Press, Louisville, Kentucky

This book is printed on acid-free paper that meets the American National Standards Institute Z39.48 standard.

Printed in the United States of America

Library of Congress Cataloging-in-Publication Data

Brackenridge, R. Douglas.
    The Presbyterian Church (U.S.A.) Foundation : a bicentennial
history, 1799–1999 / R. Douglas Brackenridge. — 1st ed.
       p.   cm.
    Includes bibliographical references and index.
    ISBN 0-664-50043-9 (alk. paper)
    1. Presbyterian Church (U.S.A.) Foundation—History.   I. Title.
BX9189.5.B73   1998
267′185137—dc21   98-41835

Contents

Acknowledgments

The origination of the project to write a history of the Presbyterian Church (U.S.A.) Foundation came from William B. Miller, then director of the Department of History in Philadelphia in 1989. Anticipating the bicentennial anniversary of the Foundation in 1999, Miller suggested to President Geoffrey Cross that a scholarly historical narrative of the corporation's two hundred years of service to the denomination be commissioned. Because of close historical ties between the Foundation and the Board of Pensions, Miller recommended that the assignment be offered to R. Douglas Brackenridge and Lois A. Boyd, who had collaborated on a history of the Board of Pensions.

After consulting with the potential authors and securing approval from the Board of Trustees in 1990, Cross authorized the Foundation history to be completed in time for its anniversary celebration. The Foundation agreed to give the authors access to all relevant archival materials in Philadelphia, Montreat, and Jeffersonville, including those of predecessor denominations and to provide opportunities for interviews with present and former staff and trustees. Although commissioned by the Foundation, this history is not an official publication of the corporation. The authors are solely responsible for the structure and content of the narrative and interpretations of events.

During the extended period of research and writing, Brackenridge assumed primary responsibility for the writing and Boyd for the editing and preparation of the manuscript for the publisher. They have received splendid cooperation and assistance from the staffs of the Foundation and the Departments of History in Philadelphia and Montreat. From the Jeffersonville office, Larry Carr, Bob Langwig, Dennis Murphy, Tom Drake, and Doug Yeager gave generously of their time to assist the research process. Becky Maple coordinated travel arrangements and interviews and answered a myriad of questions. Jan Hamblen gathered photographs from Foundation files for the book. Staff from the Department of History in Philadelphia and Montreat under the direction of Frederick C. Heuser, Jr. assisted in the search for archival materials and photographs, including Margery Sly and Amy Roberts (Philadelphia) and Bill Bynum and Diana Ruby Sanderson (Montreat).

We also appreciate the support of Trinity University in providing an academic leave for Professor Brackenridge that enabled him to conduct several research trips and to complete work on the early chapters of the history. Margaret Miksch, secretary in the Department of Religion, and Renee Rodriguez, a Trinity student, assisted in the preparation of the list of trustees and handled many photocopying assignments. Philip L. Cooley, the Dick and Peggy Prassel Distinguished Professor of Business Administration, helped interpret some of the financial information produced in early General Assembly Minutes. Mark Camann ably expedited the preparation of the camera-ready copy.

Although the research for this history has focused on primary sources such as official minutes, reports, and correspondence, much use has been made of oral interviews. We acknowledge the people whose names are listed as interviewees in the bibliography. Their willingness to relate memories of past events and to point in the direction of other sources of information has greatly enriched our understanding of people and events. In particular, Terry Young, in addition to his own interview time, set up interviews with other trustees and offered gracious hospitality during a visit to Charlotte and Montreat. Many other people with whom we have had brief conservations and incidental contacts have added much to the understanding of the work of the Foundation and its linkage to General Assembly, middle governing bodies, and local sessions.

We acknowledge with gratitude the permission of Westminster John Knox Press to utilize some material from *Presbyterians and Pensions: The Roots and Growth of Pensions in the Presbyterian Church (U.S.A.)*, published by John Knox Press in 1988. This material is found in Chapters 1 and 3 and is cited in the endnotes.

Finally, we wish to thank the many people over the years whose service and financial contributions to the Foundation have enabled Presbyterians to engage effectively in mission at home and overseas. To trustees, staff, and donors, past and present, we express our appreciation for a job well done. Without their sustained efforts, there would be no history to describe.

R. Douglas Brackenridge and Lois A. Boyd
San Antonio, Texas

Preface

Apart from the General Assembly, the Presbyterian Church (U.S.A.) Foundation is the oldest continuing national entity in the denomination, antedating even the first Standing Committee on Missions. The Foundation traces its origins to 1799 when the Commonwealth of Pennsylvania approved a request by the General Assembly of the Presbyterian Church in the United States of America to establish a corporation of trustees charged with the responsibility of receiving donations and bequests "for benevolent and pious purposes."

This early corporation, limited by charter to receive a maximum annual income of $10,000, accepted and managed gifts for various missionary and educational projects. The corporation's board of trustees, composed of an equal number of laymen and clergy, came primarily from Philadelphia and New York and were distinguished philanthropic, civic, and religious leaders in their communities. As managers of the denomination's sole incorporated body, the General Assembly trustees assumed influential roles in the evolving national church during the first decades of the nineteenth century.

In the course of its two-hundred year history, the Foundation has been related to seven denominations: the Presbyterian Church in the United States of America (PCUSA), including both the Old School and New School divisions, the Cumberland Presbyterian Church (CPC), the Welsh Calvinistic Methodist Church, the Presbyterian Church in the United States (PCUS), the United Presbyterian Church of North America (UPCNA), and the United Presbyterian Church in the United States of America (UPCUSA). The reunion of the PCUS and UPCUSA in 1983 led, four years later in 1987, to the integration of all predecessor corporations into the Presbyterian Church (U.S.A.) Foundation.

Further, by virtue of its fiduciary responsibilities, the Foundation is linked to virtually every aspect of past, present, and future mission programming. Gifts and bequests dating back to the early 1800s are still managed today by the Foundation and provide income for contemporary ministries. They will continue to do so in the coming millennium. The Boudinot Book Fund, established in 1821 to supply religious reading materials to "weak and feeble congregations," still today fulfills the purposes specified by its donor, statesman and Presbyterian elder Elias Boudinot IV. The small sum bequeathed by Boudinot has generated more than $100,000 in interest for the educational benefit of churches scattered throughout the United States.[1]

The Foundation also services other legacies received from boards and agencies whose functions were absorbed by new entities as the result of denominational mergers and reunions. Gifts made more than 125 years ago still contribute to the millions of dollars and grants and loans that are allocated each year by the General Assembly to support new church development. Several gifts to the PCUSA Board of Church Erection, dating back to the late nineteenth century, are pooled in two sundry building aid funds as part of the Evangelism and Church Development Unit's portfolio managed by the Foundation. One historic fund within that portfolio is the John S. Kennedy Building Aid Fund, established in 1911 to aid "feeble congregations in erecting houses of worship" and to assist in the establishment of schools and chapels among "the exceptional populations of Mormons, Indians, and Spanish-speaking people of the United States." Together, the principal values of the Kennedy Fund and the two building funds total $3.78 million and generate income of approximately $250,000 annually for new church development.[2]

The Foundation has had a special relationship with the Board of Pensions and its predecessor organizations. One of the primary motivations to form a corporation at the General Assembly level in 1799 was to provide a vehicle by which funds could be gathered to aid aged and destitute ministers and their families. During the first half of the nineteenth century, the cause of ministerial relief, as it was then termed, rested with the trustees of the General Assembly. When the General Assembly created a special fund for ministerial relief prior to the Civil War, it assigned the trustees the task of soliciting and managing gifts and bequests received for that cause. In 1875 these permanent funds provided the initial operating capital for the Board of Ministerial Relief and were carried over into the Board of Pensions when the PCUSA approved a ministerial retirement plan in 1927. Even after 1875, the General Assembly trustees continued to manage most of the Board of Ministerial

Relief's permanent funds.[3] In addition, many Presbyterian laymen and clergy served concurrently as trustees on both the General Assembly and Relief corporations in the nineteenth and twentieth centuries.

From its inception, the corporation and the General Assembly have dealt with issues related to mission support, fiduciary responsibility, and investment policies. When the denomination authorized such boards and agencies as Home Missions, Foreign Missions, Education, and Publication to incorporate in the 1840s and 1850s, however, the General Assembly trustees became less prominent in denominational stewardship activities. The emergence of the Presbyterian Church in the United States (PCUS) in the southern states following the Civil War further decreased resources available to the national church. At the time of the Old School-New School reunion in 1870, the General Assembly trustees accounted for an accumulation of only about $250,000 in endowment funds.

As the country moved from an agrarian to an industrial society during the latter part of the nineteenth century, the church emphasized national and international missions. This effort required increasingly large expenditures, which in turn demanded promotion of benevolence giving. In 1906, the Cumberland Presbyterian Church reunited with the PCUSA, partially healing a division that dated back to 1810, which expanded the numbers of programs and constituents. Boards and executive committees in the PCUSA and PCUS denominations provided much of the capital required to support mission operations, but the Assembly trustees in each denomination also continued to administer the donations and bequests directed to their corporations.

Rapid economic expansion that resulted in the accumulation of personal wealth in the late 1800s and early 1900s encouraged Protestant denominations to systematize stewardship efforts and explore the establishment of national foundations modeled after those created by industrial scions such as Rockefeller, Carnegie, and Morgan. During the 1920s, General Assemblies appointed committees to undertake feasibility studies, but these attempts met with resistance from denominational boards and executive committees who considered such foundations redundant appendages and undesirable competition. Coupled with the devastating effects of the Depression of the 1930s and World War II, this opposition curtailed the denominations' initiatives to establish a national foundation for more than two decades. During this time, the trustees of the General Assembly primarily received donations and bequests for designated causes, such as the education of African Americans, the provision of ministerial relief, and the support of higher education.

The period from 1950 to the present began with the post-war economic recovery that renewed an interest among major Protestant denominations to tap into the nation's growing wealth and prosperity. Presbyterians proposed to establish a central fund-raising body with a full-time professional staff. Studies conducted by interdenominational stewardship organizations in the early 1950s revealed that approximately 70 percent of church members in the U.S. died intestate. Consequently, their estates were highly taxed and not fully used for benevolent purposes. To address this, the PCUSA and PCUS created and staffed foundations to develop stewardship education programs designed to increase awareness of the importance of deferred giving through annuities and bequests. Although relationships with existing boards and agencies initially were tense, the two foundations' ability to raise money allayed doubts about the viability of the process. A merger between the PCUSA and the United Presbyterian Church of North America to form the United Presbyterian Church in the U.S.A. in 1958 resulted in a new corporation known as the United Presbyterian Foundation (UPF).

As a result of denominational reorganizations in the early 1970s, the PCUS Foundation in Charlotte and the United Presbyterian Foundation in New York were designated custodians of all denominational funds in each denomination with the exception of the pension boards, the PCUS Board of Annuities and Relief and the UPCUSA Board of Pensions respectively. They expanded their staffs for more efficient and orderly cultivation of potential donors and more creative use of advertising and investment strategies. Within the environment of rapid growth, foundation trustees in each of the two denominations addressed the issue of the use of investment policies as a means of social witness and responsibility. Following extended and substantive discussions, both the Charlotte and New York foundations reached mutually satisfactory agreements with their denominations that enabled them to maintain the integrity of their funds and to affirm their commitment to the mission of the church.

After years of intense negotiations, the PCUS and UPCUSA denominations agreed on the principles of reunion at concurrent General Assemblies held in Atlanta, Georgia, in June 1983. The affirmative votes brought into motion a process of mission design that culminated in the melding of southern and northern traditions into one corporate entity, the Presbyterian Church (U.S.A.) Foundation. Originally slated to be housed in the denominational headquarters in Louisville, Kentucky, the Foundation actually located its offices across the Ohio River in Jeffersonville, Indiana, because of more favorable state tax laws. During the first decade of its existence, the Foundation experienced phenomenal growth. At the time of this writing, with assets in excess of $1.6 billion, it is the largest denominational foundation in the United States.

Although the activities of the Foundation involve issues of finances, investments, fiduciary responsibilities, development, and marketing, its wider philanthropic, historical, and religious contexts provide a description of Christian stewardship. The Foundation's emphases are rooted in a humanitarian concern for members of society whose circumstances necessitate either material or spiritual sustenance. Its theological traditions derive from the sixteenth-century reformer John Calvin who advocated a principle of stewardship in which everything that one has—time, talents, possessions, and spiritual resources—is a sacred trust received from God. While Calvin did not consider riches to be an evil or deem poverty to be a mark of Christian piety, he believed that material prosperity carries an obligation for one to share with the poor and support the gospel ministry. Christians must recognize, he insisted, that whatever they have has been entrusted to them by God and that someday they will be asked to give an account of their stewardship.[4]

This spirit of Christian philanthropy continues to motivate twentieth-century Presbyterians who give to the ongoing mission of the denomination through various opportunities administered by the Foundation. Their stories personalize the summary figures found in financial reports. Following her retirement in 1971, Edith Buhler, a retired art teacher and member of the Los Gatos Presbyterian Church, Los Gatos, California, was inspired by the career of Dr. Ida Scudder, a medical missionary in Vellore, India, during the early decades of the twentieth century. Scudder oversaw the construction of a forty-bed hospital and a school of nursing which eventually became known as the Christian Medical College and Hospital. By 1980 the need for affordable eye care led to the establishment of the Schell Eye Hospital as part of the medical complex in Vellore. Responding to calls for assistance, Buhler donated several thousand dollars to purchase hospital beds and other ophthalmology equipment and, working through the Foundation, she gave $10,000 to establish a permanent fund with income paid directly to the Mobile Eye Clinic. Buhler periodically added to the fund through proceeds from her art exhibits and maintained close contacts with the eye clinic that she helped to start.[5]

Ethel Hawkins, born into a farming family, was the oldest of seven children. She received a scholarship from the denomination to attend Barber Scotia College in Concord, North Carolina. Later she expressed her gratitude to the Presbyterian Church by making it possible for others to enjoy the same opportunity she once had. In addition to several generous contributions for scholarships, Hawkins also established three revocable life income gifts through the Foundation. Each will eventually benefit both Barber Scotia College and Johnson C. Smith University by providing scholarships for minority students.[6]

Foundation trustees have historically been generous contributors to the denomination that they served. The philanthropy of Elias Boudinot, a charter trustee, has previously been mentioned. Many others, some anonymously, have through their Christian stewardship supported the work of the Foundation in a variety of ways over the years. Alex Booth, a former trustee and retired businessman from Huntington, West Virginia, made an initial gift of $15,000 in 1982 to help build Kingabwe Church in Kinshasa, Zaire. Deeply moved by a visit to Zaire to attend the dedication of the church building, Booth provided financial support to establish the Project for Evangelism and Church Growth in Africa. As a result, four new churches were developed in the city of Inshasa, one of the largest Christian populations in Africa. In 1987 Booth underwrote the cost of founding a Pastoral Institute to provide training for pastors in Kinshasa and funded construction costs of a new library and dormitories for students at the Presbyterian Seminary in Ndesha in the Kasai. In addition to his support of leadership training, Booth assisted in establishing twelve Presbyterian schools in Kinshasa to provide schooling for nearly 10,000 students.[7]

When Trustee Irene Nunemaker died at age 98, she left a legacy to support a variety of Presbyterian organizations. Born in 1897 to a farm family in Colorado, Nunemaker earned a degree from the University of Kansas in 1922. A writer, editor, and cosmetics executive, Nunemaker was an active member of the Fifth Avenue Presbyterian Church in New York and later joined the First Presbyterian Church in Topeka upon her return to Kansas in the 1980s. Having considerable success in the stock market, she gave funds for a variety of philanthropic purposes, many of them Presbyterian-related. In 1987, for example, she gave a substantial gift through the Foundation to the Synod of Mid-America to benefit Presbyterian Children's Services, Presbyterian Center at Holmes, New York, the Heartland and Northern Kansas Presbyteries. The contribution also established a scholarship for minorities and children of farm families. Described by a friend as "unpretentious and unassuming," Nunemaker was a disciplined giver who from the beginning of her career set aside 10 percent of her gross income into a gift account.[8]

Closely related to the stewardship of financial assets is that of time and talents. During the past two hundred years, lay and clergy volunteers have played key roles in elected and staff positions within the corporate structure. Their expertise in various aspects of foundation activities, including investment management, stewardship interpretation, and legal counsel, has provided timely and invaluable assistance to the corporation.

The inclusion in an appendix to this book of the names of trustees who have served the church from 1799 to the present provides a permanent record of faithful service. Although the responsibility of investing and managing large sums of money today requires professionally trained and experienced business and finance people, volunteerism continues to be an important factor in the implementation of Foundation programs. History indicates that lay and ordained leaders working in concert with trained professional staff members can be productive and innovative partners who have the potential to enhance the viability of a denominational enterprise.

This is not to say that tensions have not existed between the General Assembly and the incorporated bodies responsible for the investment and distribution of funds designated for various agencies and projects. From its inception in 1799, the corporation and General Assembly committees have clashed over differing interpretations regarding fiduciary responsibility and disbursement of denominational funds. These controversies reflect a continuing pattern focusing on meeting the church's needs while honoring the instructions of donors. In recent years, the Foundation and the General Assembly Council have disagreed on interpretations of *The Structural Design For Mission* of the Presbyterian Church (U.S.A.) and other official documents that regulate relationships between the two bodies. There has been progress in resolving conflict over specific issues, but the task of maintaining a creative balance between mission priorities and fiduciary responsibilities appears ongoing. Nevertheless, although both groups have occasionally articulated different visions and strategies, they remain bound together through their faith, belief, and sense of belonging to a common institution.

Tangentially, these relationships reflect the country's checkered economic history and shifting cultural attitudes toward philanthropy. Economic developments such as the Panics of 1837 and 1873, the Depression of the 1930s, the post-World War II boom, and the recent bull stock market trends greatly impact the availability of funds and exacerbate tensions between asset-allocating and asset-acquiring organizations. Because the trustees of the General Assembly had a mandate to invest funds in "good and safe" securities, their success or failure frequently depended on their ability to predict not only economic change but the mood of those contributing to the denomination.

Cultural attitudes toward making large donations and bequests have in the past been colored by a belief that each generation should take charge of its own needs and that the accumulation of endowment monies fosters fiscal irresponsibility on the part of subsequent generations. In more recent times, discussions have concentrated on the validity of unified or designated giving and the appropriateness of national or local control of mission funding. Within this context, an unprecedented intergenerational transfer of wealth is presently taking place. Estimates suggest that between $10 to $20 trillion will be transferred over the next twenty years, with billions by Presbyterians alone. A recent report from the General Assembly predicts that unified giving will not survive to the close of the century and concludes that the denomination must respond to this paradigm shift with theological integrity and without fear.[9]

Although this narrative covers two hundred years of history, it is a work in progress. At this time, decisions are being made that will have bearing on the future of the Presbyterian Church (U.S.A.), its mission agencies, and its related bodies. The Foundation unquestionably will play a key role in implementing these decisions. Based on its past performance and projected activities, it is strategically placed to greatly enhance the denomination's fiscal future. At the same time, the Foundation, in seeking to fulfill its motto, "Serving the Church in all its Work," faces the challenge, as does the church at large, of maintaining a theological continuity with the Reformed tradition that motivated its founders and shaped its historical development.

NOTES

1. Presbyterian Church (U.S.A.) Foundation *Annual Report*, 1992:2.

2. "Building Aid Funds From Last Century Still At Work Today," *The Cornerstone* (April 1990): 4.

3. For example, the General Assembly trustees in 1887 reported managing funds of $212,011.76 for the Relief Fund. Trustee Minutes (PCUSA), February 8, 1887.

4. John T. McNeill, ed., *Calvin: Institutes of the Christian Religion*, 2 vols. (Philadelphia, 1960) I:721-22.

5. "A Story of Giving," Foundation *Annual Report*, 1990:2.

6. "The Gift of Giving," Foundation *Annual Report*, 1991:2.

7. "The Gift of Giving," Foundation *Annual Report*, 1991:2.

8. "Spreading Joy Through a Lifetime and Beyond," *The Cornerstone* (April 1990): 4.

9. Report of the Comprehensive Strategy for Mission Funding Work Group to the General Assembly Council, September 22-27, 1997: 21.

The
Presbyterian Church (U.S.A.)
Foundation

1

Benevolent and Pious Purposes

Inasmuch as the General Assembly are assiduously labouring to promote the gospel throughout our extensive and growing frontiers, and in those places most destitute of the means of grace, it be earnestly enjoined on each Presbytery to use their most diligent endeavours to collect voluntary and liberal contributions from every congregation, and to obtain pious donations and bequests in order to supply the funds which are absolutely necessary to carry on with advantage the great and charitable work.—The General Assembly, Report on the State of Religion, 1799

Colonial Presbyterianism began as a missionary enterprise rather than an established denomination. Its constituents represented diverse groups of Calvinistic refugees who had emigrated to America from various European countries seeking freedom from religious persecution and economic misfortunes. Many Presbyterians from Scotland and northern Ireland and those of Huguenot, Dutch, Welsh, and German origins reached the shores of the new world to swell the ranks of Reformed Christians. Although some arrived with substantial financial resources, others did not. The indigents settled on unoccupied land, engaged in agriculture, and faced hazards of frontier life that could be relieved only by neighborly generosity and community compassion.[1]

Presbyterians were most visible in New Jersey, Pennsylvania, New York, Delaware, and Maryland. Francis Mackemie helped mesh disparate elements of Presbyterianism to form the Presbytery of Philadelphia in 1706.[2] In 1716, bolstered by additional emigration from northern Ireland and Scotland, the Presbytery of Philadelphia established a general synod to be composed of four presbyteries: Philadelphia (Pennsylvania), Long

Island (New York and New Jersey), New Castle (Delaware), and Snow Hill (Maryland). As it organized, with approximately three thousand communicants scattered among some forty congregations, "the church in the wilderness" struggled to gain a foothold in the new world.[3]

In this context, Presbyterian clergymen emphasized charitable and benevolent activities within their communities of faith. Sermons frequently stressed Christian benevolence and exhorted church members to share their material blessings with less fortunate fellow citizens. Alexander McWhorter, pastor of the First Presbyterian Church of Newark, preached on "True Religion," reminding that the truly pious "are disposed to everything that is kind, benevolent, charitable, and good; feel compassion for the miserable—inclined to relieve those that want, and forgive those who offend."[4] Other prominent Presbyterian clergy as well encouraged people of wealth to avoid avarice and seek the favor of God by contributing to charitable and religious causes. William Tennent claimed that the love of money "is especially injurious to the soul, as it vitiates all its moral powers. It raises a wall of separation between God and the sinner, which it is difficult, and next to impossible, to overpass or demolish."[5] Discoursing on the Parable of the Talents, James Muir observed that powerful and wealthy men should be stewards of God for the advantage of others. "Being faithful in this office and universally beneficial, they shall enjoy present peace of mind, and be afterwards heirs of better things than this world can bestow."[6]

Since many donations were made privately—described in the terms of the time as for the elderly, poor, infirm, widows, and orphans—most fiscal gifts cannot be documented. An example of personal philanthropy might be Catherine Steel, a Presbyterian in Derry, Pennsylvania, whose only known record of her humanitarianism rests on her tombstone: "In her lifetime raised 19 orphan children."[7] Some presbyteries and local sessions solicited aid more systematically. For example, Margaret Wright's husband died in an accident, and she was left with several children and a large debt. The Presbytery of Donegal decided that she was "justly an object of Christian charity" and urged every congregation within its bounds to raise money for her support.[8] The minutes of the Presbytery of New Castle contain similar references. In 1731 an entry noted that "the Brethren who have not collected for ye widow and her son in Nottingham be mindful of it at our next meeting," and on another occasion presbyters reported that they had made "a Collection for ye relief of Margaret McAdam, a distressed girl at Upper Elk."[9]

To support ministers and other charitable projects, Presbyterians expected members to make subscriptions, or pledges, on a sliding scale according to their financial status. In some instances presbyteries recommended that failure to pay subscriptions could be considered "a disorderly act" and might warrant disbarment from the communion table unless the congregant could document genuine poverty. Pew rentals, a tradition carried over from European churches, donations of cash, land, or agricultural products, and bequests provided other sources of income.[10] Provincial assemblies, by special enactment, authorized some Presbyterian congregations to raise money by lotteries to build or refurbish meeting houses and parsonages. In 1749 the Trenton Presbyterian Church in New Jersey held a lottery for the completion of their church building, and in 1760 the Carlisle Presbyterian Church in Pennsylvania sponsored a lottery to "enable them to build a decent house for the worship of God."[11]

Such uncoordinated efforts by individual presbyteries, however, failed to meet the needs of a rapidly expanding constituency. The Synod of Philadelphia at its initial session in 1717 designated a "Fund For Pious Uses" that became a source of revenue for missionary, educational, and charitable activities and would lay the groundwork for the formation of national boards and agencies in the nineteenth century. The Synod directed ministers to raise money among their congregations for the Fund and further designated an offering for charitable purposes at each synod meeting. The Fund for Pious Uses commenced with a modest sum of eighteen pounds, administered by a synodical committee composed of ministers and elders. Jedidiah Andrews, pastor of First Presbyterian Church in Philadelphia, served as treasurer. The Synod designated Fund revenues to assist ministers and their families, build new churches, and support frontier missionaries, and the initial disbursements were small and infrequent. The first reference to charitable giving in 1718 specified a sum that did not exceed three pounds awarded to three persons named by the Synod "to be disposed of according to their discretion suitable to the design of the Fund."[12] The following year the Synod voted to give the widow of John Wilson "four pounds and not more than three additional pounds at the discretion of the committee." She and other widows raising families with primitive shelter on a small plot of land received like sums for a number of years.[13]

Although the Fund provided personal assistance, it primarily facilitated missionary activities, including itinerant evangelism and congregational nurture. In a pastoral letter in 1719, the Synod appealed for money "for carrying on of the said noble and pious design of planting and spreading the everlasting Gospel in these Provinces." The Fund awarded grants of three pounds each to the Octorara and Hanover congregations in 1723 and a similar one the following year to "the people of Broad Creek" to sustain their small congregation. In 1741 the Synod gave ten pounds to Wilmington Presbyterians to erect a meeting house and also loaned them an additional twenty pounds interest free repayable at ten pounds a year for three years. On other occasions, the Synod reported that it had "disposed of funds for the relief of indigent places" in scattered locations within its bounds. The Fund also aided ministerial candidates, sent missionaries to frontier settlements, and instructed Native Americans in the Holy Scriptures. From time to time, the Synod provided compensation to the Fund's treasurer as well as to the janitor of the church in which the Synod met.[14]

Despite pleas for contributions to the Fund For Pious Uses, churches were not consistently able to meet requests. Occasional gifts from Presbyterian governing bodies in Scotland provided some resources, but the Synod could not rely on overseas aid to underwrite its colonial missions. To motivate clergymen to canvas their constituencies for contributions in 1738, the Synod proposed that each minister assess himself ten shillings which he could pay personally or raise from congregational donations. Records indicate that several ministers failed to make annual contributions and were billed ten shillings. At the same time the Synod directed presbyteries to elect a minister and elder to serve on the Fund committee so that each governing body might participate in disbursement of grants. By the early 1740s these aggressive tactics combined with generous donations from the Church of Scotland enabled the Fund to assemble assets of approximately six hundred pounds.[15]

The Fund For Pious Uses did not include salary supplements for ministers in frontier congregations. Traditionally, church members remunerated clerical services on a basis approved by presbytery. Prior to 1750 any congregation extending a pastoral call was required to have sufficient pledges to guarantee a minister an annual income of about sixty pounds, the equivalent of the average income of a Philadelphia seaman.[16] Attitudes and fiscal conditions complicated salary issues. Many Presbyterian congregants were reluctant to pay a minister from their own small incomes, especially those who had come from Scotland and northern Ireland where the Crown subsidized their pastors. Often clergy received compensation other than currency. In the Presbytery of Donegal, one of its congregations paid a minister sixty pounds annually and supplemented the stipend with linen yarn or linen cloth at market price.[17] Ministers in the New York presbyteries of Oneida and Utica usually received part of their salary in firewood by annual contract, but records indicate that congregations rarely delivered the full amount of wood.[18] Contributions of whiskey were commonly noted on subscription papers for ministers in amounts up to 100 gallons annually.[19] Not uncommonly presbyteries dissolved pastoral relationships between ministers and congregations because of nonpayment of salaries.[20]

Since the Fund For Pious Uses was not a factor in recruiting and supporting ministers and their families in local churches, Francis Alison, pastor of the First (Market Street) Presbyterian Church of Philadelphia, using the principle of life insurance, proposed the creation of a Widows' Fund to provide for the families of deceased ministers. Alison learned of individual life insurance through correspondence with Scottish clergy who had established a Widows' Fund in the Church of Scotland in 1744. Using actuarial research, the Fund promised a guaranteed annuity for survivors based on participants' annual rate of contributions prior to their death.[21] Following "the laudable example of the Church of Scotland," the Old Side Synod of Philadelphia petitioned Thomas and Richard Penn, the sons of William Penn, to obtain a charter for the American version of the Widows' Fund and recorded the charter on May 2, 1759. The complete title was "The Corporation for Relief of Poor and Distressed Presbyterian Ministers and of the Poor and Distressed Widows and Children of Presbyterian Ministers." Commonly used were abbreviated titles such as the "Widows' Fund," or simply the "Corporation."[22]

The Widows' Fund offered a whole life insurance policy with survivorship annuities. For a payment of from two pounds to seven pounds a year, a minister could provide his widow and/or children with an annuity about five times the amount contributed.[23] Frontier conditions and impoverished congregations precluded mandatory membership in the Widows' Fund; consequently, with no guaranteed clientele and no capital funds, the Corporation launched an endowment campaign for start-up funds to issue policies. Trustees solicited support among individuals and congregations and received a variety of contributions including cash, real estate, and personal goods. One individual gave "twelve pounds twelve shillings and sixpence and two lottery tickets in ye lottery for the Presbyterian Church in Lancaster." Another entry in Corporation minutes notes that Colonel Peter Boyard "generously bestowed ten pistoless [sic]" along with a small sum of money. Nevertheless, the Corporation did not generate sufficient capital to commence operations.[24]

American Presbyterians turned to Great Britain for assistance. In 1760 the Corporation dispatched Charles Beatty to Scotland and England to solicit funds. Because the Corporation's charter contained provisions both for issuing life insurance policies and for supporting missionaries in frontier settlements, Beatty was free to emphasize the Fund's missionary and charitable features and received gifts amounting to nearly four thousand pounds, some of which the donors designated for missionary work rather than capital income. Because the Corporation had been successful in raising money for frontier missions and because its activities overlapped the Fund For Pious Uses, the Synod turned over the Fund's assets to be administered "in trust" by the Corporation, specifying that the money be disbursed to those who had been receiving assistance before the institution of the Widows' Fund. To avoid conflict over allocation of funds, the agreement between the Synod and the Corporation stipulated that the Synod be consulted before missionary funds were distributed.[25]

Twenty-one Presbyterian ministers applied for insurance on May 22, 1761, and received the first policies issued in colonial America. Available data indicate the average age of the initial policyholder was 42.7 years and the average death was 66.6. Of the initial group, there were five lapsed policies. A sixth participant paid premiums until 1792 at which time he cashed his policy, and the remaining fifteen paid premiums until their death and their families received full annuities. After the initial enrollment, the Corporation was not successful in recruiting new members. Between 1763 and 1789 only thirty-six Presbyterian ministers became policyholders. The original register book of subscribers to the Fund shows that before 1789 thirty-two entries had the word "lapsed" written in red ink beside their names. The inability or unwillingness of ministers to keep their policies active created a financial burden for the Fund throughout its early history.[26]

One reason the Fund could not attract a large clientele was the low salary scale of ministers compared to other professionals. Secondly, many Presbyterians opposed life insurance, asserting that it undercut the Christian principle of the ultimate dignity of human life and turned a person's worth into an "article of merchandise." Women, although often beneficiaries of insurance policies, were especially sensitive to this argument. According to some insurance brokers, women frequently referred to life insurance proceeds as "blood money" and rejected the concept of benefitting from calculations on their husbands' life expectancies.[27] Others considered life insurance a form of gambling, a lottery in which people wagered upon life expectancy. Perhaps the most frequent argument was that life insurance indicated a rejection of trust in God's providential care. To rely on actuarial statistics rather than a merciful God suggested confidence in human calculations rather than certainty regarding the mercy of the Almighty. One Presbyterian author concluded, "The Widows' Fund was originally a charitable institution but ceased to be either charitable or Christian when it incorporated the principle of Life Insurance in its terms."[28]

Corporation trustees also supported missionary and charitable projects, including ransom payments to free people taken captive by Indian tribes. In 1763 the Corporation reported contributions to the "Christian friends and their children who have long endured a most distressing captivity among Savage and Barbarous Nations." In the same year it gave twenty-five pounds to Moses Tuttle, "a poor distressed Presbyterian minister, who was driven from the Frontiers in the late Indian War." In 1764 a woman who had escaped from captivity applied for assistance because her husband had been scalped and murdered and her four children remained incarcerated. The Corporation awarded her money to avoid foreclosure on the family homestead.[29]

The Corporation also assisted missionaries in establishing churches in remote frontier settlements. The Corporation enjoined them, however, from preaching to colonists who had settled on lands not yet legally acquired from the tribes, deeming the practice "Unjust in its Self and likely to prevent the Success of the Gospel among these people."[30] With money raised in England and Scotland in 1766, representatives of the Corporation undertook one of the first missionary expeditions west of the Alleghenies. They provided support for Charles Beatty and George Duffield who traveled to the Muskingum River in Ohio where they interacted with several Native American tribes and distributed religious literature to the scattered settlers in the area. Another missionary, David Brainard, received forty pounds to assist Native American converts build cabins and clear land to support their families.

For a number of years the Synod and the Corporation clashed over dispensing money not specifically designated for insurance. When the Synod asked for clarification of disbursements, the Corporation either responded with inconclusive generalities or disregarded the requests. They did not resolve their differences until 1771 when the Corporation agreed to set aside six hundred pounds of the Scottish money "to end all debates and for the sake of peace" and empowered the Synod to use interest from the money to support missionary ventures of its choosing. The Corporation reserved the right to utilize the principal, however, if other funds were unavailable to fulfill annuity obligations.[31] At the same time, the Synod created a new "Fund For Pious Uses" primarily for missionary purposes, similar to the one that had been given over in trust to the Corporation. In a pastoral letter the Synod specified that the Fund would give priority to assigning missionaries, distributing religious literature, and "propagating Christian knowledge among the Indians—And for such other Pious Uses as may occur from time to time."[32]

The Synod occasionally disagreed with the Corporation over the treatment of widows whose husbands' coverage had lapsed. Even though the Corporation had no legal obligation to provide a survivors' annuity in such circumstances, the Synod frequently requested exceptions in hardship cases. In 1768 the Corporation denied a appeal from the widow of Adam Boyd who at his death was three years' delinquent in premiums, noting that "to relax this point would be inconsistent with our obligation to the Public." On appeal the Corporation voted to give the widow twenty pounds, citing her deceased husband's role in promoting insurance annuities. Following similar cases, however, the Corporation announced that henceforth it would not grant exceptions that were inconsistent with insurance principles and encouraged delinquent payments.[33]

External financial problems related to the Revolutionary War affected the Widows' Fund. Inflation, undervaluation of property, nonpayment of taxes, and a weakened currency jeopardized investments and drained capital. The unsettled economic environment caused the Corporation to rely heavily on unsecured personal bonds and mortgage bonds secured on real estate, or it used funds to finance business ventures or purchase local real estate. Two so-called "directors' loans" resulted in losses to the Corporation, and another investment in the Continental Loan Office was equally unproductive.[34] In 1780 the Corporation reported to the Synod that it was unable to make full annuity payments and encumbered the six hundred pounds of Scottish money in order to remain financially solvent. Bordering on bankruptcy, it became impossible to recruit new members. Newly ordained ministers elected not to participate in the Widows' Fund, and many policyholders defaulted on their annual payments. Whereas the Synod affirmed its support of the Corporation, it declined to discipline delinquent members or to take action to make membership in the Widows' Fund mandatory for married clergy.[35]

Toward the formation of a General Assembly, Synod committees worked on a *Constitution and Directory of Worship*. Although the Synod lacked confidence in the Corporation and some denominational leaders feared that the Fund could not maintain its financial equilibrium, support for ministers and their families remained high on the denomination's agenda. The initial draft of a *Plan of Government*, published in 1786, awarded the Widows' Fund official status. The *Plan* specified that neither ordination nor installation could take place until congregations agreed to contribute an annual sum designated by the minister to be considered part of his salary. This proviso would mandate membership in the Widows' Fund for every minister and provide the organization with constitutional authority to conduct its business. No account of the debate regarding the Widows' Fund exists, but the result does: the Synod voted to omit the mandatory membership in the 1787 draft of the *Plan of Government* and in its place granted the Corporation permission to publish its terms of membership in the *Constitution and Directory of Worship*. For all practical purposes, the Fund functioned as an independent insurance company with only an informal relationship to the General Assembly.[36]

The creation in 1789 of a General Assembly, the highest governing body in Presbyterianism, marked a new era for American Presbyterians. Under the leadership of John Redman, a Philadelphia physician and civic leader, the Widows' Fund sought to broaden its financial base and increase denominational participation. Redman inaugurated "The Plan of 1792," which permitted any ordained Presbyterian minister to join the Fund, thus removing the restriction that policyholders had to reside within the bounds of the Synod of New York and Philadelphia. The plan also opened membership to unordained ministerial candidates and enabled older clergy to become policyholders by paying an additional sum calculated on age at entry. Robert Patterson, a mathematician and trustee since 1785, calculated these new insurance rates, the first such actuarially based set of premiums for various ages published in the United States.[37] Despite inclusiveness, liberalized conditions, and endorsement by the General Assembly, however, the plan failed to attract policyholders. Only eleven ministers joined between 1794 and 1801, and during the next decade just ten new names appeared in the Corporation's register book. Between 1800 and 1825, thirteen of forty-two new policies lapsed. Although the Corporation eventually became known as the Presbyterian Ministers' Fund and functioned successfully as a commercial insurance company, it never fulfilled denominational efforts to furnish financial support for clergy and their families.[38]

In place of a denomination-wide life insurance program for clergy, the General Assembly relied on voluntary contributions from synods, presbyteries, or, more typically, local congregations to assist ministers and their families. In frontier areas where the needs were greatest, however, resources often proved inadequate. Small struggling churches that could not provide for active pastors could not support indigent clergy and their dependents. In order to sustain and expand the denomination's ordained clergy, the General Assembly in 1794 endorsed an overture that proposed a plan to nationalize ministerial relief efforts. Unlike the Widows' Fund, which functioned as a life insurance company, the new Relief Fund was to be available to all Presbyterian ministers, even noncontributors, solely on the basis of need. Each minister with a salary of eighty pounds or more would be required to contribute 30 shillings annually through the presbytery treasurer to the General Assembly for "the relief of distressed Presbyterian ministers and their families." Presbyteries would then identify worthy recipients within their bounds, and the General Assembly would apportion the money "in the most equitable and prudent manner." In keeping with Presbyterian polity, the proposal was referred to the presbyteries for final approval or rejection.[39]

When the General Assembly met in 1795, the overtures committee reported that while presbyteries had affirmed the concept of ministerial relief in general, they had overwhelmingly rejected the proposed relief plan as being "inexpedient and improper to be adopted." Although the report did not include the specific objections, it is likely that opposition to the measure centered on its arbitrary and mandatory fee structure and on its public charity feature that would be considered demeaning and embarassing by many recipients. The Presbytery of Philadelphia, which voted negatively, offered a substitute proposal that emphasized voluntarism rather than compulsory participation and broadened the scope of benevolence to include a variety of denominational causes.

The Presbytery proposed that the General Assembly form a legal corporation in order to receive and invest funds "for the cause of ministerial relief and other pious or charitable uses." Responding affirmatively, the Assembly appointed a committee consisting of clergymen John Ewing, Ashbel Green, John B. Smith, Nathaniel Irwin, and laymen David Jackson and Ebenezer Hazard to prepare a draft of the charter for consideration at a future Assembly.[40] In 1798 the General Assembly approved the proposed charter and directed the committee to submit the petition to the Pennsylvania Legislature for adoption.[41] On March 28, 1799, the Senate and the House of Representatives of the Commonwealth of Pennsylvania ratified the request for incorporation, and the Trustees of the General Assembly of the Presbyterian Church in the United States of America came into existence.[42]

The final draft of the incorporation petition was presented to the General Assembly in 1799. It contained no mention of ministerial relief but specified only that money raised by donations and bequests would be used for "benevolent and pious purposes." It is surprising that financial support of ministers and their families, which was the impulse for incorporation, was not emphasized in the charter and that the reason for this omission is nowhere discussed or reported. Ministerial relief never became a priority in subsequent trustee activities, and no mention of the subject appears in corporation minutes prior to the establishment of a national Ministerial Relief Fund in 1849. The draft also limited to $10,000 the amount of money that could be received annually from bequests, annuities, and real estate; a higher figure of $150,000 requested by the trustees had been rejected by the Pennsylvania legislature.[43]

The charter also delineated relationships between the new corporation and the General Assembly. While granting the trustees authority to receive and hold properties, gifts, and bequests devised to the General Assembly and empowering them to act on behalf of the Assembly in all legal matters, including the ability to bring suit and plead cases in secular courts, the charter placed limitations on the corporation. So long as the Assembly met in Pennsylvania, it had the right to change one-third of the trustees' membership at any annual meeting. The corporation was mandated to keep accurate accounts of financial transactions and present the records annually to the General Assembly for examination and approval. Most important, the General Assembly retained the power to determine how the denomination would utilize the income generated from permanent funds and otherwise undesignated bequests and contributions. In short, the trustees were the servants of the General Assembly and could resist only when the corporation interpreted Assembly directives to be in conflict with the Constitution of the United States or commonwealth laws. If the General Assembly and the trustees could not resolve their differences, they would turn to the secular courts for adjudication.[44]

The eighteen charter members of the board of trustees of the General Assembly had been selected from a slate of thirty-six nominees by popular vote of General Assembly commissioners.[45] Divided between clergy and lay members, most of whom resided in Philadelphia or New York, the board consisted of former and future moderators of the General Assembly, distinguished pastors and educators, prominent business and professional leaders, and nationally known public officials noted for their civic, religious and philanthropic activities. Among the clergy members was John Rodgers, moderator of the first General Assembly in 1789, pastor of the Wall Street Presbyterian Church in New York, a trustee of the College of New Jersey, a close friend and associate of George Washington, and the first vice-chancellor of the Regents of the University of New York. The chair of the committee to draft an incorporation petition was Ashbel Green, pastor of the Second Presbyterian Church in Philadelphia and later president of the College of New Jersey, who would play a prominent role in the development of denominational programs.[46]

Alexander McWhorter, the pastor of the First Presbyterian Church in Newark, was appointed by Congress in 1775 to visit North Carolina to win "independents" over to the American cause. In 1802 he led a successful campaign to raise funds for the rebuilding of Princeton College which had been destroyed by fire. Samuel Stanhope Smith served as Professor of Moral Theology at the College of New Jersey and succeeded John Witherspoon as president of the College in 1794. With Ashbel Green, he was instrumental in persuading the General Assembly to establish Princeton Theological Seminary where future denominational leaders such as Charles Hodge and Archibald Alexander would receive their theological training. William M. Tennent, pastor of Abingdon (Pennsylvania) Presbyterian Church, was elected moderator of the General Assembly in 1797. Joseph Clark, pastor of Presbyterian Church in New Brunswick, served as a Princeton trustee and a member of the Committee of Missions. Andrew Hunter, former army chaplain and schoolteacher in New Jersey, later became Professor of Mathematics and Astronomy at the College of New Jersey.[47]

Prominent lay members of the new corporation included lawyer Jared Ingersoll, who was a delegate from Pennsylvania to the Continental Congress in 1780-81 and for many years Attorney General for Pennsylvania and Judge of the District Court of the United States. Robert Ralston, a Philadelphia shipping merchant and chief magistrate of the city, was a director of the Second Bank of the United States and a founder and trustee of the Philadelphia Exchange. Elias Boudinot, patriot, financier, and philanthropist, was elected president of the Continental Congress and later appointed a director of the First Bank of the United States and director of the United States Mint by George Washington. Andrew Bayard, a Philadelphia insurance broker, served on the board of directors of the Widows' Fund and the Insurance Company of North America and was a member of the national correspondence committee of the Federalist Party. An author of several scholarly treatises on American history, Ebenezer Hazard held the position of Postmaster General from 1782 to 1789 and later was appointed curator of the American Philosophical Society.[48]

The incorporation of General Assembly trustees set in motion the machinery to launch a comprehensive benevolence program by which the denomination could provide the human and fiscal resources to meet the demands of a rapidly growing constituency. The trustees of the General Assembly represented proven leaders whose status in the denomination and the nation evoked respect. They had the potential to influence and shape the future of American Presbyterianism as it entered a new century.

NOTES

1. Leonard Trinterud, *The Forming of an American Tradition: A Re-examination of Colonial Presbyterianism* (Philadelphia, 1949), and Guy S. Klett, *Presbyterians in Colonial America* (Philadelphia, 1937).

2. For a description of the organization of the Presbyterian denomination in America, see *Encyclopedia of the Reformed Faith*, ed. by Donald K. McKim, 1st ed., s.v. "Presbyterianism in America." Elwyn A. Smith describes "a form of church government by elders (the session) elected by members of a congregation and associated with elders and ministers of other congregations in a body called the presbytery." The Presbytery is empowered among other things to "sponsor, ordain, and discipline the clergy; to establish, combine, and dissolve local congregations; and to hold property on behalf of all member congregations." Synods are regional associations of presbyteries, and the General Assembly is the national body.

3. Trinterud, *The Forming of an American Tradition*, ch. 1; James Smylie, *A Brief History of Presbyterians* (Louisville, Ky., 1996), 1-20. Snow Hill was never organized.

4. Alexander McWhorter, "True Religion," *The American Preacher* 3 (1791): 47.

5. William Tennent, "On the Love of Money," *The American Preacher* 3 (1791): 241.

6. James Muir, *Selected Sermons* (Princeton, New Jersey, 1787), 148. See also Samuel Stanhope Smith, *Sermons on Various Topics* (Newark, New Jersey, 1799), 83-111, in which he discusses the rich man and Lazarus.

7. Klett, *Presbyterians in Colonial America*, 182.

8. Minutes of the Presbytery of Donegal, October 5, 1737, Department of History, Philadelphia, Pennsylvania, hereafter PHL Archives.

9. Minutes of the Presbytery of New Castle, April 14, 1731, PHL Archives. Presbyteries responded when they received appeals for aid in a number of instances when individuals lost houses, barns, and personal belongings by fire. They also assisted congregations to erect houses of worship. Several congregations within the Presbytery of Philadelphia made contributions to complete a church in Schenectady, New York, as well as assisting other groups in their own vicinity. See Klett, *Presbyterians in Colonial America*, 110-11.

10. Klett, *Presbyterians in Colonial America*, 115-16.

11. Luther P. Powell, *Money and the Church* (New York, 1962), 144-45.

12. Guy S. Klett, ed., *Minutes of the Presbyterian Church in America 1706-1788* (Philadelphia, 1976), 36. Hereafter Klett, *Minutes of the Presbyterian Church*.

13. Klett, *Minutes of the Presbyterian Church*, 40.

14. Klett, *Presbyterians in Colonial America*, 188, and *Minutes of the Presbyterian Church*, 58-59, 61, 77, 134, 142, 160, and 369.

15. Klett, *Minutes of the Presbyterian Church*, 151, 159-60, and 164.

16. Klett, *Presbyterians in Colonial America*, 109. One pound sterling (London) was worth 1.58 pounds in Pennsylvania currency in 1760. John J. McCusker, *Money and Exchange in Europe and America 1600-1775* (Chapel Hill, North Carolina, 1978), 185.

17. Klett, *Presbyterians in Colonial America*, 111.

18. John Boyce, ed., *The Presbytery of Utica Centennial 1843-1853* (n.p.,n.d.), 22-23.

19. William W. Sweet, *Religion on the American Frontier: The Presbyterians*, 2 vols. (New York and London, 1936), II:65.

20. The Congregation of Big Springs in Pennsylvania, during a period of eight years (1759-1767), fell in arrears to their pastor George Duffield by 213 pounds. Klett, *Presbyterians in Colonial America*, 112.

21. A. Ian Dunlop, "Provision for Ministers' Widows in Scotland—Eighteenth Century," *Records of the Scottish Church History Society* XVII (1967): 233. For background on Alison, see Alexander Mackie, *Facile Princeps: The Story of the Beginning of Life Insurance in America* (Lancaster, Pa., 1956), 31-41. Hereafter cited as *Facile Princeps*.

22. Minutes of the Corporation for the Relief of Poor and Distressed Presbyterian Ministers, and of the Poor and Distressed Widows and Children of Presbyterian Ministers, 12 (n.d.), PHL Archives. Hereafter cited as Corporation Minutes.

23. Corporation Minutes, May 22, 1761. See also, Mackie, *Facile Princeps*, 1-6. The Fund also imposed a penalty of one year's premium on ministers who remarried because the second wives usually were younger than the first ones.

24. Corporation Minutes, December 20, 1760; May 18, 1761.

25. Klett, *Minutes of the Presbyterian Church*, 245-46, 254, and 368; Corporation Minutes, May 22, 1761; Guy S. Klett, *Journals of Charles Beatty 1762-1769* (University Park, Pa., 1962), 3-39.

26. Widows' Fund Membership Register, 1761-1785, PHL Archives. See also Mackie, *Facile Princeps*, 7-8.

27. Zelizer, Viviana A. Rotman, *Morals and Markets: Life Insurance in the United States* (New York and London, 1979), 45-46.

28. "A Plea in Behalf of the Widows and Orphans of Deceased Ministers of the Presbyterian Church in the United States," *The Southern Presbyterian Review* (April 1869): 192. See also, "Life Insurance," *The Presbyterian Magazine* (May 1857): 219.

29. Corporation Minutes, November 17, 1762, May 19 and 26, 1763, and July 8, 1763.

30. Corporation Minutes, November 17, 1962, May 26, 1763, and July 29, 1766. See also Klett, *Journals of Charles Beatty 1762-1769*, xxiii-xxiv.

31. Klett, *Minutes of the Presbyterian Church*, 447-48; Corporation Minutes, May 27, 1767. After this, the Corporation relinquished responsibility for missionary activities, but continued to administer the old Fund for Pious Uses until the funds were exhausted.

32. Klett, *Minutes of the Presbyterian Church*, 423; 433-44.

33. Corporation Minutes, May 26, 1768, May 23, 1771, and October 12, 1773. Earlier the Corporation agreed to give the widow of a delinquent policyholder thirty pounds "out of compassion for her situation." Corporation Minutes, May 21, 1765.

34. Corporation Minutes, May 24, 1779. See also Mackie, *Facile Princeps*, 149-50.

35. Klett, *Minutes of the Presbyterian Church*, 572, 579, and 594-95. See also Corporation Minutes, May 17, 1781, May 22, 1784, and May 28, 1787.

36. *A Draught of a Plan of Government and Discipline for the Presbyterian Church in North-America* (Philadelphia, 1786), 24, and Klett, *Minutes of the Presbyterian Church*, 638. See also Trinterud, *The Forming of an American Tradition*, 290-91. Most likely a combination of opposition to life insurance and added expense to congregations were important factors in defeating the Plan.

37. Mackie, *Facile Princeps*, 191-96.

38. Widows' Fund Membership Register, 1761-1875, PHL Archives. For a popular history of the Corporation, see John Baird. *Horn of Plenty: The Story of the Presbyterian Ministers' Fund* (Wheaton, Ill., 1982).

39. *Minutes of the General Assembly in the Presbyterian Church in the United States of America 1789-1820* (Philadelphia, 1847), 1794:90; 1795:97. Hereafter *GAMPCUSA*.

40. *GAMPCUSA*, 1795:102-3.

41. *GAMPCUSA*, 1798:152.

42. *GAMPCUSA*, 1798:152, and *The Presbyterian Digest* (1930) 2:376-79.

43. *GAMPCUSA*, 1799:173-75. The amount was increased to $50,000 in 1864 and $250,000 in 1910. *The Presbyterian Digest*, op. cit.:379.

44. *GAMPCUSA*, 1799:174-75.

45. *GAMPCUSA*, 1798:144.

46. The names of the charter trustees are listed in *GAMPCUSA*, 1798:145-46.

47. Biographical sketches of these trustees can be found in Alfred Nevin, ed., *The Presbyterian Encyclopedia* (Philadelphia, 1884).

48. Information on lay trustees is derived from biographical references in the PHL archives.

2

Comparatively Small Things

> Let us not despise the day of comparatively small things. Let us give God the glory for what he has done, and look to him, and trust in him for what we hope he will farther do. This small cloud, which as yet appears but as a man's hand, may overspread our horizon, and plentifully water the churches with showers of heavenly grace.—*Pastoral Letter, The General Assembly of 1799*

Poised on the threshold of a period of remarkable denominational growth and expansion, commissioners to the 1799 General Assembly listened attentively to reports of events that were occurring in frontier settlements. Spontaneous revivals, accompanied by emotional public conversions, outbursts of glossolalia, and testimonies of physical healings swept across the young nation in what proved to be the vanguard of the Second Great Awakening.[1] The General Assembly issued a Pastoral Letter that year that delineated the denomination's spiritual needs and exhorted church members to higher levels of Christian commitment. It deplored what it termed "the lukewarmness and formality in religion" that prevailed in many communities and extolled "the glad tidings of the outpouring of the Spirit" being reported throughout the country. The General Assembly called on church members not to disparage "the day of comparatively small things" but to envision a new century during which the Christian gospel would be universally proclaimed.[2]

Within the context of this evangelical fervor, the General Assembly trustees gathered in the Second Presbyterian Church in Philadelphia on June 26, 1799, to organize their new corporation. After reading the Act of Incorporation, the group elected Elias Boudinot president, Ashbel Green vice-president, John B. Smith secretary, and Isaac Snowden, Jr.

treasurer. Snowden's salary was set to be 5 percent of annual receipts. A committee on investment composed of Robert Ralston and Andrew Bayard was to consult with Snowden in placing the money transferred from the former General Assembly treasurer "in some productive fund." The board established a policy that, with the exception of annual offerings from congregations, gifts and bequests would be treated as capital stock and only the interest employed for benevolent purposes. At the initial meeting the board received its first contribution, twenty-five pounds, eleven shillings, and sixpence in New York currency from Dr. John McKnight of New York City.[3]

The selection of Boudinot and Green as executive officers established the pattern of combined lay-clergy leadership that continues to this day. These men, who would play decisive roles in defining and shaping the corporate image of the new organization, first became acquainted at Princeton in 1783 when Boudinot was presiding over the Continental Congress and Green was a student at the College of New Jersey. A threatening encounter with a mutinous group of soldiers led the Congress to move temporarily from Philadelphia to Princeton, where it remained in session in Nassau Hall from late June to early November. At a gala celebration of the Fourth of July attended by George Washington, members of Congress, and local citizens, Green delivered a student oration on the superiority of a republican form of government and was invited to attend a lavish banquet held on Boudinot's nearby estate. Although with twenty-two years' difference in age, Green and Boudinot developed a longstanding personal and professional friendship.[4]

During his lifetime, Ashbel Green (1762-1848) was dominant in denominational activities as a pastor, educator, and theologian. He served as chaplain to Congress from 1792-1800 where he had frequent contact with George Washington and other national leaders. Courtly, dignified, and respected, he was the last of his era to wear the powdered clerical wig and remained a pre-Revolutionary figure in deportment and manners. One of his peers acknowledged that Green had "an air of something magisterial or repulsive," which kept strangers at a distance and irritated friends.[5] An honors graduate of the College of New Jersey, Green taught mathematics and natural philosophy there before entering the ministry in 1787 as an assistant to James Sproat at the Second Presbyterian Church in Philadelphia. He was also Stated Clerk of the General Assembly from 1790 to 1802. As president of the College of New Jersey (1812-1822), Green played a prominent role in the establishment of Princeton Theological Seminary and was a member of its board of trustees for more than twenty years. Following his resignation as college president, Green returned to Philadelphia where he edited a religious periodical called *The*

Christian Advocate. Elected moderator of the General Assembly in 1824, Green was president of the Trustees of the General Assembly from 1836 until the time of his death in 1848.[6]

The layman Elias Boudinot (1740-1821) was born into a French Huguenot family that immigrated to the new world in 1687 following the revocation of the Edict of Nantes under the reign of Louis XIV. Boudinot's father, a silversmith, first settled in Philadelphia a few houses down from the residence of Benjamin Franklin. There his wife, Susannah Le Roo, gave birth to Elias on April 21, 1740. He was baptized by George Whitefield, the renowned itinerant evangelist of the Great Awakening, during one of his frequent visits to Philadelphia. The Boudinot family joined the Second Presbyterian Church in 1743, at that time under the leadership of Gilbert Tennent, a New Light revivalist noted for his fiery evangelical sermons. Later the Boudinots moved to Princeton, New Jersey, where the elder Boudinot served as postmaster and managed a copper mining company. During Elias's formative years, the family worshiped at the Presbyterian Church of Elizabethtown, at which the minister, James Caldwell, a pulpiteer of the Whitefield tradition, reportedly rarely spoke without weeping and at times would melt his audience into tears also. Elias was elected president of the board of trustees of the Elizabethtown church at the age of twenty-five.[7]

Boudinot studied law, entered practice in New Jersey, and quickly became a well-connected member of his profession and active participant in community affairs, serving as a trustee of the local academy and the nearby college in Princeton. As an aide-de-camp to the commander of the New Jersey militia, Boudinot developed a friendship with George Washington that would prove pivotal in the development of his political career. In 1777 Congress appointed him Commissary General of Pensioners and in the same year he was elected a delegate to Congress. As congressional president, he signed the peace treaty with Great Britain in 1782 that ended the Revolutionary War and introduced the resolution in Congress that established the first Thanksgiving Day. Returning to law practice, Boudinot was reelected to Congress in 1789 and served six years in the House of Representatives until Washington designated him Director of the Mint, a position he held until retirement in 1805.[8]

In his opening address to the initial meeting of the corporation, Boudinot called for accelerated missionary activity on the frontier that would include itinerant evangelism, distribution of religious literature, erection of church buildings, and the recruitment and financial support of ministerial candidates. While acknowledging the importance of attracting European immigrants, Boudinot urged the General Assembly to give special attention to Native and African Americans who were often neglected or abused by frontier settlers.[9] A fervent advocate for emancipation, Boudinot supported the Pennsylvania Society for Promoting the Abolition of Slavery and frequently defended *pro bono* African Americans involved in litigation over manumission. On the basis of his personal research, he concluded that Native American traditions and customs were connected to the Ten Lost Tribes of Israel, and, with many of his contemporaries, believed that Native Americans were part of the Jewish Diaspora who made their way to the new world.[10]

To underwrite missionary programs, Boudinot proposed an annual fund-raising campaign to be coordinated nationally by the General Assembly trustees and regionally by presbyteries. Its target goal would be twenty-five cents per capita. He also urged the General Assembly to commission ordained ministers as field agents to solicit and receive donations and bequests and to stimulate interest in denominational programs. To complement the field agents, he suggested that lay catechists be appointed "for the instruction of the Indians, the black people, and other persons unacquainted with the principles of our holy religion."[11] He also encouraged donations from persons of "property, piety and benevolence." In that connection, Boudinot announced his gift of 20,000 acres of land in Buncomb County, North Carolina, the income from its sale or rental to be used for "promoting learning, civilization, and religion among the American Indians." Acknowledging generosity of their president, the trustees endorsed Boudinot's missionary mandate, promising to promote "such important and interesting objects of benevolence" as described in his address, and forwarded this to the General Assembly for its approval and implementation.[12]

The 1800 General Assembly accepted Boudinot's proposals "as the views and wishes of the highest judicature," but thought it inexpedient to implement the projects immediately. Commissioners did agree, however, to appoint five ministers, including Ashbel Green, to solicit donations on behalf of the Trustees of the General Assembly to assemble capital for a mission endowment fund. The Assembly also designated Jedidiah Chapman to be the first "stated missionary to the frontier" for a period of four years. Chapman received subsequent appointments and some supervisory authority over other missionaries, anticipating the later appointments of mission superintendents and synodical executives.[13]

At the 1801 General Assembly four of the five clergy reported that they had secured more than $12,000 in cash and pledges, a considerable amount in that the entire denomination had only 152 churches and that a missionary's monthly salary was $33.33. Their expenses were $550 against that sum.[14] With these funds available, this General Assembly assigned ten missionaries, including John Chavis, an African American freedman who had been educated at Princeton under John Witherspoon and licensed by the Presbytery of Lexington, as a missionary "among the people of his own colour." Chavis was the first African American to be ordained in the Presbyterian Church in the United States of America.[15] Although the General Assembly did not designate specific missionaries to seek Native American converts, it directed the presbyteries to investigate and report the willingness of local tribes to receive religious instruction. It also asked for a report on "what means may have been used with them and the success of those means."[16] The Synod of the Carolinas reported to the 1802 General Assembly that nine missionaries had spent some time instructing tribes in agriculture and presenting the gospel. One convert, a young boy known as Blue Jacket, had been received into church membership and was serving as an interpreter.[17]

With this promising start, Boudinot encouraged the trustees to become more involved as agents of the General Assembly, especially in regard to the evangelization of Native Americans. In his presidential address of 1802, Boudinot reiterated his vision to have a denominational missionary enterprise among diverse populations and rapid geographical expansion. He urged the trustees to recruit "influential ministers of the gospel" to conduct revival meetings in frontier communities and to solicit donations and bequests in settled areas. Boudinot also recommended that the denomination set aside specified periods of prayer "for the revival and progress of true religion." He suggested that increasing fiscal and programmatic responsibilities demanded that the corporation's trustees meet more frequently to discuss mission and financial strategies.[18]

Electing not to respond directly to Boudinot's ambitious agenda, the trustees appointed a committee chaired by Ashbel Green to make a formal reply. Following a consultation with his peers, Green reported that the committee members thought that the trustees already had done as much as "expediency and propriety dictates" and that they could recommend no further measures to improve what already had been implemented by the General Assembly. Rather than the trustees becoming more proactive, as Boudinot envisaged, Green and his colleagues proposed that the General Assembly appoint a Standing Committee on Missions who would supervise the missionary enterprise on behalf of General Assembly. In effect, this proposal marked the beginning of an organization of competitive boards and agencies and a move away from a centralized fund-raising organization of the denomination as a whole.[19]

The fourteenth General Assembly of 1802 was sparsely attended because of the inability of frontier governing bodies to send commissioners, but the meetings nevertheless lasted for thirteen days. Much of the business related to missionary activities and the establishment of three new presbyteries, bringing the total to thirty-one, and three new synods. In response to the initiative from the trustees, the Assembly agreed to appoint a Standing Committee on Missions with wide ranging authority to supervise and configure the denomination's missionary enterprise. Although the General Assembly reserved the right to appropriate funds and to make annual reviews, the Standing Committee on Missions would designate field assignments, distribute available funds, and nominate missionaries to the General Assembly.[20]

General Assembly trustees constituted a majority of the original committee of seven, chaired by Ashbel Green, including elders Elias Boudinot, Robert H. Smith, and Ebenezer Hazard. Boudinot's influence is reflected in the emphasis given to missions among African and Native Americans. In addition to Chavis, who had been on the field since 1801, the committee commissioned John Gloucester, a freedman, to conduct revival meetings in Philadelphia. Gloucester had been ordained by the Presbytery of Union in Tennessee though the intercession of Archibald Alexander, the pastor of Third Presbyterian Church in Philadelphia. In 1811 Gloucester reported that he had organized a church, purchased a lot, and started work on a meeting house. The following year the African Presbyterian Church was taken under the care of the Presbytery of Philadelphia and remains an active congregation to this day.[21]

In 1803, the Standing Committee appointed Gideon Blackburn as its first missionary to Native Americans, designating him their missionary to the Cherokee Nation, a tribe that then numbered about 15,000. Blackburn opened a school in Hiwassee, Tennessee, which briefly flourished but closed in 1810 due to insufficient funds. Another mission to the Wyandot tribe in the Synod of Ohio taught agricultural skills and other practical courses to attract potential converts. When the tribe moved westward beyond the Mississippi, however, that enterprise came to a close.[22]

As missionary work increased, the Assembly enlarged the Standing Committee to seventeen, providing for members who were residents of Philadelphia or the vicinity and the others from each of the seven synods. The 1816 General Assembly elevated the Standing Committee to board status and provided for full-time staff members. Although Ashbel Green continued to serve as president of the Standing Committee for a number of years, the Assembly trustees became peripheral figures in the formulation of mission strategy. For the most part, they simply disbursed funds to the Standing Committee as directed by the General Assembly.[23] At times this routine task had presented problems for corporation officers. In 1810 treasurer Snowden reported to the Assembly that the missionary funds had experienced loss of value because some contributions had been made in nonnegotiable bank notes from unincorporated institutions or entities too distant from Philadelphia to be accepted as legal tender. Snowden also acknowledged the receipt of some counterfeit bills that were included in funds derived from the annual presbytery mission offerings. Snowden recommended that contributions designated for the General Assembly treasury be limited to notes of $5 or more from incorporated banks in New York, Baltimore, or Philadelphia.[24]

Questions regarding the authority to disburse funds for missionary operations emerged. As early as 1801 the trustees asked the General Assembly to appoint a committee to recommend guidelines for the transaction of business between the corporation and the General Assembly and its committees. The committee concluded that the trustees were responsible for the management and disposal of all assets including cash, land, and bequests unless the General Assembly, in writing through the stated clerk, issued special instructions. In addition, the committee recommended that the trustees' treasurer provide a detailed annual report and that any actions taken by either body that might possibly involve the other be communicated as quickly as possible.[25] Although approved as a policy, such did not always work in practice. The following year the trustees reported that their treasurer had paid missionary Jedediah Chapman $262 with no written confirmation from the stated clerk to do so because the payments were "necessary and proper." The trustees requested the General Assembly to appropriate funds to cover the expenditure which it subsequently approved.[26]

Although their responsibility for missionary operations gradually diminished, the trustees were assigned other fiduciary tasks by the General Assembly, including paying the stated clerk and providing janitorial services at the annual meetings.[27] Until 1808, each presbytery assumed responsibility for defraying the expenses of commissioners to the General Assembly. Because the Assembly met annually in Philadelphia during the early years of its existence, remote governing bodies incurred high costs while nearby ones had virtually no expense. To address this inequity, the General Assembly constituted a special travel fund to be raised from monies contributed by local congregations and managed by the Assembly's trustees. It was specified to be maintained as a separate account, distinct from benevolent funds.[28]

During the early decades of the nineteenth century, before the creation of the Board of Publication, the trustees provided governing bodies and congregations with a variety of official documents and worship aids. In 1801 the General Assembly directed them to supervise the transcription, printing, and distribution of the *Minutes of the General Assembly* to each presbytery and to arrange for the distribution of copies of the *Confession of Faith, The Longer and Shorter Catechisms, The Book of Discipline and*

Directory of Worship, and *The Plan of Government* in frontier settlements.[29] In 1804 trustees reported that they had purchased books "suitable for distribution among the poor and on the frontiers" and requested guidance from the Assembly regarding their disposition. The following year they disbursed $35 for the purchase of religious books "to be distributed among the people of colour within the bounds of Hanover Presbytery."[30] When colporteurs employed to sell books and pamphlets failed to render their accounts, the Assembly directed the trustees to collect what was owed. Later, the trustees assumed responsibility for providing congregations with Psalters and hymnbooks.[31]

The trustees played important roles in establishing theological seminaries during the first half of the nineteenth century. Ashbel Green headed a committee appointed by the General Assembly in 1810 to "digest and prepare the plan of a Theological Seminary" and became the first president of the Board of Directors when Princeton Theological Seminary was established in 1812. Other trustees, including Samuel Stanhope Smith and Elias Boudinot, also served on the seminary board and assisted in procuring endowment funds for scholarships and faculty chairs.[32] The trustees of the General Assembly were appointed custodians of the Princeton Seminary funds and authorized to receive contributions and invest the money in productive stock. For a number of years the trustees managed the funds of Union Theological Seminary in Virginia that had been organized by the Synods of Virginia and North Carolina. At the request of the synods in 1836, however, the General Assembly authorized the trustees to transfer the funds to the governing bodies so that "they may be safely invested in the South at a much higher rate of interest than they now bear."[33]

The trustees acted on behalf of the General Assembly as legal counsel or in cases of litigation. Throughout the nineteenth century, lawyers who served on the board provided their services to the church either gratis or expenses only. Bequests of land often involved acquiring valid deeds, dealing with contested wills, and managing the property until it could be disposed at a reasonable profit. One example was when John Postly bequeathed three hundred acres of land "to cultivate and instruct the Indians of North America," but stipulated that his son could hold the property following his death and that "several families of people of colour" could continue to occupy the land during the interim.[34] Another occurred in 1819 when Eleazar Wheelock, president of Dartmouth College, donated property in New Hampshire estimated to be worth $20,000 for the benefit of Princeton Seminary. Four years later, the family contested Wheelock's will, and "as an example of Christian moderation," the trustees made an effort to bring about an amicable settlement before resorting to a legal tribunal.[35]

Acreage in North Carolina donated by Elias Boudinot engaged the attention of the Assembly trustees for nearly four decades. Agents appointed to supervise the property reported that squatters refused to leave the property despite efforts to have them evicted. Periodically agents resigned their positions citing threats of violence and their inability to control the influx of unauthorized immigration. The trustees were forced to suspend sales of land until the matter could be settled.[36] On numerous occasions, the trustees also provided legal counsel and services to presbyteries and local congregations who encountered problems with contested property rights. In a few instances, General Assembly instructed the trustees to investigate allegations of irregular appointments of professors at Presbyterian-related seminaries or on matters dealing with revisions or modifications of institutional charters.[37]

These varied responsibilities were secondary to the primary task of receiving and disbursing money derived from gifts and bequests that had been directed to the corporation and designated for denominational causes. During the early decades of the nineteenth century, most donors designated their contributions either to domestic missions or theological education. Gifts ranged from $25 to $10,000, but most were between $500 and $2,000. Often the benefactors sent detailed instructions regarding the utilization and investment of funds, although occasionally they left much to the discretion of the trustees and the General Assembly. One legacy received by the trustees stated simply that it was to be applied "to the objects and purposes that will most extensively advance the Redeemer's cause and kingdom in the world."[38] Trustees referred ambiguous or potentially problematic bequests to the General Assembly to be the arbiter of such matters. For example, John Colt of Paterson, New Jersey, offered the trustees a promissory note for $2,500 with five percent interest payable in ten years to be used for scholarships at Princeton Seminary. During his lifetime Colt requested the right to designate recipients of the scholarship. Trustees initially refused to accept the offer but did so upon a directive from the General Assembly.[39]

One of the earliest bequests was from Margaret Sherman in 1812. Her will reflects the evangelical piety of nineteenth-century American Presbyterianism. To her niece, Sherman left a watch, the family Bible, items of wearing apparel, and a bed and mattress. Her collection of religious books were given to the Presbyterian Church of Abington, Pennsylvania, to be used as a lending library. She designated half of her estate to create a fund for supporting the pastor's salary and gave the other half to the trustees of the General Assembly to promote "spreading the gospel on the frontier of the United States." When in the opinion of the General Assembly frontier missions were no longer necessary, Sherman specified that the money be employed to educate "poor and pious youth for the ministry and no other use." She ended her will with these words: "Into the hands of my saviour, the Lord Jesus Christ, whom, I believe to be both God and man, in one divine and adorable person, I commend my spirit, and to the dust I commit my body, in humble hope of the resurrection through gospel grace to eternal life."[40]

Although many legacies were small, the corporation received them graciously and meticulously observed the instructions of the donors. One unidentified donor gave $25 designated for missions to American Indian tribes and another $50 to support "the preaching of the gospel."[41] Catharine Nagle gave stocks and bonds amounting to $372.13 for the sole use of Princeton Seminary "to be disposed of as the gentlemen see fit." Because Nagle had no immediate family and no residue in her modest estate, the trustees deducted $150 to cover her funeral expenses.[42] In 1820 Thomas Lindsay donated $121.60 for the evangelization of American Jews who were settling in eastern port cities. Although the General Assembly accepted the money and directed the trustees to create a permanent fund for Jewish evangelization, subsequent Assemblies displayed little interest in the project.[43] In 1839 the General Assembly approved the intention of the Board of Foreign Missions to begin mission work for "the ancient people of God" and the trustees transferred the Lindsay Fund to the Foreign Board for the evangelization of the Jews.[44]

Presbyterian women's organizations supported various missionary, educational, and social causes. During the early nineteenth century, the groups were called cent, sewing, praying, or charitable societies, but later the term missionary society or missionary circle became widespread. The General Assembly noted with approval in 1815 "the exertions of pious and benevolent females" who had organized local societies to raise funds for the support of indigent seminary students.[45] Reference to such groups first appears in the Trustee Minutes in 1818 when the Presbyterian Female Education Society of Charleston, South Carolina, established a scholarship fund for students at Princeton Theological Seminary. Other Princeton contributors included women's groups in Augusta, Georgia, Orange, New Jersey, and Camden and Salem, South Carolina. The latter group gave $300 in 1821 but they requested the following year that their money be returned "in order to invest it at more productive interest for the same object." Honoring their request, the trustees returned the $300 but applied the accrued interest to the general scholarship fund.[46]

The bequest of Joseph Eastburn, founding missionary of the Mariners Church in Philadelphia who died in 1828, featured a unique ministry to seamen. In his will, Eastburn left money and property worth approximately $9,000 to provide a manse and a stipend for a missionary to the mariners.[47] A carpenter by trade, Eastburn was denied ministerial ordination by Philadelphia Presbytery in 1783 because of educational deficiencies, including an inability to master Latin grammar. Ashbel Green later persuaded the presbytery to appoint Eastburn as a chaplain to city institutions such as the jail, hospital, and almshouse, although the presbytery continued to withhold full ministerial privileges. During service as city chaplain, Eastman became acquainted with the sailors who crowded the streets of the bustling port of Philadelphia. Feeling kinship to these men considered by many to be socially unredeemable, Eastburn in 1819 procured a sail loft and raised the Bethel Flag which signified a place of worship to attract the attention of passing mariners. When a group of sailors approached the loft they would call out "Ship Ahoy" and Eastburn would return the greeting. They would then ask, "Where are you bound?" to which Eastburn would respond, "To the Port of New Jerusalem. We sail under the Admiral Jesus, a good commander. We want men. We have several ships—the ship Methodist, the ship Baptist, the ship Episcopalian, the ship Presbyterian. You may have a choice of ships." Here, commented Eastburn in his *Memoirs*, marked the beginning of the Mariners' Church which became a refuge for sailors and a fixture in Philadelphia Presbyterianism for more than a century and a half.[48]

When Elias Boudinot died in 1821, his will consisted of twenty-six manuscript pages. After bequeathing personal property and various sums of money to relatives and servants, Boudinot distributed the remainder of his estate to various educational, religious, and humanitarian causes. To the New Jersey Bible Society he gave two hundred dollars to purchase reading glasses for "poor old people" so that they could read the Bibles being distributed to them. He also gave 6,800 acres of wooded area in Pennsylvania to provide firewood for indigent citizens of Philadelphia. He gave money to the Moravians at Bethlehem, Pennsylvania, to "civilize & gospelize the Indian Nations, or any other destitute of a gospel ministry." The Public Hospital of Philadelphia was granted the use of 3,270 acres in Bradford County to enable poor foreigners and persons from states other than Pennsylvania to meet the requirements for admission. The Magdalene Societies of Philadelphia and New York received $500 each, and stock dividends from the Burlington Aqueduct Company were to be devoted to the relief of "poor females" in New Jersey.[49]

Boudinot's bequests that were to be administered by the trustees included endowment funds for urban missions and the circulation of religious literature. The Boudinot Mission Fund reflected his longtime concern for people with a marginal existence amid the prosperity of an expanding economy. Boudinot specified that the interest derived from a bequest of $5,000 dollars be used to support catechists in Philadelphia and New York "to instruct aid & assist the poor & distressed by visiting, advising & yielding them spiritual comfort in the Hospitals, Magdalenes, Alms Houses, Bettering Houses, Public Prisons & places of Confinement, for Crimes & Misdemeanors." Boudinot also bequeathed two houses in Philadelphia, their rent to be used to purchase books for "weak and feeble" congregations, a fund that continues to be administered today by the Presbyterian Church (U.S.A.) Foundation. One of the first disbursements from this fund, in the amount of $168.03, was divided equally among three New Jersey congregations, "all of which are feeble and have stated pastors."[50] On several occasions, trustees made awards to the Episcopal Church in Burlington, New Jersey, in which the Boudinot family frequently worshipped.[51]

Incapacitated during the last years of his life, Boudinot was unable to perform the duties of president of the trustees. Three years prior to his death, the trustees accepted his resignation with regret and elected another layman, Robert Ralston. A self-made man in the model of Benjamin Franklin, Ralston was a Philadelphia merchant noted for his business expertise and wide-ranging philanthropy. His clipper ships sailed as far as China to bring back silk, spices, and other exotic goods for sale in eastern cities. As an elder in the Second Presbyterian Church, Ralston instituted the first Sunday school in the city, organized the Philadelphia Bible Society and served as its treasurer, and founded the Philadelphia Orphans and Widows Asylum. He was one of the earliest and most munificent benefactors of the Mariners' Church, and he also contributed to a variety of seamen's missions in other eastern port cities.[52]

Ralston's tenure as president of the trustees, 1818-1836, was marked by allegations of misuse of endowment funds, poor performance of investment strategies, and unsatisfactory maintenance of financial records. Although Ralston's personal integrity was never questioned, his apparent lack of supervision over the performance of treasurer Isaac Snowden led to a series of inquiries conducted by General Assembly committees that impacted negatively on the public image of the trustees. Snowden accepted responsibility for much of the criticism leveled at his peers during Ralston's administration. He was involved in work for the Bank of the United States, served as treasurer of a number of civic and religious organizations including the Presbytery of Philadelphia, and suffered ill health in his declining years. Snowden admitted in 1827 that he was not able "to present the accounts and vouchers in the regular and accurate manner which heretofore have been characteristic of his character." In his annual financial report for that year, Snowden acknowledged a deficit of approximately $5,000 due to poor returns on stock investments and noted that he could not vouch for the accuracy of the financial statement, although he believed it to be "substantially correct." The trustees and the General Assembly nevertheless accepted Snowden's report, requesting that he submit a more detailed statement of individual investments at the next annual meeting.[53]

The issue of fiduciary responsibility resurfaced in 1829 when the trustees approved a request from the executive committee of the Mission Board to release designated missionary funds for such expenses as printing the *Minutes*, paying the Stated Clerk, and reimbursing travel expenses for commissioners. Previous General Assemblies had ruled that no capital or interest from permanent funds were to be allocated for operational expenses. In a written dissent, Ashbel Green argued that funds designated by donors solely for missionary endeavors were a sacred trust that even the Assembly itself could not violate without a breach of faith. Green felt the trustees should contract loans from outside sources rather than intrude into endowment capital.[54] As a result, the trustees recommended that the annual collection for missionary funds be changed to a collection for a contingency fund that would provide a steady flow of cash for Assembly expenses. The Assembly endorsed this idea and directed the presbyteries to so inform sessions.[55]

Despite the new ruling, Snowden continued to have difficulties allocating resources to meet the requests for funds that were channeled to him through the General Assembly. Because presbyteries were erratic in reporting and disbursing collections, the treasurer often could not ascertain precisely how much money was available for travel expenses, salaries, and missionary operations. The General Assembly routinely established budgets and authorized Snowden to release funds based on projected receipts rather than on actual cash in hand. As a result, when he lacked resources to pay the salaries of professors at Princeton Seminary, Snowden transferred money from the permanent fund to cover the shortfall, anticipating that he would replace it with subsequent contributions. This practice apparently went unnoticed until 1833 when a General Assembly committee's audit of the treasurer's books revealed that approximately $15,000 had been expended and never restored from endowment capital funds over a period of five years.[56] Although the committee expressed regret that any part of the permanent fund had been used for current expenses, it exonerated the treasurer from any criminal negligence or maleficence. To recoup the losses, however, the committee suggested that the trustees consider whether safe investments of funds could be made "so as to produce a higher rate of interest than they now yield." It also recommended that the composition of the board be changed "especially on account of the advanced age of some of the members."[57]

Challenged to monitor the denomination's assets more carefully and to diversify their investment portfolio, the trustees appointed a permanent finance committee to make recommendations regarding new investment strategies. From its inception, the corporation had invested conservatively, usually on the initiative of the treasurer and the president, placing the bulk of its assets in government and Bank of the United States stock. One of the earliest published financial reports indicated that in 1826 the trustees held assets of $111,532, virtually all of which were invested in Government certificates and stock (at 6 percent interest) and had only a few thousand dollars in the Steam Boat Company, Schuykill Permanent Bridge, and mortgages on Philadelphia property.[58] Following the directive of the General Assembly, the trustees began to include stock in western banks and in canal and railroad companies that were experiencing rapid growth. The resulting dividends were so high that the board signed promissory notes in order to purchase additional shares of the Bank of Vicksburg in Mississippi. Reporting to the General Assembly in 1836, the trustees announced that the seminary professors' salaries had been paid in full and that $2,600 of capital that had been taken previously from the permanent mission fund had been replaced.[59]

Although the General Assembly expressed satisfaction in the increased productivity of the new investment policies and approved the actions taken by the corporation, the standing committee assigned to review the report expressed caution regarding risking capital in speculative ventures in order to secure high short-term returns. Emphasizing the importance of safety and permanency, the committee reminded the trustees to take no greater risk than "would be incurred by a prudent man whose family with himself might be dependent upon the investments." It also recommended that the trustees dispose of certain stocks, including the United Passaic and Hackensack Bridge Company, unless they deemed such action to be inconsistent with the terms of the bequest.[60] Trustees themselves questioned some actions. Thomas Bradford entered a written protest against the policy of investing in unregulated western banks, which he thought too risky for mission funds. Fearing the future of economic prosperity, Bradford advocated a return to investments in United States stock, Pennsylvania banks, and Philadelphia real estate.[61]

On these notes the first period of trustee history came to a close. Along with major modifications in investment policies, the trustees underwent a generational shift in membership and in leadership positions. New laymen elected to membership between 1833 and 1836 included James Bayard, Solomon Allen, Ambrose White, and Matthew Newkirk. Robert H. Smith, a Philadelphia merchant, succeeded Isaac Snowden as treasurer following the latter's death on December 15, 1835.[62] Upon the death of President Ralston in 1836, trustees selected Ashbel Green to refurbish the corporation's image and lead it into a new era.[63] As he assumed the presidency, however, Green was deeply involved in a theological controversy within the Presbyterian Church that would trigger the Old School-New School schism in 1837 and produce two competing denominations each with their own set of General Assembly trustees.

NOTES

1. Baptists and Methodists benefitted most from the revivalistic milieu, but Presbyterians and Congregationalists also shared in the dramatic growth of church membership in the early nineteenth century. Presbyterians would enter into a "Plan of Union" with the Congregational Church in 1801 that designated geographical areas for which each of the two denominations had specific mission responsibility.

2. *GAMPCUSA*, 1799:178-79.

3. Minutes of the Trustees of the General Assembly of the Presbyterian Church in the United States of America, June 26, 1799, PHL Archives. Hereafter cited as Trustee Minutes (PCUSA).

4. Mark Noll, *Princeton and the Republic* (Princeton, N.J., 1989), 83-84. Later in the summer Boudinot presided over a reception for George Washington at the college, climaxed by Princeton's graduation exercises. As valedictorian, Green led the seniors in the customary series of speeches and debates. Green's praise for Washington apparently was so flattering that the first president reportedly colored with embarrassment, but the following day he shook Green's hand and complimented him on the address.

5. William B. Sprague, "Biographical Sketches," in *Presbyterian Reunion: A Memorial Volume 1837-1871* (New York, 1870), 103-09.

6. For further assessments of Green's career, see Sprague, "Biographical Sketches," 103-10; Mackie, *Facile Princeps*; and his biographical file, PHL Archives.

7. George Adams Boyd, *Elias Boudinot: Patriot and Statesman* (Princeton, 1952), 16-17. Elias was already a public figure by that time, having published a broadside in opposition to the Stamp Act.

8. The *Presbyterian Encyclopedia*, 89. See also Boyd, *Elias Boudinot: Patriot and Statesman*, 216-51. Ecumenical in his approach to denominational Christianity, Boudinot had a wide range of friends and acquaintances. He was noted for his hospitality, frequently entertaining guests in his spacious mansion in Burlington, New Jersey. In later life Boudinot was the first president of the American Bible Society, founded in 1816 under his leadership, and contributed generously to its permanent endowment fund.

9. Although the text of Boudinot's remarks was not preserved in the trustees' papers, its contents can be deduced from the report submitted by the trustees to the General Assembly which alludes to the presidential address. See *GAMPCUSA* 1800:195-97.

10. Boyd, *Elias Boudinot: Patriot and Statesman*, 181-83 and 254.

11. *GAMPCUSA*, 1800:197.

12. *GAMPCUSA,* 1800:193-96, and Trustee Minutes (PCUSA), May 4, 1800.

13. *GAMPCUSA*, 1800:208-09.

14. *GAMPCUSA*, 1801:227-28. The General Assembly recommended at this meeting that in presbyteries in which there were no General Assembly agents, the governing bodies appoint their own agents to obtain "voluntary contributions as God may put into their hearts to make."

15. *GAMPCUSA*, 1801:229.

16. *GAMPCUSA*, 1801:229.

17. *GAMPCUSA*, 1802:238.

18. Trustee Minutes (PCUSA), May 19, 1802. The substance of Boudinot's remarks are derived from the subsequent report to the General Assembly rather than the address itself which the author has been unable to locate.

19. Trustee Minutes (PCUSA), May 19 and 27, 1802.

20. *GAMPCUSA*, 1802:238. See also Clifford Drury, *Presbyterian Panorama* (Philadelphia, 1952), 21-40.

21. Drury, *Presbyterian Panorama*, 24.

22. *GAMPCUSA*, 1806:361, and Drury, *Presbyterian Panorama*, 26-27.

23. Despite efforts to create a national church, the General Assembly rejected a request from the Presbytery of Baltimore that the Assembly occasionally meet outside of Philadelphia, because the trustees and members of the standing committee on missions resided in Philadelphia and could only hold their sessions there. *GAMPCUSA*, 1804:317

24. *GAMPCUSA*, 1810:445-46.

25. *GAMPCUSA*, 1801:232-33.

26. *GAMPCUSA*, 1802:239.

27. *GAMPCUSA*, 1806:346.

28. *GAMPCUSA*, 1807:385-86. Commissioners received two dollars for every thirty miles of travel to and from meetings of the Assembly.

29. *GAMPCUSA*, 1802:220-21.

30. *GAMPCUSA*, 1804:297; 1805:340, 345.

31. *GAMPCUSA*, 1806:346. For a period of time the trustees also published the General Assembly's magazine, *The Evangelical Intelligencer. GAMPCUSA*, 1807:392.

32. *GAMPCUSA*, 1810:453-55. For background on the founding of the seminary, see Mark Noll, *Princeton and the Republic 1768-1822* (Princeton, N.J., 1989), 244-71.

33. *GAMPCUSA*, 1836:522. Beyond fund management, the trustees occasionally were given authority by the General Assembly to evaluate proposals for the establishment of new theological seminaries. See, for example, *GAMPCUSA*, 1824:119.

34. Trustee Minutes (PCUSA), May 30, 1819.

35. Trustee Minutes (PCUSA), May 30, 1823.

36. Trustee Minutes (PCUSA), May 20, 1806. As late as 1836 the land still constituted a problem for the trustees. They were paying $400 annually for taxes and not generating any income. A local presbytery requested that some of the land be given to them for church expansion, but the trustees ruled that because the devise was for the entire denomination, it would not be proper to give it to one of its parts. Affirming that it would establish an "injurious precedent," the trustees rejected the request. Trustee Minutes (PCUSA), June 3, 1836.

37. For some examples, see *General Assembly Minutes of the Presbyterian Church in the United States of America (Old School) 1838-1869* (Philadelphia, n.d. [c. 1888] 3 vols., I:221, 224; II:135. Hereafter cited as *GAMPCUSA[OS]*.

38. *GAMPCUSA[OS] 1838-1869*, I:277.

39. Trustee Minutes (PCUSA), October 18, 1828, June 1, 1830, and *GAMPCUSA*, 1830:301.

40. Trustee Minutes (PCUSA), May 29, 1812.

41. Trustee Minutes (PCUSA), June 5, 1830 and May 18, 1832.

42. Trustee Minutes (PCUSA), October 2, 1851.

43. *GAMPCUSA*, 1820:733. In 1835 Jonathan Winchester requested permission to use the funds but the Assembly declined to make an appropriation. *GAMPCUSA*, 1835:467 and Trustee Minutes (PCUSA), June 18, 1835.

44. *GAMPCUSA[OS]*, I:168. It was not until 1846 that the Board dispatched evangelists to New York, Philadelphia, and Baltimore. At the beginning of the twentieth century, the General Assembly assigned responsibilities for Jewish evangelization to the Board of Home Missions. See Drury, *Presbyterian Panorama*, 149-50.

45. *GAMPCUSA*, 1815:600. For background on early societies, see Lois A. Boyd and R. Douglas Brackenridge, *Presbyterian Women in America: Two Centuries of a Quest for Status*, 2d ed. (Westport, Conn. and London, 1996), 3-23.

46. Trustee Minutes (PCUSA), May 21, 1820 and May 21, 1822.

47. Ashbel Green, *Memoirs of Joseph Eastburn* (Philadelphia, 1818), 176-80, and Trustee Minutes (PCUSA), March 1, 1828.

48. Green, *Memoirs of Joseph Eastburn*, 112-13. See also Lester E. Paul, "Joseph Eastburn—Preacher to Mariners," typescript, Record Group 124-1-3, PHL Archives.

49. Barbara Clark, *Elias Boudinot: The Story of Elias Boudinot IV, His Family, His Friends, and His Country* (Philadelphia, 1977), 456-57. Boudinot also played a key role in establishing the American Society for Ameliorating the Condition of the Jews which was organized in New York on February 8, 1820 with Boudinot as president. The main purpose of the society was to "colonize and evangelize" Ashkenasic (German) Jews who were facing persecution in Europe. In his will Boudinot left the society four thousand acres of land in Warren County, Pennsylvania, so that arriving immigrants could receive fifty acre plots. As an alternative, the group elected a cash sum of $1,000. The group's tenuous existence ended around 1860 "for want of Jews" interested in investigating Christianity. Boyd, *Elias Boudinot, Patriot and Statesman*, 262.

50. Trustee Minutes (PCUSA), May 19, 1829.

51. Trustee Minutes (PCUSA), May 30, 1821 and June 6, 1831.

52. Ashbel Green, *Believers, Sojourners on Earth, and Expectants of Heaven: A Sermon Occasioned by the Death of Robert Ralston, Esq.* (Philadelphia, 1836), 1-5, and Mackie, *Facile Princeps*, 244-45.

53. Trustee Minutes (PCUSA), May 26, 1827, and GAMPCUSA, 1830:290. Snowden continued to maintain inaccurate records. In 1831 he reported to the trustees that so many stocks had been sold and reinvested that he could not pinpoint how much money was coming from particular stocks. Trustee Minutes (PCUSA), May 23, 1831.

54. Trustee Minutes (PCUSA), August 4, 1829. Following Green's protest, the trustees began to borrow money from local banks to cover deficits rather than tapping into the endowment funds. Trustee Minutes (PCUSA), May 18, 1832.

55. Trustee Minutes (PCUSA), June 5, 1830 and *GAMPCUSA*, 1830:305.

56. Trustee Minutes (PCUSA), May 31, 1833, and *GAMPCUSA*, 1833:411-12.

57. *GAMPCUSA*, 1833:412.

58. *GAMPCUSA*, 1826:188. On a number of occasions the trustees discussed the possibility of diversifying their investment portfolio but invariably decided to keep their funds in government stock and Bank of the United States stock. See Trustee Minutes (PCUSA), May 19, 1802, June 7, 1807, and May 18, 1808.

59. *GAMPCUSA*, 1836:522-23.

60. *GAMPCUSA*, 1836:522-23.

61. Trustee Minutes (PCUSA), June 30, 1836.

62. "Obituaries," *The Presbyterian*, 17 December 1835:103, and Trustee Minutes (PCUSA), June 18, 1835. Snowden, an elder in the Second Presbyterian Church of Philadelphia, also served as treasurer for local voluntary societies such as The Humane Society, The Magdalen Society, and The Evangelistic Society. A collection of his papers can be found in Record Group 218, PHL Archives.

63. Trustee Minutes (PCUSA), October 5, 1836. In his will, Ralston gave $2,000 for a scholarship at Princeton Seminary to be administered by the trustees of the General Assembly. The incumbents were to be nominated by his children and their heirs or the Presbytery of Philadelphia. Trustee Minutes (PCUSA), November 8, 1837.

3

Division and Controversy

The Church is now fairly divided into two separate and independent denominations. Of this secession we only complain as to the manner in which it was effected, for we hold it to be the unalienable right of all Christians—a right which duty requires them to exercise—to separate themselves from other Christians with whom they cannot conscientiously agree on subjects of Christian doctrine and church order.—*Pastoral Letter, The General Assembly (Old School) of 1838*

At the opening session of the General Assembly in Philadelphia on May 19, 1837, commissioners anticipated unity but prepared for controversy. The "era of good feelings" of the American Revolution was giving way to sectional tension exacerbated by the slavery issue. For a number of years there had been tension in Presbyterianism in the United States regarding matters of governance and doctrine. Before the 1837 General Assembly recessed, the Presbyterian Church had divided into Old School and New School parties, both retaining the name of the Presbyterian Church in the United States of America and both claiming to be custodians of the denomination's assets.[1]

The majority party, the conservative Old School members, opposed the Plan of Union of 1801 with the Congregational Church, charging that "Presbygational" churches were anomalies and not subject to the discipline of Presbyterian judicatories. They also believed that the denomination should constitute its own church boards, subject to the General Assembly, rather than participate in nondenominational agencies such as the American Education Society and the American Home Missionary Society. On the other side, New School adherents supported the Plan of Union and contended that denominational growth confirmed the efficacy of cooperative missionary programs. Doctrinally, the New School party was inclined to modify Calvinism to accommodate a growing liberal theological climate while the Old School adherents resisted pressures to deviate from traditional orthodoxy.[2] At the 1837 Assembly, the Old School majority abrogated the Plan of Union and ruled that the four Synods organized under the Plan of Union were no longer part of the denomination. After being refused seats in the Old School Assembly, the exscinded synods and sympathetic followers formed a rival General Assembly of about equal size of the Old School Assembly in 1838. Both Old School and New School groups maintained a separate and at times hostile existence until they reunited in 1870.[3]

A trying period for Old School trustees, they found their effectiveness as custodians of denominational funds questioned by General Assembly commissioners and their legal status challenged by New School officials. Over nearly two decades, the Old School General Assembly investigatory committees audited the loss of capital funds attributed to risky investments made in a highly volatile market and raised charges of erratic record keeping. Although the General Assembly exonerated the trustees of negligence, many Old School commissioners questioned the trustees' organizational skills and financial expertise. Concurrently, denominational growth fostered the incorporation of programmatic boards and agencies, all of which not only competed for benevolence funds but also managed their assets independently of the General Assembly trustees. By mid-century these boards and agencies surpassed the General Assembly trustees in total denominational fund raising.

The New School General Assembly initially confronted the Old School trustees in 1838 by electing six trustees to replace the incumbents. They also designated James Todd president in place of Ashbel Green. The Old School General Assembly declined to seat the New School appointees and instructed the sitting trustees to "take all such measures as to them shall seem needful for asserting, defending, and securing the rights and interests of the Church confided to their care." Additionally the Assembly pledged to indemnify the trustees from any loss or damage of assets in the course of implementing the Assembly's directive.[4] Litigation costs in procuring a favorable settlement for the Old School Assembly amounted to $4,000. Rather than encumber General Assembly funds, the trustees borrowed money from private sources. A grateful Old School General Assembly commended the trustees for "their wise, firm, faithful and successful administration of the trust committed to them."[5]

Of more significance were fiscal issues following the Panic of 1837. As indicated previously, the trustees capitalized on a bull market in 1836 by purchasing large quantities of stock of banks in the western states that at first paid off handsomely and enabled them to restore lost capital to the permanent mission fund. Many of these banks, however, loaned money too freely on inadequate security and often issued more bank notes than their reserves warranted. President Andrew Jackson intervened in 1836 and issued the famous "Specie Circular" that required that public lands must be paid for in specie, an act that helped curb speculation but precipitated panic among investors. In May 1837 New York banks suspended specie payment, and banks in other parts of the country collapsed. Following a brief recovery in 1838, the country entered a decade-long depression during which investors disposed of stocks at a loss or held them in hopes of increased valuations.[6]

A detailed financial report to the General Assembly in 1837 from treasurer Robert H. Smith gave commissioners good news and bad news. On the one hand, the trustees' investment dividends during 1836 and the first quarter of 1837 averaged 10 percent, an amount that permitted them to meet the denomination's financial obligations, including full payment of the professors' salaries at Princeton Theological Seminary. On the other hand, trustees had purchased additional western bank stock early in 1837 that suddenly dropped in value. Acknowledging that "what the event of these changes will be is impossible to be foreseen," Smith indicated that the trustees intended no alterations in their current investments until the market settled. Smith expressed confidence that if income from the ensuing year failed to meet current expenses, the deficiency could be covered by the previous year's surplus.[7]

By 1840 the country was experiencing economic collapse. Business stagnation resulted in a steady downward trend in crop and commodity values and created widespread unemployment among the growing urban population. Confronted with chronic financial shortfalls, General Assembly commissioners increasingly criticized the trustees' management of the denomination's permanent funds. The General Assembly's standing committee on finance questioned the investment in western banks and advised the trustees to sell their unproductive bank stock "as soon as it may be judiciously done" and to invest in securities that were "less fluctuating and less hazardous." The committee also regretted that previous General Assemblies had approved an investment strategy that anticipated more than 6 percent annual interest. Noting a budget deficit of $3,900, the committee recommended that contributions be solicited from the church-at-large to balance the budget.[8]

Of long-term importance to General Assembly trustees, the 1840 General Assembly granted authority to seek incorporation to the Board of Foreign Missions, the Board of Home Missions, and the Board of

Education. With their full-time executives and staffs, the boards expanded their fund-raising activities. In 1839 the boards had requested the Assembly trustees to issue bonds of indemnity so that they could receive legacies directly rather than through the denominational corporation.[9] As earlier in the century, Ashbel Green opposed extending the fiscal duties of the trustees to include transactions conducted by the various boards. Such a step would require modifying the original charter, an act which Green deemed inappropriate and unwise. Following Green's lead, the trustees advised the General Assembly to authorize the Boards of Education and Foreign Missions to incorporate in New York and the Board of Home Missions to incorporate in Pennsylvania.[10] The General Assembly concurred, and the following year the incorporation processes were complete. The trustees thus were no longer the sole custodians of denominational endowment funds and consequently would have a diminished role in procuring and managing legacies and bequests.[11]

During the next two years, the General Assembly scrutinized the trustees' annual financial reports. In 1841 the Assembly's Standing Committee on Finance reported that the treasurer's records were "kept in a confused state so as to render it impossible to investigate them with the minuteness the subject demands." While noting that the incumbent treasurer, Matthew Newkirk, was not to blame for his predecessor's mistakes, the committee recommended that Newkirk close the treasurer's books and open new ones that would accurately reflect the current status of the funds. At the same time the committee directed the trustees to transfer endowment funds in their possession designated for Princeton Seminary to the trustees of that institution.[12]

The 1842 General Assembly commended the trustees for keeping accurate financial accounts but criticized them for not transferring all the funds to the seminary, implying that the Assembly trustees were less competent than their Princeton counterparts. "As far as we understand, the condition of the funds of the Seminary, managed by its own Board of Trustees, seem to have escaped the wreck of our other funds." According to committee calculations, stocks estimated to be worth $93,022 in the 1841 market declined to $44,032 during the ecclesiastical year. Chastising the trustees for not heeding advice and instead exposing the funds to loss, the committee concluded, "This expose [sic], it must be confessed, is most deplorable. The instruction it communicates is so emphatic that the committee forbear to make any comment." A reference to the integrity and good intentions of the trustees did little to alleviate the negative assessment of the corporation's performance.[13]

The General Assembly adjourned shortly after the condemnatory report, so the trustees could not respond until 1843. In a carefully crafted rebuttal, Ashbel Green addressed what he described as "several statements and remarks, calculated to make an erroneous impression on the public mind" regarding the conduct of the Assembly trustees. On investment policies, Green pointed out that in seeking higher returns from western bank stocks the trustees had complied with directives from the General Assembly to generate more income from the permanent funds. He reminded commissioners that Assemblies from 1833 through 1839 had commended them for astute investments. Only after the market went into an extended decline, Green noted, did the Assembly raise serious objections to the trustees' investment strategies. In estimating losses incurred by speculative investments, Green observed that as disastrous as they appeared, they would have been much greater had the trustees continued to operate on pre-1833 strategies. He reported that the trustees had disposed of some of the bank stock as urged by the General Assembly, but that they also took seriously the directive to do so only when it could be done "with advantage and safety." From the trustees' perspective, to sell additional stock would have greatly diminished the total value of the permanent fund. Since the 1842 General Assembly, Green noted that market prices had begun to rise, and stocks estimated to be worth $46,705 were now valued at $63,614.[14]

Finally, concerning transfer of endowment to Princeton Seminary, Green reported that the trustees had made all legal transferrals. Since donors bequeathed most of the seminary funds to the corporation in trust for the objects named, an unwarranted transfer would constitute a breach of trust. Replying to the charge that Princeton Seminary funds appeared to be better managed that those of the Assembly trustees, Green stated that the Princeton trustees had "next to no permanent funds to be wrecked." He noted that, according to their last report to the New Jersey legislature, Princeton Seminary had only $500 in permanent funds vested in Princeton bank stock. Concluding his report, Green asked the General Assembly to take measures to "remove the erroneous impressions, which the action of the last Assembly is calculated to make and perpetuate."[15]

The General Assembly's Standing Committee on Finance re-examined corporation and Assembly documents and reached several conclusions. First, it acknowledged that the General Assembly, not the corporation, was responsible for investment policies that led to a loss of capital of approximately $70,000. The General Assembly had initiated, encouraged, and endorsed efforts to increase the return on money invested in stocks and had accepted responsibility for the results. Second, it sustained the trustees' decision not to sell off all the western bank stock, concurring that losses could be reduced by waiting for the stock market to improve. "Though we regret the decision then made by the Trustees, we cannot pronounce it to have been unwise, when we consider the light under which they acted." The committee recommended a policy that the Presbyterian Church rapidly move its funds into government stock or into bonds and mortgages. Third, it agreed that the corporation acted responsibly when it refused to transfer funds to Princeton Seminary, agreeing that it would have been a breach of fiduciary responsibility to do so. Although the committee noted that the corporation could appeal to a secular court to secure a change in trusteeship, it concluded that there was no adequate reason for doing so.[16]

Even though vindicated by their peers, the trustees recognized that the General Assembly continued to recommend investment policies and to monitor their record keeping. In particular, it repeatedly urged the trustees to sell the remainder of their bank, insurance company, and turnpike stocks, although it left it "discretionary with the Trustees to act in this matter." In each instance the trustees informed the Assembly that they were continuing to hold the stocks in question until they reached a profitable selling price.[17] In the future, the corporation reported that it would adhere to the guidelines approved by the General Assembly and limit its portfolio to U.S. government stock, bonds, and mortgages.[18]

With the death of Ashbel Green in 1848, who had been president for more than a decade, the corporation lost its last member of the original group of trustees appointed in 1799. Ill health had confined him to his home except for a brief public appearance in 1846 on the floor of the General Assembly in Philadelphia. Although Green's conservatism in theology and economics had heavy impact on corporation policies, including its reluctance to accept more responsibility for denominational stewardship activities, his reputation for integrity and prudent conduct served the corporation well during some of its most difficult days.[19] Green's successor, William Neill, a clergyman who had served as president of Dickinson College and as secretary of the Presbyterian Board of Education, represented the same conservatism. A trustee since 1817 and seventy years old at the time of his election, Neill was highly regarded in denominational circles for his integrity and administrative acumen. During his ten-year tenure, he provided stability and continuity during turbulent times. He gradually disposed of the controversial bank stocks so that, by the time of his death in 1861, virtually all of the corporation's investment portfolio conformed to the standards recommended by the General Assembly.[20]

On several occasions during Neill's presidency, General Assembly committees charged that the corporation's accounting procedures failed to identify the source and the amount of interest attributed to individual accounts. As previously, the 1854 General Assembly directed the trustees to close the current ledgers and open a new set of books that maintained detailed accounts of each trust fund under the corporation's jurisdiction. While the trustees might blend trusts for investment purposes, they were instructed to note the percentage and amount of interest credited to each account.[21] In 1856 the General Assembly reported that the corporation books were in order with the various funds clearly distinguished and that investment policies conformed to those previously recommended by the standing committee on finance. After almost a quarter century of tension, annual financial reports became routine items.[22]

The Old School trustees received only scattered bequests between 1837 and 1870, most of which were amounts under $1,000 because of the depressed economy and the aggressiveness of the program boards. Mission causes predominated as the church moved westward. In 1838 the General Assembly recommended that missionaries be dispatched to the Republic of Texas. Shortly thereafter, the trustees received $200 to initiate a "Fund for the Conversion of Texas," but no subsequent donations to the cause were ever reported. For almost half a century the account languished, accumulating only a small amount of interest, until in 1886 the trustees turned the fund over to the Board of Foreign Missions "to be devoted to the purposes above mentioned" even though Texas had by then attained statehood.[23] Other small bequests included $500 for "the support of poor and pious young men for the gospel ministry under the care of the Presbytery of Cincinnati," $50 "for the general interests of religion in connection with the Presbyterian Church," and $100 to support superannuated ministers.[24] Typically, however, larger bequests directed that income be apportioned among various boards such as Education, Foreign Missions, and Domestic Missions, according to specific percentages or at the discretion of the General Assembly.[25]

Although designated for specific causes, most donations and bequests gave the trustees and the General Assembly latitude in dispensing funds. An exception was the Holland Trust that contained explicit doctrinal qualifications. A devise of $2,500 by Mary Holland in 1845 provided income for scholarships for indigent students at Princeton Seminary. In her will, however, Holland stipulated that if the following doctrines ceased to be taught at the seminary, the money was to go to the American Bible Society: "Doctrines as comprised in the Confession of Faith and Catechism of the Presbyterian Church in the United States such as the doctrine of the Trinity, the doctrine of universal and total depravity, the doctrine of election, the doctrine of the atonement, the doctrine of the imputation of the guilt of Adam's sin to all his posterity and the imputation of Christ's righteousness to all his people for their justification, the doctrine of human inability, the doctrine of the necessity of the influence of the Holy Spirit in the regeneration, conversion, and sanctification of sinners as these doctrines are understood and explained by the aforesaid Old School General Assembly."[26]

The trustees acquired new responsibilities when the General Assembly created the Fund For Disabled Ministers in 1852. The Assembly originally assigned the presbyteries and congregations the task of administering and promoting the cause of ministerial relief. Notices in church newspapers suggest that occasionally local congregations were attentive to their retired ministers and that some presbyteries negotiated small retirement settlements between clergy and congregational representatives before dissolving pastoral relationships. When Eli Cooley of Trenton, New Jersey, ended his pastorate, *The Presbyterian* noted that he retired "to abide in the midst of an affectionate people who cannot and will not forget that he has given to them the strength of his manhood, and the maturer wisdom of his advancing years."[27]

Other sources, however, indicated that many superannuated clergy spent their final years in poverty, unnoticed and unappreciated by the church-at-large.[28] Efforts at the presbyterial and congregational levels to cope with clerical poverty were largely ineffective. In 1849 the Presbyteries of Steubenville and Elizabethtown presented overtures to General Assembly requesting a national fund to care for the growing number of retired clergy, some of whom lacked the basic necessities of food and shelter. The Assembly authorized the creation of such a fund to be raised from annual collections from synods and presbyteries and approved the establishment of an endowment fund derived from special contributions and legacies as an additional source of income.[29] Initially administered by the Board of Publication, the General Assembly transferred the responsibility for receiving and distributing relief funds to the trustees in 1852. The corporation appointed President Neill and trustees Joseph H. Jones and Thomas Janeway as a committee of three to assume responsibility for administering the relief program.[30]

The Fund for Disabled Ministers held its first meeting in 1853 and appropriated funds totaling $675 to two widows and six ministers. The Fund originated during a period when board agencies were competing among themselves for congregational support and the General Assembly was scrutinizing its unorganized and often chaotic benevolence procedures. One minister complained that board representatives descended upon congregations like the frogs of Egypt and disrupted the routine of worship with their impassioned pleas for money. The Assembly appointed a Special Committee on Systematic Benevolence in 1853, but it produced no satisfactory solution.[31] In this context, the Fund for Disabled Ministers made its first report to the General Assembly in 1856, which triggered an extended debate that received front-page coverage in many denominational papers and reflected a social ambivalence about national welfare projects, especially those that relied wholly or partially on endowments and bequests. In an address to the Assembly, Ebenezer P. Rogers, chair of the Standing Committee on Ministerial Relief, criticized the denomination for inadequate financial support by noting that contributions to ministerial relief averaged less than seventy-five cents for every Old School congregation in the country. In response, the Assembly appointed a committee to draft a proposal for the creation of a permanent ministerial relief fund. When the committee reported the following day with a recommendation that relief funds be secured by assessing ministers 5 percent of their annual salary (1 percent over a five-year period) and by requiring congregations to make a single deposit of 20 percent of their ministers' salaries, commissioners engaged in a heated debate that extended over several days and ended inconclusively.[32]

Some opponents of the proposal claimed that the vast majority of ministers required no financial aid and the few who did were adequately cared for by their former congregations and families. Others argued that there was no need for a national relief fund because "A minister ought to preach as long as he is able to stand, and then lie down and die." One argument was that even if ministers had financial needs, they could never bear the public shame in revealing such dependency.[33] Another group opposed the fund because of the danger of mismanagement of such large sums of money and because of the potential abuse of power in the centralization of wealth. But the most prominent objection was that each generation should bear its own burdens and that the present generation had no obligation to provide for the future. James H. Thornwell, an educator from South Carolina, believed that "heroism, courage, and energy" are produced by economic suffering. Thornwell said that by providing economic resources for needy clergymen, the denomination would be contributing to the weakening of ministerial fortitude.[34]

In contrast, lay persons endorsed the proposal, applauding efforts to relieve the economic burdens of parish ministers either before or during retirement. They stressed that financial assistance should be viewed as a reward for service and not as a charitable handout and that without sustained financial support only the wealthy would choose the ministry for a profession. One elder used the precedent of government pensions for military personnel, "The government has provided for her old soldiers and the church should do the same for her aged soldiers of the cross."[35]

Following a year of study, a clergy and lay committee recommended that the proposal to tax clergy and congregations be dropped, and the Assembly of 1857 reaffirmed its previous decision to raise money for ministerial relief through annual offerings and contributions to a small endowment fund.[36] Despite the importance given to the issue of ministerial relief, governing bodies and local congregations did not support the idea of contributing to the Fund For Disabled Ministers. Initially fewer than one hundred congregations forwarded offerings, and many presbyteries failed to file an annual report to the General Assembly regarding efforts to promote the cause of ministerial relief within their bounds. During one year, total presbytery receipts amounted to $1,580, or an average of seventy-five cents from every congregation in the country. Two presbyteries, among the denomination's wealthiest, drew more money from the treasury than they contributed. For the Fund For Disabled Ministers to attain a foothold in the denomination's benevolence program, it required direction and leadership from its administrators, the trustees of the General Assembly.[37]

The appointment of Stephen Colwell as president of the trustees in 1861 following the death of William Neill marked the beginning of a new period for ministerial relief in the Old School Presbyterian denomination. A graduate of Jefferson College in Pennsylvania, Colwell practiced law in Ohio and Pennsylvania but changed professions at age thirty-six to become an iron manufacturer, first in New Jersey and later at Conshohocken on the Schuylkill near Philadelphia. His extensive civic activities included serving as trustee of the Universities of Pennsylvania and Princeton, a member of the Presbyterian Board of Education, and a charter member of the Union League of Philadelphia. A colorful and controversial figure who championed the cause of the working class and criticized both the federal government and organized religion for their lack of concern for the nation's poor, Colwell wrote prolifically on business ethics and had a large collection of books and pamphlets dealing with money and religious values which he bequeathed to the University of Pennsylvania. His *New Themes for the Protestant Clergy*, was issued in several editions and generated editorial response in prominent secular and religious periodicals. Colwell charged that both Roman Catholics and Protestants had neglected the religion of Jesus who went about helping the poor. "The poor must be sure of the disinterestedness of the teacher," wrote Colwell, "before they will receive his teachings."[38]

Colwell's influence concerning care for the poor was reflected in the trustee's annual report to the 1861 Old School General Assembly that called for deeper commitment to the Fund for Disabled Ministers. The report criticized the denomination for its lack of participation in the Fund, reiterated previous calls for annual collections in local churches, and requested separate reporting for contributions toward the relief fund in the General Assembly benevolence statistics. It also recommended that each presbytery appoint ministerial relief committees to encourage participation in the Fund. The General Assembly approved the report and endorsed the appointment of Joseph H. Jones as chairman and full-time promotional agent of the Fund, the first such position in American Presbyterian history. In his capacity as chairman, Jones visited synods and presbyteries, spoke in local churches, and corresponded with denominational leaders to promote participation.[39] The following year, the Assembly established a standing committee on the report of the Trustees and the Fund for Disabled Ministers, to be appointed by the moderator in connection with other standing committees.[40]

These efforts soon showed results. Despite the loss of southern constituents at the beginning of the Civil War, contributions to the Fund For Disabled Ministers increased dramatically. Between 1861 and 1869, annual receipts rose from approximately $1,500 to $37,196, and the number of contributing congregations increased from fifty in 1849 to more than a thousand in 1869.[41] The permanent endowment fund, which opened with a $13 dollar contribution in 1851, reached $77,551 in 1870.[42] Anticipating large contributions to the Fund for Disabled Ministers, in 1864 the trustees successfully petitioned the Pennsylvania legislature to raise the annual limit of permissible income from trusts and bequests from $10,000 to $50,000. The Old School General Assembly, however, rejected a proposal to appoint paid agents to solicit funds for ministerial relief, affirming that "support for that cause should be left to the zeal of its many friends, leaving it a voluntary agency."[43]

Following their expulsion in 1837, New School Presbyterians were by 1852 developing a network of denominational boards and agencies similar to those of their Old School counterparts. In 1855 the New School General Assembly also incorporated as the Presbyterian House with a board of ten trustees equally divided between ministers and laymen. Between 1855 and the consolidation of the Old School-New School corporations in 1885, three laymen served as president: John A. Brown (1855-1868), Samuel H. Perkins (1868-1874), and Samuel C. Perkins (1874-1885). During that time the board handled thirty-five trusts amounting in aggregate to $113,483.[44] Emulating the Old School Assembly, the New School Assembly in 1864 approved "The Ministerial Relief Fund" and entrusted the reception and disbursement of the fund to the trustees of the Presbyterian House. In the first year of operation, the Fund received $3,638 and made appropriations to two families for a total of $250. The overall denominational support of the Fund, however, was limited. In 1866, only 130 out of 1,147 churches contributed; subsequent gifts improved little. Between 1864 and 1870 the Fund collected and disbursed $96,610, and the permanent fund contained $34,750. With these resources, about 200 individuals received various levels of support.[45]

In the 1850s, with the impending outbreak of civil conflict, the constituencies of both Old and New School Presbyterians began to subdivide along sectional lines. When the New School General Assembly pressed the issue of slavery in 1853 and 1855, southern commissioners withdrew in 1857 and organized the United Synod of the Presbyterian Church in the United States of America. Fewer than five weeks after the bombardment of Fort Sumter on April 12, 1861, the Old School General Assembly met in Philadelphia, still formally united but on the verge of schism. After five days of heated debate, the General Assembly adopted resolutions supporting the Federal cause, and the southern commissioners withdrew to form what would become the Presbyterian Church in the United States (PCUS), a denomination of about 70,000 members.[46]

The new denomination was almost totally absorbed in supporting war-related activities that depleted both human and financial resources. When peace returned in 1865, Southern cities lay in ruin, currency was valueless, cotton crops were destroyed, and congregations were scattered and devoid of leadership. Nevertheless, southern Presbyterian leaders created a network of executive committees to implement missionary, educational, and benevolence activities. Sensitive to the danger of independent boards and agencies, they endorsed a policy that would appoint such executive committees on a year to year basis and limit their power. The General Assembly would have direct supervision and regulatory authority over them. Although the committees eventually acquired more status, operating in a similar manner to other denominational boards, the PCUS administrators resisted changing the nomenclature for nearly a century.[47]

Guided by the administrative philosophy of a strong General Assembly and ad interim executive committees, southern Presbyterians established only one incorporated body to serve the entire denomination. After several abortive efforts to obtain a charter, representatives of the General Assembly obtained permission from the state of North Carolina on February 19, 1866, to incorporate pending their formal organization in Charlotte and payment of a $100 organization fee. The charter specified that the incorporation was responsible directly to the General Assembly and that any executive committees or other agencies formed by the General Assembly were considered "branches of the corporation." Executive committees were granted ex officio representation on the board but possessed no legal power to hold or receive gifts, grants, and bequests. Because the trustees possessed no funds, a group of lay commissioners took up a collection among their peers to pay the organization fee required by the laws of North Carolina.[48]

Although the General Assembly approved the proposed charter in 1866, the trustees failed to hold their organizational meeting until May 15, 1868, because of inability to muster a quorum of five from their widely scattered membership. At their initial session, the trustees elected Thomas C. Perrin president and Jesse H. Lindsay secretary and treasurer, adopted bylaws, and approved a standard Form of Bequest for denominational use.[49] One of the first bequests received by the trustees came from Judge W. E. Kennedy of Columbia, Tennessee, who left $10,000 to be divided among the American Bible Society, American Tract Society, American Colonization Society, and the various General Assembly executive committees. In his will, Kennedy spelled out precisely which General Assembly he had in mind: "I mean the Old School Presbyterian Church in the South, and should any part thereof reunite with the Northern Church, I mean the part that shall remain as a separate Body in the South."[50]

The Kennedy bequest precipitated a debate between the trustees and executive committee secretaries regarding the dispensing of funds during the interval between General Assemblies. Executive committee secretaries argued that they were de facto the General Assembly when it was not in session and therefore should have immediate access to designated gifts and bequests. The trustees on the other hand insisted that they were obligated to make no application of funds until directed to do so by the General Assembly at its annual meeting. In order neither to hinder the work of the executive committees nor to render the trustees powerless, a committee appointed by the General Assembly worked out a compromise policy that satisfied both parties in the dispute. Undesignated gifts would be retained until the next meeting of the General Assembly. Designated gifts to executive committees would be disbursed immediately unless they exceeded $3,000, in which case the trustees would pay only interest until the next meeting of the General Assembly.[51]

During the remainder of the nineteenth century, General Assembly trustees and executive committee secretaries enjoyed amicable relationships. Gradually the executive committees secured permission from the General Assembly to incorporate and subsequently established autonomous development programs similar to those of their northern counterparts. Meanwhile, the General Assembly trustees maintained a low profile in Charlotte under the volunteer leadership of laymen Thomas Perrin (1866-1873), James H. Hemphill (1873-1889), E. Nye Hutchison (1889-1908), and George E. Wilson (1908-1920). Some years no monies were received and in others the amount minuscule. In 1875, for example, the treasurer reported that he had received no money since his last report and that the treasury contained $84.07. The only sizable legacies were those of William Hugh and Margaret Guthrie of Tinkling Springs Presbyterian Church in Augusta, Georgia, who in 1889 designed approximately $20,000 to be used for domestic and overseas missions.[52] By the end of the century, the trustees reported only $13,105.04 in permanent funds, and as late as 1920 their investment policy consisted solely of lending money on real estate located in Mecklenburg County.[53] The Charlotte corporation would play a minor role in mission program funding until the second decade of the twentieth century when it achieved Foundation status and began to advertise and solicit funds.

NOTES

1. For background on the Old School-New School division, see George M. Marsden, *The Evangelical Mind and the New School Presbyterian Experience* (New Haven and London, 1970), 59-88.

2. Smylie, *A Brief History of the Presbyterians*, 95-97.

3. Ibid., 97-98.

4. *GAMPCUSA[OS]*, 1838:42-43. When the General Assembly subsequently instructed the trustees to borrow money on the security of "funds held by the board" to cover expenses for the pending suit, trustee John Kane secured an amendment to read "funds of the General Assembly" thus clarifying the ultimate ownership of the financial resources. Minutes of the PCUSA[OS] Trustees, March 15, 1839.

5. *GAMPCUSA[OS]*, 1839:95, and Trustee Minutes (PCUSA[OS]), May 31, 1839. In another interdenominational suit, the Old School General Assembly in 1838 ordered the trustees to pay $1,401.17, a judgment obtained by the Associate Reformed Church against the Trustees of Princeton Seminary. Initially the trustees declined but later acquiesced. Trustee Minutes (PCUSA[OS]), September 11 and 17, 1838.

6. For an economic history of the period, see Gilbert C. Fite and Jim E. Reese, *An Economic History of the United States*, 2d ed. (New York, 1969), 133-49.

7. *GAMPCUSA[OS]*, 1837:661-64.

8. *GAMPCUSA[OS]*, 1840:138.

9. Trustee Minutes (PCUSA[OS]), December 17, 1839.

10. Trustee Minutes (PCUSA[OS]), January 8, 1840.

11. *GAMPCUSA [OS]*, 1840:139.

12. *GAMPCUSA[OS]*, 1841:184-85.

13. *GAMPCUSA[OS]*, 1842:241-42.

14. *GAMPCUSA[OS)*, 1843:231-32.

15. *GAMPCUSA[OS]*, 1843:231-34.

16. *GAMPCUSA[OS]*, 1843:225-28.

17. *GAMPCUSA[OS]*, 1845:405; 1848:23; 1849:80.

18. Trustee Minutes (PCUSA[OS]), May 12, 1846. The incorporated boards also adhered to the investment guidelines established by the General Assembly.

19. *GAMPCUSA[OS]*, 1848:20-22.

20. The *Encyclopedia of Presbyterian History*, s.v. William Neill.

21. *GAMPCUSA[OS]*, 1852:228-29; 1854:337. At the same time, the corporation successfully combined disparate Princeton Seminary endowments into three professorship so that the funds could be invested more efficiently. Although the loss of capital in the

seminary account was never fully restored, the funds became more productive as the century progressed.

22. *GAMPCUSA[OS]*, 1856:432. As late as 1861, however, a standing committee reported that the Corporation was still carrying a few worthless stock on the books and should discontinue doing so. *GAMPCUSA[OS]*, 1861:160.

23. Trustee Minutes (PCUSA[OS]), February 8, 1887. No indication of its final disposition has been discovered by this author.

24. Trustee Minutes (PCUSA[OS]), May 26, 1843, and May 3, 1860.

25. Trustee Minutes (PCUSA[OS]), June 16, 1868.

26. Trustee Minutes (PCUSA[OS]), June 18, 1845. When reviewing the status of endowment funds in 1905, legal counsel informed the trustees that once the seminary ceased to teach these doctrines, the trustees could no longer administer the fund. Trustee Minutes (PCUSA[OS]), November 9, 1905.

27. *The Presbyterian*, 25 July 1857:116.

28. In 1842 several Old School presbyteries requested that the General Assembly formulate a uniform policy regarding the care of elderly and infirm clergymen and their families. In their requests, the presbyteries cited numerous examples of clerical poverty within their bounds. *GAMPCUSA[OS]*, 1842:217.

29. *GAMPCUSA[OS]*, 1849:254.

30. Trustee Minutes (PCUSA[OS]), November 4, 1852.

31. Ernest Trice Thompson, *Presbyterians in the South*, 3 vols. (Richmond, Va., 1963), I:524-28.

32. *GAMPCUSA[OS]*, 1856:531, and *The Presbyterian*, 31 May 1856:80.

33. *The Presbyterian*, 31 May 1856:85-86.

34. *The Presbyterian*, 31 May 1856:86.

35. Ibid.

36. *GAMPCUSA[OS]*, 1857:218.

37. *GAMPCUSA[OS]*, 1856:455. Statistics for 1857-1861 were not published in the *Minutes of the General Assembly* and do not appear in the trustees' minutes.

38. Stephen Colwell, *New Themes for Protestant Clergy: Creeds without charity, Theology without humanity, and Protestantism without Christianity*, 2d ed. (Philadelphia, 1853), 222. For information on the life of Colwell, see Henry C. Carey, *A Memoir of Stephen Colwell read before the American Philosophical Society* (Philadelphia, 1871), 1-10, and "Stephen Colwell," *The Presbyterian*, 28 January 1871:2. Colwell also established a chair of Christian Ethics at Princeton Theological Seminary.

39. *GAMPCUSA[OS]*, 1861:142-43.

40. *GAMPCUSA[OS]*, 1862:232. Jones resisted efforts to create a separate Board of Ministerial Relief with a full professional staff. "Every instrumentality for collecting, receiving and disbursing this money is furnished by the Trustees, who make an annual report to the Assembly." *GAMPCUSA[OS]*, 1863, Appendix:106.

41. *GAMPCUSA[OS]*, 1862:261, and 1869:497.

42. *An Historical Sketch of the Presbyterian Board of Ministerial Relief* (Cincinnati, Ohio, 1888), 12-13.

43. *GAMPCUSA[OS]*, 1864:289; 1865:641.

44. *Manual of the Trustees of the General Assembly of the Presbyterian Church in the United States of America* (Philadelphia, 1908), 31-35. The charter New School trustees were Albert Barnes, Thomas Brainerd, Henry Darling, and David H. Ribble. To this board by successive election and in order of their election between 1855-1870 were clergymen

George Chandler, John Patton, Thomas J. Shepherd, John Jenkins, Ezra E. Adams, Daniel March, William T. Eva, David A. Cunningham, Alexander Reed, Villeroy D. Reed, Charles A. Dickey, Thomas L. Janeway, and William Brown, and laymen William Darling, Charles S. Wurts, Alexander Whilldin, William E. Tenbrook, Samuel C. Perkins, John B. Gest, William G. Crowell, Charles M. Lukens, T. Charlton Henry, George Junkin, and Enoch Taylor.

45. *GAMPCUSA[NS]*, 1864:295-98; 1865:339. For additional information, see *An Historical Sketch of the Presbyterian Board of Ministerial Relief,* 8-10.

46. Loetscher, *A Brief History of Presbyterians,* 104-06

47. For a survey of the history of the Southern Presbyterian Church, see Thompson, *Presbyterians in the South.*

48. *Minutes of the General Assembly of the Presbyterian Church in the United States,* 1866:24-25. Hereafter, *GAMPCUS.* In 1861 the General Assembly approved a proposed charter and appointed a committee to seek incorporation in one or more of the Confederate States. Impeded by war-time conditions, the committee was unable to complete its assignment until 1863 when it reported to the General Assembly that it had formed a board of trustees under an Act of Incorporation granted by the Tennessee State Legislature. The board convened at a meeting held in Columbia, South Carolina, on May 21, 1863, and elected Thomas C. Perrin as president. General Assembly counsel deemed the terms of incorporation to be inadequate and recommended that incorporation be sought in North Carolina. Even though trustees obtained a new charter in 1864, additional complications arose when the General Assembly of 1865 changed the name of the denomination to the Presbyterian Church in the United States. As a result of these events, legal counsel advised that the Assembly reapply to North Carolina for a new charter. The charter trustees were Thomas C. Perrin, B. M. Palmer, Samuel McCorkle, Joseph H. Wilson, Jesse H. Lindsay, Robert Adger, J. A. Ansley, J. A. Crawford, James B. Walker, J. A. Inglis, John Whiting, R. M. Patton, George Howe, J. L. Kirkpatrick, and William L. Mitchell. See *GAMPCUS,* 1861:31-33; 1862:13; 1863:131-33; and 1864:247.

49. *GAMPCUS,* 1868:270, 298. A native of Abbeville, South Carolina, Perrin studied law and was admitted to the bar in 1828. In 1853 he became president of the Greenville and Columbia Railroad, serving in that capacity until 1866. For many years a member of the state legislature, Perrin presided over the first mass meeting held to consider the question of secession and was the first to sign the roll of the Ordinance of Secession. An elder in the Upper Long Cane Presbyterian Church, Perrin took great interest in the American Bible Society and other benevolent causes. See "The Late Honorable Thomas C. Perrin," *The Southern Presbyterian,* 12 May 1878: 2.

50. Minutes of the Trustees of the General Assembly of the Presbyterian Church in the United States, May 9, 1872. Department of History Archives, Montreat, N.C. Hereafter Trustee Minutes (PCUS).

51. *GAMPCUS,* 1873:320-22.

52. Trustee Minutes (PCUS), May 4, 1876; July 15, 1889; and April 24, 1890.

53. Trustee Minutes (PCUS), April 25, 1901, and April 29, 1920.

4

Reunited Corporations

Two bodies, bearing the same name, adopting the same Constitution, and claiming the same Corporate rights, cannot be justified by any but the most imperative reasons in maintaining separate and, in some respects, rival organizations. It is both just and proper that a Reunion should be effected by the two churches on equal terms.—*The Proposed Terms of Reunion Between the Two Branches of the Presbyterian Church in the United States of America, 1868*

The Civil War precipitated the formation of a separate and distinct Presbyterian religious tradition in the southern states and served as a catalyst for the reunion of Old and New School denominations in the northern states. A common patriotism for the Federal cause and a gradual reconciliation of theological and organizational differences enabled the two parties to initiate reunion conversations as the civil conflict drew to a close. In 1864, the retiring New School moderator, Henry Boynton Smith, urged commissioners to work towards ecclesiastical unity just as they had done for national unity. "Our nation is now vindicating its unity by the costliest sacrifices. Let the church of Christ heed the lesson, scrutinize the disease and inquire for the remedy."[1] Favorable responses from Old School officials led to five years of intense negotiations that culminated in a merger, based on the Westminster Standards "pure and simple." This ended a schism that dated back to 1837. The reunited church retained the name it had held before the separation, the Presbyterian Church in the United States of America.[2]

This reunion coincided with the beginning of a period of remarkable economic growth and significant cultural change in the United States. In the years between the end of the Civil War and the end of World War I, the country was transformed from a producer of basic agricultural commodities to becoming the leading manufacturing nation of the world. The nation's wealth multiplied at a faster rate than ever before in its history, with per capita income reaching its highest level. Furthermore, between 1870 and 1920 more than twenty-six million immigrants, with their diverse religious and cultural traditions, arrived in the United States. Population in the United States soared from forty million in 1870 to nearly 106 million in 1920 and by the turn of the century the majority of Americans were living in urban rather than rural environments.[3]

Responding to this environment, the reunited church launched an extensive missionary enterprise through a network of national boards and agencies, including for the first time national, regional, and local organizations for women. Its avowed goal was to "Christianize the whole country." To finance this undertaking, the General Assembly inaugurated a program of stewardship and systematic benevolence that set the standard for other Protestant denominations in the nineteenth century.[4] The General Assembly's Committee on Stewardship and Systematic Benevolence held its first meeting in 1871 and proposed standards for a unified budget which would provide the Board of Home Missions, the Board of Foreign Missions, and six other agencies a specified percentage of benevolence giving. Through the Board of Publication, the committee disseminated promotional materials pertaining to stewardship to congregations throughout the denomination.[5]

Despite sweeping programmatic changes, reunion had minimal impact on the structure and operating policies of the General Assembly Trustees. They functioned as one corporation, much as they had as two separate bodies during the Old School-New School schism. According to legal counsel consulted during the reunion process, bequests and gifts designated for the New School or Old School General Assemblies would not be jeopardized by the merger of the two branches. Citing precedents set by previous court decisions, corporation lawyers concluded that because there was no material difference in respect to faith or form of government between the new denomination and its predecessors, the will of the donors could be fully honored in the new structure.[6] To integrate New School and Old School representation on the Board of Trustees, the General Assembly in 1870 replaced six former Old School appointees with a corresponding number of former New School trustees. While expressing regret over the loss of six qualified members, the Assembly noted that "this course appeared least open to objection."[7]

Following the death of Stephen Colwell in 1871, the trustees selected as president James A. Bayard, a lawyer and former United States Senator, who had been a trustee since 1833 and had served for a number of years as corresponding secretary. As a United States Senator (1851-64), Bayard defended the Union cause and supported Lincoln and the Republican Party during the Civil War, but he opposed most of the anti-slavery measures enacted between 1861-64, including the emancipation of the District of Columbia. After resigning from the Senate in 1864, Bayard returned to the Senate and to the Democratic Party in 1867 following the death of his successor. He subsequently saw his son, Thomas F. Bayard, take his seat in the Senate. At age seventy-two and in declining health, Bayard had only a brief tenure as president of the trustees (1871-74) before he resigned and retired from public life.[8]

Bayard's successor, another veteran Old School trustee, George Sharswood, served as president for the next decade. Admitted to the bar in 1831, Sharswood began a distinguished career that included a term in the Pennsylvania legislature and extended service on the Pennsylvania Supreme Court, culminating in an appointment to Chief Justice. As an Associate Justice he wrote a negative opinion in 1873 on woman suffrage based on the argument that historic practice in the Commonwealth of Pennsylvania indicated that women were never intended to possess the elective franchise. As a law professor at the University of Pennsylvania, Sharswood wrote a number of books and articles on legal subjects including the famous *Sharswood's Blackstone's Commentaries* published in 1859. An active churchman, Sharswood was ordained an elder in the Tabernacle Presbyterian Church of Philadelphia in 1856 and also served as a trustee and director of Princeton Theological Seminary.[9]

The merger of the Old and New School corporations proved more formidable than initially envisioned by General Assembly counsel. The trustees presented a revised charter for approval to the General Assembly in 1874 accompanied by testimony from their legal advisors that "nothing stood in the way of implementation."[10] The following year, however, Sharswood reported to the General Assembly that the Governor of Pennsylvania had vetoed the proposed charter on the grounds that his legal advisors deemed it to be in conflict with one of the articles of the new denominational *Constitution*.[11] Because of legal obstacles not referred to in official records or to procrastination, the trustees did not resolve the legal impasse until 1885 when they successfully applied to the Commonwealth of Pennsylvania for a charter that consolidated the Trustees of the Presbyterian House (New School) with the Trustees of the General Assembly (Old School). This allowed the trust funds of both former denominations to be administered by the one corporation.[12]

Under Sharswood, the trustees continued to be a small corporation primarily of volunteers who resided in Philadelphia and surrounding areas. In contrast to other denominational boards and agencies that had professional staffs and regional field representatives, the trustees had only two paid part-time employees, a treasurer and a recording secretary, who received annual salaries of $1,000 and $150 respectively.[13] Their office consisted of a sparsely furnished room provided rent-free by the Presbyterian Board of Education in its Philadelphia headquarters and meager supplies. In 1876 when the treasurer reported that the box containing the Board's valuable papers had become too small, the trustees "resolved that a larger box be procured."[14] On another occasion, the trustees received a donation of a fire-proof safe and a desk for the treasurer, gifts that they acknowledged with grateful thanks. Two years later, however, because "they had no use for it at this time," they gave the safe to the Board of Ministerial Relief.[15]

The minutes of the trustees indicated their passivity in that they suggest that occasionally substantial sums of money languished in low interest bearing bank accounts rather than being invested in more productive securities or mortgages. One example of casual administration was a legacy of $2,000 given by Jesse M. Ash, the income from which was to be paid to her daughter Caroline until the latter's demise, that accumulated income for twenty-five years. When questioned about the account, the treasurer replied, "Nobody seems to know Caroline M. Ash, and no one knows whether she is dead or alive."[16]

Although the trustees themselves seemed not inclined to widen their scope of activities, the General Assembly in 1870 assigned them the task of managing and directing "The Relief Fund for Disabled Ministers and the Widows and Orphans of Deceased Ministers," created by combining the assets of the former Old School and New School relief programs. At this time, the trustees annually elected a secretary, treasurer, and a committee of four who were empowered to receive and dispense funds. Previous Old School and New School relief fund administrators, George Hale and Charles Brown, were retained as a symbol of unity between the former rivals. Ordinarily the committee met once a month to hear a financial report and to identify recipients of grants. During its first year, using interest from the permanent endowment fund of $85,000 and offerings from presbyteries, congregations, and individuals, the Fund disbursed $67,371 to 108 ministers, 144 widows, and orphans of 15 families. The Relief Fund inherited it predecessors' problems, however, to insufficient endowment income and erratic free will offerings.[17]

Concerned about the inefficiency of multiple financial agencies, the 1874 General Assembly appointed a special committee to formulate procedures that would harmonize the various boards and agencies then engaged in home mission activities. The committee recommended that the General Assembly authorize the creation of a central treasurer for the

Board of Education, the Relief Fund, and the Trustees of the General Assembly. According to this proposal, the trustees of the General Assembly would elect the treasurer and be responsible for overseeing the performance of his duties.[18] When commissioners discussed the proposal, the trustees objected, insisting that the Board of Education and the General Assembly Trustees were "two separate and distinct" corporations and that the present treasurer of the trustees was already overburdened and underpaid. Trustee Hale argued on the floor of General Assembly that creating a central treasury would "give a blow to the cause of benevolence which it has never felt since the foundation of the church." Hale especially opposed the merger of Education and Relief, saying the two causes differed so greatly that the incentives to contribute to one were not the same as to the other.[19] The opposition ultimately prevailed; although the General Assembly made minor adjustments to board structures, it abandoned the concept of a central treasury.[20]

Following their successful resistance to yoking the Relief Fund with the Board of Education, Hale and Brown rallied support for the creation of an independent Board of Ministerial Relief. Arguing that the Relief Fund would never be able to effectively serve needy ministers and their families until it acquired a status equal to that of other denominational boards and agencies, the two men traveled widely and corresponded extensively to convey their message. After lengthy discussion and debate, the 1876 General Assembly approved an overture that the Relief Fund "be clothed with the dignity of a separate Board of the Church, with incorporated power." Villeroy D. Reed, a member of the General Assembly in 1849 when the Fund began, was elected president, Hale served as corresponding secretary, and Brown became treasurer and recording clerk.[21] Although the General Assembly Trustees continued to receive and manage the permanent endowment monies designated for ministerial relief, their programmatic responsibilities ceased.[22]

The discussions about the Relief Fund took place during the Panic of 1873, precipitated by the failure of Jay Cooke and Company of Philadelphia and New York, which had invested heavily in railroads and overextended its debt capacity. The resulting economic panic ushered in a decade of financial and industrial depression and impacted negatively on investment possibilities. One of the worst years, 1878, saw the failure of ten thousand firms with total liabilities of $234 million.[23] Unlike the Panic of 1837, however, when trustees were heavily invested in western banks and canal and railroad companies, the Panic of 1873 had a less severe impact on the trustees' permanent funds.[24] Nevertheless, five years later at the height of the depression, the General Assembly's Standing Committee on Finance expressed concern regarding the "shrinkage of investments" and reported that they could not ascertain from the treasurer's records the precise "character, value, and worth" of all the funds. In response, the 1878 General Assembly appointed a committee of five to study the problem and to report the following year.[25] After a careful examination of the endowment funds and investment policies, the committee concluded that despite the unfavorable financial climate, the trustees were satisfactorily performing their duties. An analysis of the performance of investments indicated that interest rates varied between six and seven percent and that dividends ranged between four and eight percent. The only questionable securities in the trustees' portfolio antedated the reunion, and, in the opinion of the investigating committee, could not be attributed to the present board personnel.[26]

To eliminate one category of investments, the Board established a policy of not investing funds held by the trustees in loans to or secured upon any church property. Proponents of this policy argued that because the trustees were agents of the General Assembly, they could not hold property for individual congregations. Beyond this legal principle lay practical considerations. When churches could not make payments on a mortgage, the trustees found it virtually impossible to initiate foreclosure procedures. For example, the treasurer of North Tenth Street Church in Philadelphia informed the trustees that it would be "injurious to the church" if they were compelled to pay $2,000 on a delinquent note, and the trustees decided not to press the matter.[27] Despite this new policy, trustees occasionally approved congregational loans with notations that they were "exceptional cases" and not to be taken as precedents.[28]

During the last two decades of the nineteenth century, the trustees were led by George Junkin, Jr., one of the most influential laymen in the Presbyterian Church. A child of the manse, Junkin grew up in the educational environments of Miami University in Ohio and Lafayette College in Pennsylvania where his father was president. He graduated from Miami University in 1842 at the age of fifteen and returned to Pennsylvania where he studied law under George Madison Porter and Samuel H. Perkins. Admitted to the bar at age twenty-one, Junkin practiced law until his retirement. During most of his adult life, Junkin attended the Tenth Presbyterian Church in Philadelphia where he served as ruling elder, superintendent of the Sunday School, and choir member. Beyond service to his local church, Junkin provided legal advice and counsel to other congregations and denominations, held memberships on the Board of Ministerial Relief, the Board of Trustees of Lafayette College and Princeton Seminary, and served as president of the Executive Commission of the Alliance of Reformed Churches.[29]

When Junkin assumed office in 1883, the trustees reported assets of

$425,000 and income generated during the previous year of $22,127. Despite more than a decade of depressed economic conditions, the trustees had safeguarded their capital funds and had experienced a modest growth.[30] As the denomination continued to emphasize stewardship and to expand its missionary and educational programs, future prospects looked promising. During his first year in office, however, Junkin discovered that treasurer Eugene G. Woodward had for a number of years been embezzling money from several accounts in order to cover personal debts, including $10,000 from the Relief Fund. Although corporation bylaws specified that trustee treasurers were to be bonded, Woodward not only was not bonded but the fact had gone unnoticed by Junkin's predecessor. Woodward signed a promissory note to repay the deficiency with interest but records indicate that he never restored the lost funds. Through Junkin's efforts, however, donations were obtained from trustees and other Philadelphia churchmen to offset the loss. After consulting legal counsel, the trustees decided not to prosecute Woodward, but they instituted new bonding procedures to ensure that the incumbent and subsequent treasurers would automatically be covered.[31]

Junkin's decisive response to the Woodward situation reassured General Assembly commissioners that he had things well in hand, and it enabled the trustees to attend to their primary task of managing endowment funds. The Boudinot Book Fund continued to support the maintenance of congregational libraries by providing small sums to purchase religious reading materials. During the first half of the century, trustees made distributions primarily to congregations in the northeast and mid-west. By the 1880s, however, the funds were going to congregations coast to coast. In almost any given year, church people in states such as Oregon, Oklahoma, South Dakota, Louisiana, California, Nebraska, Florida, Tennessee, Washington, Illinois, Missouri, Kansas, and Colorado benefitted from Elias Boudinot's interest in religious education.[32]

The Boudinot Mission Fund provided support for urban ministries to the poor and homeless in Philadelphia and New York. The trustees periodically appointed committees to visit the designated ministries to ascertain that the funds were being properly utilized.[33] In 1878 the trustees voted to pay a semiannual salary of $75 to Alexander Hebreton to hold religious services in the Magdalen Society, the Blockley Almshouse, and the Rosine Reformatory Home in Philadelphia.[34] His successor, Andrew McIlvain, added hospital visitation and ministries to immigrant Jews. In 1888 he reported to the trustees that he had visited the Philadelphia Home for the Incurables to "minister the consolations of religion to the sick and dying where I could have access, and have endeavored to lead the easing into the way of rectitude and peace where opportunity offered."[35] McIlvain also distributed literature for the Philadelphia Tract Mission Society in an effort to sustain a mission among the Jews in southeastern Philadelphia and worked with the Mission of the Covenant to Israel on Lombard Street.[36] In New York City, Boudinot funds and contributions from the Fifth Avenue Presbyterian Church supported the salary of a chaplain, S. G. Law, who visited men incarcerated in Tombs Prison. Law was a Presbyterian as were a majority of members of the prison executive board.[37]

The Boudinot Mission Fund continued to be a source of income for social ministries in Philadelphia and New York during the first two decades of the twentieth century. Evangelism featured prominently in all forms of ministry. In 1908 a Boudinot missionary reported that he had "ministered to men and women of all classes, faiths, and nationalities, [in Philadelphia] many of whom had not been in a church for years, and many others unfamiliar with the fundamental truths of Christianity," and that he had conducted magic lantern services attended by "roughs of many sorts" including Jews and Catholics.[38] Because the annual interest from the Boudinot Fund amounted to less than $100, the trustees decided in 1916 to permit the income to accumulate so that the principal might eventually be adequate to employ a missionary. Two years later, however, they reversed that policy and gave the annual income from the Boudinot Mission Fund to the Presbytery of Philadelphia to be used in connection with a cooperative ministry to residents of the local almshouse.[39]

In addition to managing existing endowment funds, trustees received gifts and bequests and distributed them to various boards and agencies as requested by donors or the General Assembly. Some years the trustees received no contributions and in other years the income amounted to less than $1,000.[40] Although the funds were spread among a wide variety of educational and missionary endeavors, during the late nineteenth and early twentieth centuries they were most frequently directed to the causes of ministerial relief and African American missions.[41]

The newly formed Board of Ministerial Relief embarked on a vigorous publicity campaign in the 1880s and 1890s to highlight the plight of superannuated ministers and their families. In addition to providing annual cash payments, the Board promoted the establishment of retirement homes in which retired clergy and their spouses could live comfortably surrounded by co-workers and friends. Much of this was generated by George Junkin who had served for many years as a trustee on the Board of Ministerial Relief and knew first hand about ministerial poverty in the United States. Calls for contributions generated numerous small and several substantial gifts and bequests. By 1900 the trustees had $325,000 of relief funds in their care and were distributing approximately

$15,000 annually to the Board of Ministerial Relief.[42]

Contributions to African American educational institutions and congregations constituted a significant percentage of funds managed by the trustees of the General Assembly between 1870 and 1910. The reunited church expanded missionary work among African Americans that had begun on a smaller scale at the end of the Civil War. A committee on Freedmen based in Pittsburgh was incorporated in 1882 as the Board of Missions for Freedmen in order to facilitate ownership of property and the handling of bequests. The new board encouraged the organization of African American congregations and emphasized the importance of recruiting, educating and training ministers and teachers and placing them in leadership positions. Numerous day schools and institutions of higher learning such as Lincoln University, Johnson C. Smith University, and Barber-Scotia College provided educational opportunities for African American Presbyterians who were denied access to state institutions.[43]

Trustees began to receive gifts and bequests designated for African American ministries shortly after the Board of Freedmen was established in 1882. The earliest were in the $500-$3,000 range but several contributions of $10,000 were received in 1884, 1888, and 1894.[44] The most substantial bequest came from the estate of Phineas M. Barber, a Presbyterian layman and Philadelphia merchant who died in 1891. Referred to in a local history as an "active, energetic, and progressive man," Barber operated a distillery in Lycoming County but razed the structure in 1869 and erected a lumber mill that manufactured sashes, doors, blinds and related building materials. Early in his career Barber had been a school teacher and recognized the importance of education in elevating the social and economic status of minorities. Barber left the bulk of his estate to be used "for the erection of churches and maintaining of needy ministers of the Presbyterian congregations of colored people in the United States of America, as seems best in the judgement of the General Assembly."[45] The Barber Fund eventually totaled nearly $300,000 and was divided between the Board of Freedmen and the Board of Home Missions for educational and congregational scholarships and financial assistance.[46]

The trustees administered other funds that supported African American educational endeavors. Maryville College, which had previously accepted African American students, was compelled by state law in 1901 to bar them from attending classes. The following year the college requested the General Assembly trustees to accept a trust of $25,000, the income from which was to be used for "promoting the education of colored youth" or "colored men entering the Presbyterian ministry." The trustees accepted the money after receiving assurances from legal counsel that there were no constitutional barriers to such an arrangement.[47] In 1907 the trustees accepted a trust from Ira P. Wallace to be administered for the Board of Freedmen and known as the Bible Scholarship Fund. Designated for students in schools and colleges under the auspices of the Board of Freedmen, the Fund provided scholarships for men and women who pledged to read the authorized Bible (King James) or an accepted version from beginning to end once a year for as many years as they were receiving financial aid.[48]

Despite an economic depression during the 1890s, the trustees were able to report modest growth in the accumulation of endowment funds as the century ended. In 1896 treasurer Frank K. Hipple informed the General Assembly that the Board of Trustees were managing investments aggregating approximately $700,000 at a cost of only $1,713.00. "For those familiar with financial affairs," Hipple commented, "these facts speak volumes as to the skill and fidelity of the Trustees.[49] By 1900 endowment funds totaled $867,990 and were generating $40,758 for Presbyterian boards and agencies. Noting that oversight of such a large sum of money called for "moral faculties of a high grade," the Standing Committee on Finance congratulated the trustees on the fidelity and sagacity with which they conducted their responsibilities.[50]

As the new century began, president George Junkin was nearing the end of a long and distinguished career as churchman and jurist. Plagued by poor health and a debilitating hearing loss, Junkin offered his resignation in 1901 but the board refused to accept it. The following year, however, at Junkin's insistence, his request was honored and a new president, Samuel C. Perkins, assumed leadership of the board.[51] A Yale undergraduate and recipient of a law degree from the University of Pennsylvania, Perkins was admitted to the bar in 1851 and entered his father's law firm where he attained success in copyright cases. Active in Philadelphia civic affairs, Perkins was president of the Public Building Commission, one of the first directors of Girard College, and a leading official of the Masonic Order. He joined First Presbyterian Church at an early age and later served as a trustee and a ruling elder in that local congregation. Perkins served as a member of the Presbyterian Board of Publication and as manager of the American Sunday School Union. Referred to by his peers as "one of the most deservedly prominent men of Philadelphia," Perkins died in 1903 after only three years in office.[52]

During Perkin's brief tenure the board revised its investment policies in response to the economic growth and expansion that characterized the United States in the early decades of the twentieth century. Since the Panic of 1837, trustees had been mandated by the General Assembly to invest only in real estate mortgages and government bonds, and they had meticulously adhered to those investment directives. In 1901, however, the finance committee reported that good real estate mortgages were not readily available and that their returns did not compare to the high premiums of national, state, and city bonds. The committee wanted to know if the limitations placed on investments by the General Assembly made it impossible for them to modify the investment portfolio.[53] To respond, the trustees sought legal counsel from Charles B. Matthews, a member of the board and a highly regarded Philadelphia lawyer. In a carefully crafted written opinion, Matthews advised that so long as the trustees invested only in securities sanctioned by the Commonwealth of Pennsylvania and operated under the "prudent man" principle, they could change their by-laws without the consent and approval of the General Assembly. Matthews noted, however, that the trustees were still bound to obey all instructions regarding investments communicated to them in writing by the Stated Clerk which the General Assembly might subsequently give. Accordingly, the trustees in 1902 modified their investment policy statement to include "loans and securities of the United States and of any state, county, or city that had not within five years previously defaulted in payment of interest on its loans."[54]

Perkins was succeeded as president by John H. Converse (1840-1910), president of the Baldwin Locomotive Works in Philadelphia, at that time the world's largest manufacturer of steam locomotives. The son of a Congregational minister, Converse embraced an evangelical piety that shaped his personal life and public career. Graduating from the University of Vermont in 1861, Converse rose through the ranks of various railroad companies to become director of operations and president of the Baldwin Locomotive Works. A noted philanthropist, Converse supported various Presbyterian colleges and academies as well as mission schools and hospitals at home and abroad. After hearing a stirring address by evangelist Dwight L. Moody in 1898, Converse proposed that the Presbyterian General Assembly undertake a world-wide evangelistic crusade. The Assembly approved the venture and appointed him chairman. For a number of years Converse bore the entire cost of the endeavor ($100,000 annually) and prior to his death in 1910 created a trust fund of $200,000 to continue the work in perpetuity. An elder in the Bryn Mawr Presbyterian Church, Converse taught an adult Sunday School class for more than thirty years and served as a director of the Presbyterian Historical Society, a trustee of Princeton Theological Seminary, and a member of the Presbyterian Board of Publication.[55]

Under Converse, the first businessman to serve as president since the early nineteenth century, the General Assembly trustees modified their financial operations to conform more closely to the patterns of modern secular corporations. In 1904 they employed legal counsel, paying two lawyers a combined annual salary of $500. The lawyers were to receive extra remuneration for any court proceedings that "unduly exact[ed] the time of the counsel."[56] A professional stenographer was hired in 1908 to transcribe proceedings and minutes of meetings were typed rather than being entered in longhand.[57] Encouraged by the growth of philanthropic activity championed by industrial barons such as Andrew Carnegie, Cyrus McCormick, and John D. Rockefeller, and anticipating significant contributions from wealthy Presbyterians, the trustees in 1909 requested the approval from the Commonwealth of Pennsylvania to raise the annual limit of gifts and bequests from $50,000 to $250,000.[58] Concurrent with these changes, the trustees successfully implemented the revised investment policies. By 1910 they boasted a diversified portfolio consisting of mortgage loans, municipal, state, federal, and railroad bonds. Endowment funds topped the million mark for the first time in history and generated an annual income of approximately $50,000.[59]

Two events during Converse's presidency diverted the trustees from their usual routine of committee reports and reception of bequests. The first was a case of embezzlement that surfaced following the suicide of longtime treasurer Frank K. Hipple. Apparently Hipple had accumulated a large personal debt and used stocks from trustee endowment funds as collateral for loans amounting to approximately $20,000 that were later sold to cover his indebtedness.[60] As a result of this defalcation, the trustees engaged the Philadelphia Trust Safe Deposit and Insurance Company in 1906 to do the office clerical work for an annual fee of $1,500 and three years later officially appointed the company as treasurer. When efforts to recover money from the Hipple estate proved to be futile, the trustees charged the debt pro rata to the several trusts as they stood at the time of the shortage. Through contributions from anonymous donors, however, most of the principal was eventually restored.[61]

The second event was the union in 1906 of the Presbyterian Church in the United States of America with the Cumberland Presbyterian Church which had originated in Kentucky and Tennessee in the second decade of the nineteenth century. During those years, revivalist and anti-revivalist factions in the Synod of Kentucky clashed over ordination procedures involving four men of the Cumberland Presbytery. The Synod of Kentucky dissolved Cumberland Presbytery in 1806 because it refused to submit the candidates for re-examination and to accept the *Westminster Confession of Faith* in its entirety. On February 4, 1810, Samuel McAdow, Finis Ewing, and Samuel King reconstituted Cumberland Presbytery without synodical approval. Although the trio apparently did not intend to form a new denomination, they were unsuccessful in their efforts to effect a rapprochement with the Synod of Kentucky or any other neighboring judicatories. Growing rapidly, the Cumberland Presbyterians formed a Synod in 1813, a General Assembly in 1829, and incorporated trustees in 1841. Following the frontier westward, Cumberland ministers frequently adopted the practice of circuit-riding rather than locating in settled pastorates. By the beginning of the twentieth century, Cumberland Presbyterians numbered approximately 180,000 with 3,000 congregations scattered throughout the country, but their chief strength was in the Border States and the South.[62]

The Cumberland trustees performed tasks similar to their counterparts in other Presbyterian denominations but never acquired comparable assets because of their relatively small and impoverished constituency. During the last half of the nineteenth century, they frequently reported that "No funds or estates of any kind have come into [our] hands since [our] last report."[63] One of their few large donations was a gift of $10,000 from John A. Doherty of Warren County, Kentucky, that would provide a fund for the education of ministerial candidates.[64] In 1902 the trustees reported receipts of only $401 and cash and securities totaling $11,834. At the time of the Cumberland-PCUSA reunion in 1906, Cumberland trustees turned over assets of $13,775.36.[65] During reunion negotiations, General Assembly trustees frequently conferred with legal counsel regarding the integration of gifts and bequests. Because the PCUSA denomination had modified its *Constitution* in 1903 to eliminate some predestinarian terminology that Cumberland Presbyterians had deemed unacceptable, lawyers concluded that there were no legal or theological impediments to merging the two corporations.[66]

Following the death of John Converse in 1910, George Stevenson, a prominent Philadelphia banker and civic leader, became the eleventh president of the board of trustees, a position he would hold for fifteen years. Stevenson and John Sailer founded the banking house of Sailer and Stevenson in 1866, a partnership that lasted for more than half a century. For many years, Stevenson lectured at the Wharton School of Finance at the University of Pennsylvania and wrote financial columns for the *Philadelphia Public Ledger*. A life-long member of the Arch Street Presbyterian Church, Stevenson's pastor, Clarence Edward Macartney, honored him at a reception held in recognition of his forty-seven years of service as a trustee and his forty-five years as a ruling elder.[67] Under Stevenson's leadership the trustees adhered to their traditional policies of protecting endowment funds by investing conservatively and of maintaining a low profile at sessions of the General Assembly. Financial statements issued by the Trustees were invariably prefaced with a disclaimer, "The Trustees are restricted in their investments to the highest disclaimer, "The Trustees are restricted in their investments to the highest class of securities." Annual reports between 1910-1920 reflect only minuscule growth in endowment funds from $1,031,544 to $1,168,678. During that time period only one or two legacies were received annually, mostly of $2,000 or less, and some years the trustees reported no new contributions. Improvement in interest rates from 4 to 5 percent, however, generated increased earnings so that by 1920 the trustees were reporting an annual income of $73,919, up more than $20,000 from 1910.[68]

In 1920 the PCUSA effected a union with the Welsh Calvinistic Methodist Church, a denomination of 14,000 members located primarily in Wisconsin, Minnesota, Ohio, Pennsylvania, and New York. The denomination traced its origins to Watford, Glamorganshire in Wales where the renowned evangelist George Whitefield, one of the original organizers, presided over the first Conference in 1742. The two denominations had been in close fellowship for more than a century but were unable to agree on union primarily because of the language problem. When the Presbyterian church altered its Constitution in 1905 to provide for racial ethnic presbyteries and synods within the bounds of existing governing bodies, a major barrier was removed. The union agreement permitted the Welsh synods and presbyteries to retain their endowment funds but the legal and corporate powers of the Welsh General Assembly were assumed by the PCUSA General Assembly.[69]

The 1920 PCUSA General Assembly also appointed a committee to plan for the consolidation of the denomination's twenty boards and various committees to promote economy and efficiency. After several years of work, the committee, chaired by John Timothy Stone, pastor of the Fourth Presbyterian Church in Chicago, recommended in 1922 that the denomination have four major boards: National Missions, Foreign Missions, Christian Education, and Ministerial Relief and Sustentation, and that a General Council be formed to conduct the business of the church between annual General Assemblies. The General Assembly unanimously endorsed this structure and set in process procedures for implementation that were completed in 1923. The Stone Committee also recommended that the General Assembly appoint a committee of three clergy and four laymen to consider the adoption of a unified financial system for the consolidated boards and to examine the organizational structure of the Trustees of the General Assembly and their relationship to the trust funds committed to them for administration.[70] The status of the trustees in the new denominational configuration and the broader issues of unified finances and effective stewardship promotion would be subjects of discussion for the next decade.

NOTES

1. Henry B. Smith, "Christian Union and Ecclesiastical Reunion," in *Faith and Philosophy*, 267. Cited in Marsden, *The Evangelical Mind and the New School Presbyterian Experience*, 212.

2. Smylie, *A Brief History of the Presbyterians*, 128-29. Also, see Marsden, *The Evangelical Mind and the New School Presbyterian Experience*, 212-29.

3. Between 1879 and 1919 the total gross national product in constant prices grew at an annual rate of approximately 3.72 percent. Individual incomes also made remarkable gains. Between 1859 and 1916 there was a rise of more than 70 percent in real individual incomes. See Fite and Reese, *An Economic History of the United States*, 300-02.

4. *The Presbyterian Reunion: A Memorial Volume*, 273-75. For a historical overview of Presbyterian home missions in the nineteenth century, see Drury, *Presbyterian Panorama*, 171-302. The church simultaneously carried on an equally extensive program for foreign missions.

5. One of the most widely circulated publications was *Education, God's Rule for Christian Giving* (Philadelphia, 1875), written by William Speer, secretary of the Presbyterian Board of Education. In 1886 the *Directory For Worship* was revised to include for the first time a chapter entitled "Of the Worship of God by Offerings."

6. For a discussion of these issues, see *GAMPCUSA[OS]*, 1868:401-15. Bequests held by the trustees of Princeton Seminary, however, were considered questionable because of references to specific theological doctrines articulated by the donor.

7. *GAMPCUSA*, 1870: 98. From 1870 to the present, page numbers of the General Assembly minutes relate to individually published and bound volumes of *General Assembly Minutes*.

8. "James Asheton Bayard," *Dictionary of American Biography* (New York, 1929), II: 66-67. Bayard retired to Wilmington, Delaware, his place of birth, and died in 1880.

9. "George Sharswood," *Appletons' Cyclopaedia of American Biography, Who Was Who in History*, s.v. George Sharswood. Sharswood wrote, "We can say that we have in Pennsylvania a uniform and uninterrupted usage of nearly two hundred years, showing that women were never intended to possess the elective franchise." During his career, of some 4,000 cases, only 156 decisions were appealed. Of those only 32 were reversed.

10. Trustee Minutes (PCUSA), May 5, 1874.

11. *GAMPCUSA*, 1874:23, 145, and 147; 1875:477. See also the Trustee Minutes (PCUSA), May 4, 1875.

12. Trustee Minutes (PCUSA), May 7, 1878, and June 10, 1885. See also *GAMPCUSA*, 1885:826 and 1887:262-63.

13. In 1882, for example, the trustees had an income of $62,273 in comparison with the Board of Home Missions ($326,964), the Board of Foreign Missions ($388,427), the Freedmen's Board ($60,538), and the Board of Ministerial Relief ($61,887). *GAMPCUSA*, 1883: 640 and 815.

14. Trustee Minutes (PCUSA), May 2, 1876.

15. Trustee Minutes (PCUSA), May 7, 1888 and February 4, 1890.

16. Trustee Minutes (PCUSA), May 14, 1916. In 1878 the trustees reported that they had six vacancies, some of which dated back to 1871, and apologized to the General Assembly for their tardiness in attending to the matter. *GAMPCUSA*, 1878:62-63.

17. *GAMPCUSA*, 1871:620-21. For further background, see Brackenridge and Boyd, *Presbyterians and Pensions*, 51-62.

18. *GAMPCUSA*, 1874:26 and 33-34.

19. "Ministerial Relief," *The Presbyterian Banner*, 18 May 1873:100.

20. *GAMPCUSA*, 1874:33-34, 45, and 74; 1875:476 and 513. See also *The Presbyterian*, 6 June 1874: 3.

21. *An Historical Sketch of the Presbyterian Board of Relief*, 18-19; Minutes of the Board of Relief for Disabled Ministers and the Widows and Orphans of Deceased Ministers, February 18, 1879, PHL Archives.

22. In 1887 trustees reported that they were managing $212,011.76 for the Relief Fund. The standard rule of the board, approved by the General Assembly, was that all gifts were to be invested and interest only used unless donors specified that money was for current use. Trustee Minutes (PCUSA), February 8, 1887. For the history of the Board of Pensions, see Brackenridge and Boyd, *Presbyterians and Pensions*, 119-51.

23. Fites and Reese, *An Economic History of the United States*, 303-04.

24. In 1873 the trustees reported endowment funds worth $211,238 and in 1874, $221,338. *GAMPCUSA*, 1873:646-48, and 1874:173.

25. *GAMPCUSA*, 1878:62.

26. *GAMPCUSA*, 1879:564-67. Investments remained conservative, primarily in Philadelphia mortgages and United States Government bonds. When donations or bequests of other stocks and bonds were received, trustees usually held them only long enough to be sold at a favorable rate. See *GAMPCUSA*, 1880:177 and 1882:65.

27. Trustee Minutes (PCUSA), November 4, 1879 and February 3, 1880.

28. The trustees accepted a conveyance from the Beadle Memorial Church of Cape May, New Jersey, as an "exceptional case." Trustee Minutes (PCUSA), February 8, 1887.

29. Outside of law, theology was his chief literary occupation. An Old School Calvinist, Junkin opposed the so-called higher criticism of the Bible and proposed changes to the Westminster Confession of Faith. Marcus A. Brownson, "Address at the Funeral Service of George Junkin, April 12, 1902," 1-15. Throughout his long career, Junkin served as a preceptor for students wishing to enter the field of law. When the Commonwealth of Pennsylvania attempted to levy a tax on the income derived from denominational investments, Junkin successfully appealed the case to the Supreme Court. Trustee Minutes (PCUSA), May 1, 1890, and February 3, 1891.

30. *GAMPCUSA*, 1883:814-20.

31. *GAMPCUSA*, 1884:80 and 1885:826. See also Trustee Minutes (PCUSA), February 3, 1885.

32. Although distributions to individual churches were not large, they assisted congregations that otherwise may have been destitute of religious literature. For Boudinot Book Fund reports, see Trustee Minutes (PCUSA), June 15, 1905.

33. Trustee Minutes (PCUSA), November 6, 1883, and February 5, 1884.

34. Trustee Minutes (PCUSA), November 5, 1878, May 2, 1882, and May 6, 1884. Heberton's main source of income was from his Philadelphia parish.

35. Trustee Minutes (PCUSA), May 1, 1888. In an article describing the Philadelphia Rescue Missions, the author says that "into them are gathered a heterogeneous mass of humanity, such as is rarely or never seen within the wall of a church. The drunkard, the gambler, the profligate, and the fallen of both sexes constitute the majority of the congregations, and most of them are in rags. There is not a mission but what is doing successful, soul-saving work, and there is none whose sphere of usefulness could not be greatly enlarged by gifts of money and lives." *The Presbyterian*, 10 January 1894: 7.

36. Trustee Minutes (PCUSA), May 6, 1896. He also visited the poor and elderly in their homes, "praying with them and administering the comforts and consolations of our holy religion." Trustee Minutes (PCUSA), May 3, 1894.

37. Trustee Minutes (PCUSA), November 1, 1892.

38. Trustee Minutes (PCUSA), May 7, 1908.

39. Trustee Minutes (PCUSA), May 4, 1916, and May 2, 1918.

40. In 1897 two legacies, one for $396.89 and one for $7,123.09; 1914, one legacy for $3,000; and 1917, no legacies. See *GAMPCUSA*, 1897:297; 1914:448; and 1917:448.

41. Occasionally donors did not specify particular boards or agencies but left that decision up to the General Assembly. One legacy, for example, stated that the money was "to be used for the establishment of the Christian Religion, that the light of the Gospel may be made to shine more perfectly." Trustee Minutes (PCUSA), May 7, 1908.

42. *GAMPCUSA*, 1900:128 and 339. During the same year, the Trustees dispensed $4,060 to Princeton Seminary, $6,538 to the Board of Freedmen, $4,947 to the Board of Home Missions, and $3,245 to the Board of Education.

43. For the development of the Board of Freedmen and related activities, see Andrew Murray, *The Presbyterian and the Negro* (Philadelphia, 1966) and Inez M. Parker, *The Rise and Decline of Education for Black Presbyterians* (San Antonio, 1977).

44. Trustee Minutes (PCUSA), June 19, 1884, February 7, 1888, and May 3, 1894.

45. *GAMPCUSA*, 1895:314. For biographical information on Barber, see *Philadelphia Public Ledger*, 5 November 1891, and John F. McGinnis, *History of Lycoming County, Pennsylvania* (Chicago, 1892), 533.

46. *GAMPCUSA*, 1895:314; 1899:286. See also Trustee Minutes (PCUSA), November 6, 1894, and May 1, 1913. His wife donated funds to establish Barber College which later combined with Scotia College to become Barber-Scotia College.

47. Trustee Minutes (PCUSA), November 4, 1902, and *GAMPCUSA*, 1904:392. Income was used to pay for the education of African American students at the Swift Memorial Institute in Rogersville, Tennessee until it closed in 1953. Trustee Minutes (PCUSA), November 25, 1953. For the background on the Maryville situation, see Murray, *Presbyterians and the Negro*, 42, 44, and 60.

48. Trustee Minutes (PCUSA), August 8, 1907.

49. Trustee Minutes (PCUSA), June 18, 1896.

50. *GAMPCUSA*, 1910:127-28 and 443.

51. Trustee Minutes (PCUSA), June 21 and November 6, 1900, and May 2, 1901. Referring to Junkin's services, his peers said, "At the meetings of the Trustees he presided with dignity, geniality and with an energy and clearness of judgment which made the business of the Board a pleasure." Trustee Minutes (PCUSA), May 2, 1901.

52. *Biographical Encyclopedia of Pennsylvania* (Philadelphia, 1874); *Presbyterian Journal*, 23 July 1903: 20. Another biographical account noted that Perkins normally walked with "the regular scholarly droop of the shoulders, but when in his Presbyterian clothes, walks erect and steps with an air of purpose and authority." The *Philadelphia Sunday Transcript*, 6 July 1884: 6.

53. Trustee Minutes (PCUSA), May 2, 1901.

54. Trustee Minutes (PCUSA), May 2 and June 20, 1901, and May 1, 1902.

55. R. Douglas Brackenridge, "John H. Converse: The Man Behind the Building," *Westminster Review* (Fall, 1996): 12-15.

56. Trustee Minutes (PCUSA), November 10, 1904, and May 4, 1905. The first solicitors were Charles H. Matthews, a member of the board, and H. T. Prentiss Nichols, who was not a board member.

57. Trustee Minutes (PCUSA), June 11, 1908, and May 1, 1913.

58. Trustee Minutes (PCUSA), November 11, 1909, and *The Presbyterian Digest*, II:379.

59. *GAMPCUSA*, 1910:443-501. The average net income on investments averaged 4.5 percent.

60. Trustee Minutes (PCUSA), September 20, November 8, and December 6, 1906.

61. Trustee Minutes (PCUSA), September 20, 1906, and May 6, 1909. See also *GAMPCUSA*, 1909:427; 1910:444; and 1911:445.

62. Ben M. Barrus, Milton L. Baughn, and Thomas H. Campbell, *A People Called Cumberland Presbyterians* (Memphis, Tenn., 1972), 32-44; R. Douglas Brackenridge, *Voice in the Wilderness. A History of the Cumberland Presbyterian Church in Texas* (San Antonio, 1969), 1-11. The charter of incorporation of the Cumberland Trustees is reproduced in *Minutes of the General Assembly of the Cumberland Presbyterian Church*, 1889, 159-60. Hereafter cited as *GAMCP*.

63. *GAMCP*, 1886:142.

64. *GAMCP*, 1883:106-07.

65. *GAMPCUSA*, 1905, Appendix:39a.

66. Trustee Minutes (PCUSA), November 9, 1905. Because the union was contested in the courts by Cumberland dissidents, however, the formal uniting of the two corporations was not accomplished until 1919. See *GAMPCUSA*, 1919:447-48.

67. Ernest Spufford, ed., *Encyclopedia of Pennsylvania Biography* (New York, 1928), s.v. George Stevenson. Stevenson also served as a trustee of the Presbyterian Hospital of Philadelphia and was a member of the Union League, Scotch-Irish Society, and St. Andrew's Society.

68. *GAMPCUSA*, 1910:443-50 and 1920:428-42.

69. Smylie, *A Brief History of the Presbyterians*, 136, and *The Presbyterian Digest*, 2:135-54.

70. *GAMPCUSA*, 1922:167-68.

5

National Foundation

The Presbytery of Chicago respectfully petitions the General Assembly to instruct its Trustees to study and report to the next General Assembly upon the advisability of creating a Presbyterian Foundation. This Foundation to consist of funds now held by the Trustees and of others which would be attracted to it if the Foundation was continually held before the Church as a most worthy fund for gifts large and small and for Presbyterians and others to remember in their wills.—*Overture 33, "On a Presbyterian Foundation," PCUSA General Assembly, 1951*

The PCUSA denominational restructuring in 1923 launched a modern ecclesiastical enterprise patterned after the business world's consolidation into large corporations and industries. Although impeded by the Depression of the 1930s, the Presbyterian Church in the United States of America in the next two decades would become a nationally inclusive denomination of two and one-half million members. Noted for its progressive national and overseas educational, medical, and missionary institutions, the PCUSA in fiscal year 1950 would report receipts in excess of $94 million. As this transformation occurred, the General Assembly trustees, comprised of a small number of clergymen and laymen from the eastern United States who served as caretakers of gifts and bequests, evolved into a nationally representative, proactive Presbyterian Foundation with a full-time director and support staff. The slow and tedious changes, sometimes opposed by the trustees themselves, for the first time provided a central agency dedicated to meeting the financial needs of the whole denomination.[1]

The United States experienced a decade of economic prosperity and an increased standard of living fueled in the 1920s by the expanding production of automobiles, radios, refrigerators, and other consumer goods. From 1922 to 1929 national income increased about 23 percent, and faith in the efficacy of business and of business leadership permeated every branch of American society. Millionaire John J. Raskob wrote in *The Ladies Home Journal* that most Americans could achieve wealth simply by investing in good common stocks. Between 1920 and 1928 the estimated total number of stockholders in American corporations increased from twelve to eighteen million.[2]

In an effort to respond to this economic environment, the 1922 General Assembly appointed a Special Committee on Unified Finance with clergyman Joseph A. Vance as chair. Committee members included laymen H.S.P. Nichols, Herbert K. Twitchell, E. H. Perkins, and A. C. Ernst. During its organizational meetings, the committee agreed to investigate instituting a standard system of accounting for all denominational treasuries and creating one treasurer for the entire church responsible for promoting and managing designated gifts. Although committee members did not use the term "foundation," they envisioned a centralized financial organization that would function on behalf of all boards and agencies, hopefully ending competition for funds.[3]

After a year of intensive research and several consultations with national board executives, the Unified Finance Committee reported to the General Assembly on May 26, 1924. Noting that each board was separately incorporated, Vance stated that it would be "impossible legally" and "presently inadvisable" to appoint a central treasurer and that the committee had abandoned hopes of achieving such a goal in the foreseeable future.[4] Nevertheless, Vance reported that the committee agreed that some method of unification of finances was imperative for the sake of the management of the denomination's invested funds, amounting to between thirty and forty million dollars at that time. The committee had found that different boards had large holdings in the same corporation, and no mechanism existed by which these interests could secure better protection. As an example, Vance cited the Northern Pacific Railroad in which the Home Mission Board and the Board of Church Erection each independently had purchased considerable stock at $127 per share, only to see it shrink to $51 per share. Furthermore, the denomination possessed no complete list of endowment funds and neither designated anyone to gather and publish such data nor to make recommendations for investment strategies.[5]

Instead of a central treasurer, the committee recommended that the General Council establish the Office of Comptroller, which would supervise the finances of the four national boards, serve as the central receiving agency for benevolent contributions from individuals and churches given in support of the boards, and distribute these funds according to quotas determined by the General Council and confirmed by the General Assembly. Its responsibilities would include keeping the General Council informed regarding investment and reinvestment of denominational funds. The committee also recommended that a Finance Committee of the General Assembly be created to direct the work of the comptroller and to advise the finance committees of the four boards and the trustees regarding investment of all present and future permanent funds of the General Assembly.[6]

The General Assembly endorsed the proposals "as a statement of progress to date" and directed the committee to consult with the various board executives and bring a final report to the 1925 General Assembly. Opposition surfaced quickly, especially among board executives resistant to the idea of an Office of Comptroller, which they viewed as a threat to their financial autonomy. Their wishes prevailed, and the Office of Comptroller was replaced by a Secretary of Finance, little more than a bookkeeper who maintained records of the permanent funds, monitored the accounting and auditing procedures of various church organizations, and kept track of the operating costs of the different administrative agencies. Although the General Council retained the responsibility to prepare benevolence budgets and supervise stewardship and promotion efforts, the boards continued to direct their own fundraising efforts.[7]

During the efforts to unify the financial system, the General Assembly trustees conducted business as usual, which sometimes seemed provincial. The presidency of the board continued to be a lifetime appointment. When George Stevenson tendered his resignation in 1924 citing a hearing loss that excluded him entirely from discussions, the trustees deemed it "unwise to accept his resignation and heartily and unanimously re-elected him to the presidency of the Board."[8] In 1926 they agreed to change the date of their June meeting "because it does not seem to be a convenient one for many of the members in view of the Princeton commencement."[9] Their contacts with the Unified Finance Committee were limited to requests for information, including if the trustees could consolidate their securities into a common pool with other boards and agencies. When counsel for the trustees replied that such a move would violate the charter, the committee ended its correspondence with the corporation.[10]

Following Stevenson's death in 1925, William Adger Law assumed the presidency. Son of Thomas Hart Law, a Presbyterian clergyman and stated clerk of the General Assembly of the Presbyterian Church in the U.S., Law was born in 1864 on a cotton plantation in Hartsville, South Carolina. A graduate of Wofford College, he organized the Spartanburgh

Savings Bank in 1891 and in 1903 became assistant cashier and later president of the Merchants National Bank in Philadelphia. In 1910 he accepted the position of first vice-president of the First National Bank of Philadelphia and was later promoted to chairman of the board. Law was accidentally shot on January 21, 1936, by the president of the R. J. Reynolds Tobacco Company while quail hunting at a private club. At the time he was president of the Pennsylvania Mutual Life Insurance Company of Philadelphia and considered "one of the foremost leaders of Philadelphia's financial life."[11]

In 1923, the trustees reported to the General Assembly that they were administering sixty-one trusts valued at $1,160,965.67. Of the various trusts, twenty-seven were founded prior to 1832 and eight were more than one hundred years old. The funds were invested in securities (73 percent), mortgages (26 percent) with the balance (1 percent) uninvested.[12] In the 1920s most bequests and gifts were under $5,000, and donors usually designated them for a particular board or agency. Toward the end of the decade, however, several large bequests dramatically increased the assets administered by the trustees. In 1927 a bequest by Charles H. Harbison of Fort Scott, Kansas, "to promote the best interests of the human family" generated almost $400,000, and one by David L. Gillespie of Pittsburgh, "to be used in such manner as they [the trustees] deem proper," resulted in an increase of $337,775. Additional payments to the Harbison and Gillespie Funds enabled the trustees to reach an all-time high of $1,904,972 in 1930 before the effects of the Depression began to be experienced.[13] The trustees requested guidance from the General Assembly regarding the distribution of these undesignated funds. After consultation with the General Council, the trustees decided that after March 31, 1931, undesignated funds would be distributed according to percentages fixed annually by the General Council.[14]

In 1924 the trustees assumed responsibility for the Hubbard Press, a publishing venture started early in the century by William H. Hubbard, the colorful pastor of the First Presbyterian Church, Auburn, New York. A graduate of Amherst College and Princeton Seminary, Hubbard's pastoral ministry featured evangelistic revivals, lunch-hour meetings with factory workers, and welfare assistance programs for the poor and homeless in Auburn. Also active nationally, he served as editor and manager of *The Assembly Herald*, the official denominational publication, and for a number of years was secretary of the Committee on Systematic Beneficence. In 1908 Hubbard became a member of the Executive Commission (the predecessor of the General Council) and was appointed Executive Secretary in 1911, a position he held until his death in 1913.[15]

Hubbard was one of the first Presbyterian clergymen to see the importance of using the duplex envelope system to encourage systematic giving in local congregations.[16] At his own expense, he purchased a linotype machine and other necessary equipment and opened a printing shop in a two-story building that his sons had erected as a bowling alley at the rear of the family property. Shortly before his death, Hubbard transferred the printing operation to the General Assembly's Committee for the Every Member Plan, and the work continued under the name of the Supply Office until 1917 when the business was incorporated as the Hubbard Press and expanded to include a full line of material for use of treasurers or financial secretaries.[17] Between 1917-24 the Hubbard Press produced 3,500,000 sets of envelopes and showed a profit of $55,824. Initially the profits were turned over for distribution among the boards of the church, but the General Assembly subsequently decided that the original purpose of the enterprise could best be accomplished by rebating the profits to the purchasers.[18] When the Committee for the Every Member Plan was dissolved in 1924 and the responsibility for stewardship and promotion transferred to the General Council, the General Assembly appointed the trustees of the General Assembly as its corporate successor to conserve the property rights of the Hubbard Press. In order to preserve the organizational structure of the press, the General Assembly also instructed the trustees to conduct the annual election of directors of the press which consisted of nominees from each of the boards and a member of the General Council.[19] After World War II, the Hubbard Press moved to Findlay, Ohio, where it reorganized and resumed operations in 1949 on land donated by local Presbyterians.[20]

A fundamentalist-modernist controversy in the Presbyterian Church negatively affected the programs of its boards and agencies and resulted in denominational schism in the 1920s. Triggered by a sermon entitled "Shall the Fundamentalists Win?," delivered in 1922 by Harry Emerson Fosdick, stated preacher at the First Presbyterian Church in New York City, the clash between liberals and conservatives was played out at the General Assemblies between 1923 and 1929. Efforts by conservative leaders in 1923 to enforce doctrinal orthodoxy by requiring acceptance of five articles of faith (inerrancy of Scripture, Virgin Birth, miracles, substitutionary atonement, and bodily resurrection) were countered in 1924 by liberal clergymen who issued a document which was known as the Auburn Affirmation that deemed such requirements unconstitutional.

About the same time, at Princeton Seminary Professor J. Gresham Machen was calling for the downfall of theological liberalism. Because of tension among the faculty, the General Assembly investigated the situation at Princeton. The result was the withdrawal in 1929 of Machen and some of his followers to Philadelphia where they organized the independent Westminster Seminary. Later Machen and other conservatives organized the Independent Board for Presbyterian Foreign Missions and in 1936 formed the Bible Presbyterian Synod, the first denominational schism since the Old School-New School division a century earlier.[21] From this controversy emerged a movement, led by Minneapolis businessman and Presbyterian philanthropist George Draper Dayton (1857-1938), to establish an independent Presbyterian Foundation that was insulated from theological controversy. A graduate of Macalester College, Dayton founded the Dayton Company Department Store in 1902 and shortly thereafter established the Dayton Investment Company. In 1918 he incorporated the Dayton Foundation to promote religious and moral standards through education and to aid for the poor and homeless.[22] An active elder in his local congregation, Dayton served as a member of the Board of National Missions and as a trustee of Macalester College. He was also a leader in other organizations such as the YWCA and Goodwill Industries.[23]

Dayton presented his proposal to form a Presbyterian Foundation to the General Council in November 1927. Noting that there were hundreds of foundations in existence, but none primarily Presbyterian, Dayton envisaged a corporation of one hundred trustees from all over the United States, composed primarily of prominent business people, bankers, and other professionals. The plenary board would meet semi-annually, and a twenty-five member executive committee whose members lived in eastern cities accessible to New York would meet monthly. In addition to committees for investment, allocation of funds, and office management, the Foundation would employ a promotional staff to publicize the work of the Foundation and systematically contact potential donors. The most controversial aspect of Dayton's proposal was that the Foundation would be controlled by self-perpetuating trustees rather than by the General Assembly and that it would be free to support causes not directly related to the Presbyterian Church, such as the Red Cross and the American Bible Society. "The people must have the assurance," said Dayton, that "the management of the Foundation is free from all attacks, whether inspired by prejudice, fanaticism or well-intentioned efforts that sane, conservative, experienced, successful business men might deprecate."[24]

In his address to the General Council, Dayton cited a number of reasons why the denomination needed an independent foundation. He claimed that ministers were not promoting General Assembly causes from the pulpit as they had done in previous generations. As a result, "there is rapidly growing up a generation that does not understand the machinery of our denomination as their fathers and mothers did; that is not being taught to give for living, appealing causes." He felt that the establishment of a Presbyterian Foundation would alleviate this deficiency and encourage support of the spectrum of denominational causes. Dayton also pointed out that wealthy Presbyterians would welcome a foundation directed by prominent laymen trusted to distribute contributions wisely and, if requested, anonymously. To the objection that a foundation might secure bequests otherwise designated to specific boards, Dayton argued that the Foundation would attract more and larger legacies to be shared with all the boards. Finally, he observed that a foundation would give Presbyterians three choices when wishing to give large sums to the Church: an independent foundation, the trustees of the General Assembly, and the particular boards in which they had special interests.[25]

Although the General Council agreed to study the possibility of creating a Presbyterian Foundation, individual responses to Dayton's proposal were mixed. While many pastors and church officials lauded the concept, especially its promotional features, and praised Dayton for providing leadership at a crucial period in the denomination's history, others were less sanguine. In particular, they expressed concern that an independent foundation eventually controlling a multi-million dollar endowment would have a disruptive influence on the denomination's benevolence budget.[26] Some General Council members pointed out that a four-year $15 million dollar campaign to fund the new ministerial pension plan was nearing completion and to divert attention from that cause was unwise. Moreover, they asked, would the same donors be willing to contribute so quickly to another multi-million dollar proposition?

Other nationally known churchmen such as Henry Sloan Coffin, president of Union Theological Seminary, New York, William P. Merrill, pastor of the Brick Presbyterian Church, New York, and Lewis S. Mudge, stated clerk of the General Assembly, objected to the nondenominational features of the proposed foundation. Privately, Mudge said, "Personally, I am strongly opposed to such a plan as this. There are numerous other already existent foundations well equipped in every respect for the reception and administration of bequests, contributions and gifts for non-Presbyterian objectives. Why establish another whether Presbyterian objectives are to be a major or a minor element therein?"[27]

Dayton was not deterred by opposition to his proposed foundation. He used his considerable influence to secure the support of denominational leaders such as Charles R. Erdman, president of Princeton Theological Seminary, John H. MacCracken, president of the American Council on Education, and wealthy laymen James N. Jarvie and J. Willison Smith. Dayton apparently eventually won Mudge to his side by agreeing to grant the General Assembly the right to approve the charter trustees and by stipulating that the Foundation report annually to the General Assembly. Although he remained committed to an ecumenically oriented foundation, Dayton accepted a revision of the draft of incorporation that emphasized the primacy of organizations related to the Presbyterian Church through its boards and agencies. In the meantime, the General Council continued to explore the possibility of establishing a foundation and periodically reported progress toward achieving that goal.[28]

Only a month after the stock market crash of October 25, 1929, the General Council reported that "general opinion has been favorable to the establishment of a foundation" and directed a committee to proceed with plans for organizing and administering the new organization.[29] The following March the General Council approved a draft of incorporation of the Presbyterian Foundation to be executed in the state of New York. The Foundation initially would be managed by fifteen directors, ten of whom were "Presbyterians whose names would command the confidence of their fellow Presbyterians throughout the United States," the present moderator of the General Assembly, and one representative from each of the four boards. After a trial period of five years, the number of directors would be increased to 100 from all sections of the United States.[30] Dayton was selected to present the proposal to the 1930 General Assembly, which endorsed the creation of a Presbyterian Foundation and directed the moderator to appoint a committee to nominate a president and directors and to begin the process of incorporation.[31]

Meeting in Philadelphia in September 1930 to identify potential directors of the Presbyterian Foundation were Hugh Thompson Kerr, moderator of the PCUSA, the retiring moderator Cleland B. McAfee, Stated Clerk Lewis Mudge, and George Dayton. Dayton brought a list of 135 names that he had gathered during the past three years, including such notables as Charles B. Van Dusen, president of the Kresge Company, Captain Robert H. Dollar, president of the Dollar Steamship Lines, A. C. Ernst, president of Ernst and Ernst, Albert A. Reed, vice president of the U. S. National Bank in Denver, and Chicago industrialist Cyrus McCormick. After pruning the list to twenty names, they decided to ask Edward D. Duffield, a Presbyterian elder and president of the Prudential Life Insurance Company in New York, to head up the new organization. Duffield was noted for his philanthropic activities and had a national reputation as a judicious manager of company assets.[32]

Kerr, McAfee, and Mudge conferred with Duffield in New York City regarding his interest in the proposed Presbyterian Foundation. Duffield asked why the trustees of the General Assembly would not be competent to serve as officers of the Foundation. Mudge responded by naming the trustees and commenting that while they were thoroughly competent men so far as their present obligations were concerned, they were not the type of personalities needed to give the proposed foundation national recognition. In relating the conversation, Mudge said that Duffield was "entirely satisfied with my reply." Although Duffield did not commit to accept the presidency, he agreed to host a meeting in the near future of Presbyterian laymen who were interested in pursuing the project.[33]

Under normal business conditions, Duffield's endorsement of the project would have been sufficient to guarantee its immediate implementation and likely success. As the Depression deepened, however, enthusiasm for the Foundation among its proponents waned. Although Dayton continued optimistic that the Foundation could become a reality in the near future, Mudge, Kerr, and McAfee thought otherwise. In a letter to Duffield written in September 1931, Mudge suggested a postponement until economic conditions improved. Duffield concurred with Mudge's recommendation, noting that the disturbed financial condition would make it impossible to secure subscriptions for its establishment. "As soon as the skies clear a little bit and a spirit of optimism succeeds the present depression," Duffield assured Mudge, "I will be glad again to cooperate with you in getting together a group whom we might be able to interest in the project."[34] In 1932, however, with no sign of economic recovery in sight, the General Council disbanded the Foundation Committee and no further mention of the subject appears in the official records.[35]

Although economic panics and recessions in the nineteenth century negatively affected funds held by the trustees of the General Assembly, none matched the intensity and duration of the Depression of the 1930s. Stock prices fell a staggering $14 billion on October 25, 1929; American Telephone and Telegraph lost $449 million, and the net worth of United States Steel declined by $142 million. By September 1932, nearly 5,000 banks with aggregate deposits exceeding $3.2 billion had closed. Businesses either failed or managed to survive bankruptcy only by severely limiting their output. National unemployment rose from 3 percent to 25 percent, the highest figure in the country's history. During the depth of the Depression, more than 18 million Americans sought emergency relief. In Philadelphia, in which the General Assembly trustees held a large number of real estate mortgages, more than 80 percent of the city's 280,000 unemployed received no relief assistance whatsoever.[36]

During the 1930s, the financial records of the trustees reflected the economic malaise of the country as a whole. An appraisal of stocks and bonds, conducted on December 12, 1931, showed a book value of $1,228,112.64 and market value of only $993,604, a depreciation of 24 percent. The following year securities depreciated 27 percent and mortgages amounting to $53,800 were in default. In 1933 the market value of stocks and bonds plummeted to $796,141.25, and the treasurer noted that there were no market quotations for many of the securities and only nominal quotations for others.[37] Despite a reduction of interest rates, mortgage foreclosures were common. By 1938 the trustees had acquired title to approximately 40 percent of the properties on which they had originally held mortgages. As late as 1941, so little money was available for the Boudinot Book Fund that the trustees agreed not to publicize the fund widely "lest we be overwhelmed with applications."[38] While acknowledging that these financial problems were beyond the control of the trustees, the General Assembly nevertheless praised them for "their successful administration of the trust committed to them—especially during the difficult days of the recent past."[39]

In the midst of the prolonged financial crisis, president Law died in a hunting accident, and the corporation turned for leadership to veteran trustee J. Howard Pew, president of Sun Oil Company.[40] Pew was appointed a trustee in 1922 and had served for a number of years as the chairman of the budget and finance committee. A graduate of Grove City College, Pew was an elder in the First Presbyterian Church of Ardmore, Pennsylvania, and served as a trustee of Grove City College and Jefferson Medical College in Philadelphia. Pew and his siblings utilized their vast family fortune to reflect strongly held convictions about the importance of traditional Christian values and the American free enterprise system. Pew held the presidency until his death in 1971. His thirty-six years' tenure is the longest in the history of the trustees.[41]

As the United States emerged from the Depression and entered into World War II, financial conditions slowly improved. The market value of stocks and bonds exceeded the book value for the year ending March 31, 1944, the first time that this had occurred since the stock market crash of 1929. Although the appreciation was only .69 percent, it marked the beginning of a positive trend that would continue for decades.[42] Changes in investment policies coincided with the upturn in the stock market. The board's policy had been to invest only 20 percent of any one fund in common stocks, but in 1943 trustees raised the level to 33 percent believing "that through this method not only will more income be obtained, but a better hedge will be had on the dangers of inflation."[43] By war's end in 1945, the market value of the board's securities was 13.58 percent higher than the cost, and the board began selling off real estate as quickly as possible.[44]

From 1799 to the end of 1947, gifts received by the trustees were held and invested in separate trust accounts. In 1947 the governor of Pennsylvania approved an act of the General Assembly of Pennsylvania that authorized nonprofit corporations to establish and maintain one or more common trust funds for the collective investment and reinvestment of moneys of trusts.[45] This provision simplified investment procedures and allowed a diversified portfolio of investments that both provided protection against market fluctuations and generated higher returns. On November 25, 1947, the trustees established the Combined Trust Fund (CTF) with assets of $1,798,192. By 1958, the CTF had grown to $6,452,609, and interest during those eleven years on units deposited in 1948 averaged 4 percent after allowing for operating expenses.[46]

Improvements in the fiscal environment were accompanied by changes in denominational leadership. Stated Clerk William Barrow Pugh, who had held that position since 1938, was killed in an automobile accident near Cheyenne, Wyoming, on September 14, 1950, while returning from a speaking engagement. The position remained vacant until the General Assembly met in May 1951, and members of the General Council guided denominational activities and appointed several committees to study the duties and functions of the stated clerk and secretary of the General Council. The 1951 General Assembly commissioners elected Eugene Carson Blake stated clerk and Glenn W. Moore secretary of the General Council. Both clergymen came from leadership positions in southern California and envisioned a national church that could respond to the challenges of the post-war era.[47]

The origins of the Presbyterian Foundation are traced back to the early 1950s when mainstream Protestant denominations experienced unprecedented increases in membership due to a revival of religion following World War II. Presbyteries presented twelve overtures to the 1950 General Assembly that spoke to the immediate need for capital funds for church extension and new church development. Responding to the overtures, the General Assembly appointed a Special Committee on Capital Funds and named Samuel C. Slaymaker, an elder in the First Presbyterian Church of Lancaster, Pennsylvania and a General Assembly trustee, as chair. The committee was to study the subject of fund raising and report to the 163rd General Assembly.[48]

In its report the following year, the Committee on Capital Funds recommended that the General Assembly authorize a campaign to raise $30 million for new church development, seminary construction, and national and overseas mission projects. At the same time, the committee urged the General Council to devise a more permanent mechanism for raising endowment funds. Through a series of studies conducted by ad hoc committees, the General Council decided to hold a conference with prominent Presbyterian laymen to discuss the best way to organize an agency that would solicit gifts and legacies for denominational boards.[49]

About the same time, on its own initiative, the Presbytery of Chicago sent an overture to the General Assembly to create a Presbyterian Foundation that would administer funds currently held by the General Assembly trustees and formulate an ongoing program to attract additional contributions.[50] The Chicago overture received an ambivalent reaction from the trustees and J. Howard Pew. At their annual meeting in April 1952, the trustees agreed upon the following response which was accepted by the General Assembly. While they were capable of creating a fund known as the Presbyterian Foundation within the body of their accounts, they were unwilling to accept the responsibility for soliciting such funds. Moreover, if the Presbyterian Foundation Fund were to be established, they reckoned that neither the trustees nor the Foundation should bear the burden of promotion and staff expenses. Deeming stewardship and promotion a responsibility of the General Assembly, the trustees recommended that the General Council draw up a plan for soliciting funds and present it to the next General Assembly.[51]

In a letter to a denominational staff member, Pew stated his opposition to the proposed foundation. "Frankly, I don't see where anything could be gained by the creation of an organization known as the Presbyterian Foundation." He indicated, however, that he was willing to discuss the matter with members of the General Council.[52] Although Pew remained unconvinced, leadership on the General Council that now included Blake, Moore, and a number of progressive laymen moved forward with plans for a proactive Presbyterian Foundation.[53] One layman in particular, Rudolf J. Wig (1883-1968), played a key role in shaping the structure of the proposed foundation and in persuading Pew of the necessity and practicality of an expanded fund-raising organization. The son of a Hungarian immigrant and graduate of the Illinois Institute of Technology, Wig was an engineer with the U.S. Geological Survey and Bureau of Standards and later held executive positions with the Celite Company of Lompoc, California, a producer of diatomaceous earth, the Kelco Company of San Diego, a developer of uses for kelp and seaweed products, and during World War II, the Douglas and Timm Aircraft Corporation. Retiring at age sixty-five, Wig became active in charitable, educational, and ecclesiastical affairs. His associations included memberships in thirty different agencies, foundations, and college boards as well as church organizations on local, regional and national levels. Wig joined the Pasadena Presbyterian Church in 1921, serving as a trustee and elder under the ministries of Robert Freeman and Eugene Carson Blake. He became a member of the General Council in 1947 and was reelected for a three-year term in 1951.[54]

The General Council selected Wig to chair a special committee,

Elias Boudinot IV, Congressman, Director of the Mint, and first president of the Trustees of the General Assembly (1799-1818). (DOH-Philadelphia)

Robert Ralston, Philadelphia merchant, elder, Second Presbyterian Church, and second president of the Trustees of the General Assembly (1818-1836). (Historical Society of Pennsylvania)

Ashbel Green, pastor, educator, theologian, president of the College of New Jersey (1812-1822), and third president of the Trustees of the General Assembly (1836-1848). (DOH-Philadelphia)

William Neill, clergyman, president of Dickinson College, secretary of the Board of Education, and fourth president of the Trustees of the General Assembly (1848-1861). (DOH-Philadelphia)

These are, however, more than just stories about Earl ...olton. His book is also an important addition to Grand ...apids history. At a time when the community and its ...onomy are booming, many commentators seek to ...derstand that success. They can find many of their

conference, and there was less need than previously for him to supplement his income with outside work. We lived in a nice house in a pleasant, middle class neighborhood, three blocks from the elementary school where I attended fifth and sixth grades.

Living across the street from a Catholic convent, school, and church gave me the opportunity to develop a new sense of the kindness and friendliness of these neighbors. I remember playing softball in a vacant lot next to the convent and breaking a window. I had seen those women in black clothing, but didn't know much about them, and thought, "Oh, boy, I'm in trouble." One of the

Earl, in middle school

Learning to Lead

My Life and Meijer

1/4" HT

ped find several key documents and illustrative
otographs.

Michelle O'Brien patiently transcribed several of the
ed interviews, and Sharon Pawloski of the Cedar Springs
torical Society provided photographs from Earl's high

INTRODUCTION

Gordon L. Ol...

I said, "Yeah, sure."

"Okay," she said, "I've got this stuff on the board. Why
n't you sit in the back row where you've been sitting and
ll me what it says?" So I stumbled through it. "Now sit in
e front row and tell me what it says." I read it easily. She
id, "I think you better tell your parents you need your
sion checked."

It wasn't an especially memorable incident, but it did
lp me realize that there are many people like me who are
luctant to ask for help, and it is important to be observant
see those needs and offer assistance. Miss Burns did me a
al favor.

After one year, I dropped Latin in favor of geography,
nich was taught by football and baseball coach John

J. Howard Pew, president of Sun Oil Company, elder, Ardmore (Pennsylvania) Church, and thirteenth president of the Trustees of the General Assembly (1936-1971). (Hagley Museum)

E. Nye Hutchison, physician, businessman, elder, First Presbyterian Church, Charlotte, and president of the Trustees of the General Assembly (PCUS) (1889-1908). (DOH-Montreat)

Philip F. Howerton, General Agent, Connecticut Mutual Life Insurance Company, elder, First Presbyterian Church, Charlotte, and president of the Board of Trustees of the PCUS Foundation (1960-1964). (DOH-Montreat)

James E. Spivey, clergyman, synod executive, and Director (staff) of the United Presbyterian Foundation (1972-1977). (DOH-Philadelphia)

W. Terry Young, businessman, Associate Director, PCUS Foundation (1982-1986), Acting President of the Presbyterian Church (U.S.A.) Foundation (1986-1988). (Foundation)

Fred R. Stair, clergyman, Executive Director, PCUS Foundation (1981-1985), and Associate Director, Presbyterian Church (U.S.A.) Foundation, (1987-1988). (Foundation)

Aaron E. Gast, President of the UPCUSA Foundation (1981-1986) and Chairperson of the Presbyterian Church (U.S.A.) Foundation (1986-1989).

Geoffrey R. Cross, President and CEO of the Presbyterian Church (U.S.A.) Foundation (1988-1992). (Foundation)

had promise. Certainly Hendrik Meijer and his son Fred saw this. Earl knew they saw it, and from that mutual awareness arose a mutual trust that stayed with him throug different jobs and different stores, and through supervisors not always as appreciative of his talents as Hendrik and Fred proved to be.

e "we" of a team. The company's achievements belong to of our team members. Earl knows that in his bones. It is ny he is so reluctant to place himself in the spotlight. And ny it might be more accurate to think of him as first nong equals.

Earl Holton was born in Manton, Michigan, in 1934, e same year Hendrik Meijer opened a small grocery store miles south in Greenville. As Earl recounts in these ges, he began his career at Meijer in the chain's second, d smallest, store. (There were a total of six in 1952.) This s in Cedar Springs, Michigan, half an hour north of and Rapids before the US 131 expressway was built. He s eighteen, just out of high school, and newly married to a vivacious young woman who had worked across the eet at the Cedar Café when he first met her. Cedar rings was one of a string of small Michigan towns Earl

CHAPTER

EARLY LESSONS:
1934-1952

CHRONOLOGY

ndfather's illiteracy had probably spurred my mother to
ss on a love of reading to me.

Perhaps because of my mother's interest in books, I
veloped varied reading interests. Depending on my mood,
ead everything from history and biographies to mysteries.
e book that has had a strong impact on me is *Ladies'*
radise, written by Emile Zola. Despite its peculiar name,
e book is about Bon Marché, the first great department
re in Paris. The book gives a detailed description of Bon
arché, the entrepreneur who built it up, and its impact on
e small shopkeepers competing with it. I discovered the
ok through Hendrik Meijer. He read it as a young man in
e Netherlands and it affected his thinking about retailing,
e treatment of workers, and even competitors. Mr.
eijer's appreciation of that book helped me realize the
ights that can be gained from all types of books.

CONTENTS

First Presbyterian Church, Philadelphia, Pennsylvania, site of the union of the former PCUS and UPCUSA Foundations on January 6, 1987. (DOH-Philadelphia)

First Presbyterian Church, Charlotte, North Carolina, site of the organization of the PCUS Trustees of the General Assembly in 1866 and for many years the location of Foundation offices. (First Presbyterian Church, Charlotte)

A bequest by Joseph Eastburn in 1828 left money and property to support the Mariners Church in Philadelphia, a unique ministry for seamen. (DOH-Philadelphia)

Princeton Theological Seminary in the early nineteenth century. For many years seminary endowment funds were managed by the Trustees of the General Assembly. (DOH-Philadelphia)

the opening of the first three Thrifty Acres stores, the first of the modern Meijer supercenters.

Earl has never waited for challenges to come his way. He has anticipated them, prepared for them, surrounded himself with people who could surmount them — or who would give their all trying, without having to fear recrimination. It has been the company's good fortune, and Earl's, too, that the big idea Hendrik and Fred started with along with the supercenter concept, was to trust other people to do their jobs and welcome those who could do them better than they could do them themselves. That made this company a ready arena for Earl. Soon the standards he met were the ones he set.

In 1980, Earl became president of Meijer. As his responsibilities expanded, he became — in an evolution th appears almost seamless — a teacher. He showed the company the importance of superior logistics and technology, and how to not just survive but flourish, despi a unionized environment, through sensitive labor relations When negotiations got heated and tempers frayed, it was Earl who reminded the bargainers that their real task was not to win a battle of egos across a table, but to think of th best interests of Meijer team members. From his early day in operations, when the boy whose parents were teetotaler took charge of the company's liquor licenses, he came to understand the importance of government relations. As the company grew and public policy decisions affected it mor and more, those early lessons informed his judgment.

Fort Defiance Navajo Presbyterian Mission in Arizona, c. 1940, Board of National Missions, PCUSA. (DOH-Philadelphia)

Goodland School for Indians, Indian Territory (present day Oklahoma), nineteenth century, Executive Committee on Home Missions, PCUS. (DOH-Montreat)

Miss Caroline V. Lee, teacher missionary, with students at the James Sprunt Academy, Kiangyin, China, early twentieth century, Executive Committee on Foreign Missions, PCUS. (DOH-Montreat)

Dr. Alexander A. McFadyen at work in a China eye clinic conducted by PCUS missionaries, early twentieth century. (DOH-Montreat)

moved up the corporate ladder to store manager, district manager, vice president, and finally, in 1980, company president. His is a classic success story of starting at the bottom and rising to the top.

"I've had one of the more unusual careers in the retail industry," he says. "I have worked for three generations of the same family." In these days of executive mobility, such a strong and long-lasting bond between employer and employee is remarkable.

In some privately held companies, the owners pressure non-family officers to move on if they draw the spotlight. But Earl's relationship with the Meijer family completely avoids these kinds of tensions. Throughout his 46 years at Meijer, Earl has wholly embraced the key components the company was founded on — unwavering commitment to guest service, quality merchandise, the well-being of all Meijer team members, and community organizations.

So close that outsiders often assumed he was a membe of the Meijer family, Earl learned many of his managemen values over coffee sessions with Hendrik Meijer, who taught lesson after lesson through stories of how he grew the business from a single grocery store in Greenville into regional chain of supermarkets. Later, Earl worked closely with Fred Meijer and other top executives as the company developed its Thrifty Acres model and expanded beyond West Michigan.

many experiences that it is hard to know where to start an
when to stop.

Earl and I come from very different backgrounds.
However, we've never had a problem reaching a consens
on a multitude of issues.

Some of my most enjoyable times were Saturday
mornings at the office, when we would just talk, often no
concerning our jobs. These conversations gave us a great
understanding of each other.

From my point of view, working with Earl has been a
extraordinary exercise in decision making. We've never h
a problem saying, "We may not agree, but let's go your
way. It won't kill the company." Often when we reached
decision, that understanding went unsaid.

My father was a tremendous business mentor and
teacher. I have always tried to follow his example of how
deal with people and reach objectives. I hope I've been a
good mentor to Earl. However, as with families, you star
out being their teacher and mentor; then, in later years, th
become your mentor and teacher. The same is surely true
with Earl. He has been one of my best mentors — advise
— for many years now, as Harvey Lemmen was before
him.

I've been very lucky to have fine family and busines
associates, people of intelligence, quality, and dedication.
But Earl particularly has played a significant role. So it is

ichigan's quality of life, including the support given
cial service and cultural organizations. Locally owned
mpanies, Earl says, are more likely to support their
mmunity because doing so directly benefits their
mpanies, employees, and customers. It is a simple
ncept, but one well worth remembering.

Whether your interest is Grand Rapids history, business
anagement generally, or Meijer specifically, *Learning to
ead* has something to offer. Earl Holton tells a good story.

Atrium of the Presbyterian Church (U.S.A.) office building in Jeffersonville, Indiana. (Foundation)

consisting of Stewart J. Cort and Rush Taggart with Blake and Moore as ex officio members, to develop a plan of operation for the foundation. Although Wig's financial expertise and previous experience as a trustee of the Southern California Foundation qualified him for the position, his infectious enthusiasm, unbounding confidence, and relentless drive also were essential in winning over Pew, without whose support the project would flounder. At a meeting in Pew's Ardmore home, Wig convinced him that rather than forming a separate corporation, the trustees of the General Assembly should reincorporate as the Presbyterian Foundation, arguing that the trustees' years of experience and admirable reputation would lend continuity and stability to the Foundation. Moreover, Wig contended that without aggressive solicitation of funds, the denomination would not be able to meet educational and evangelistic programmatic needs, both priorities with Pew. According to Wig's biographer, Wig spent the night in the Pew home, and the two men talked late into the evening over the details of reorganization.[55]

Assured of Pew's cooperation, Wig's committee drafted a series of recommendations regarding the new foundation to be submitted to the General Council at its meeting in March 1953. Emphasizing the need of a nationwide organization that would operate in cooperation with existing boards and agencies, the committee proposed to enlarge the corporate powers of the trustees of the General Assembly in order to enable them to receive gifts both from individuals as well as corporations, foundations, trusts, and other organizations. The new corporation, known as The Presbyterian Foundation of the Presbyterian Church in the United States of America, would be empowered to receive funds from local churches and other governing bodies that would be invested and administered in the combined trust fund.[56]

In order to broaden representation, the number of trustees would be increased to thirty with a provision for six additional members when deemed appropriate and their service limited to six-year terms rather than for an indefinite period. Anticipating concerns of donors that funds given without restriction might be spent by the General Assembly during a time of "emotion and strain" and possibly without adequate reflection, the committee requested that the General Assembly adopt a standing rule that no more than 25 percent of unrestricted capital funds could be disbursed in any one calendar year until approved by the next succeeding General Assembly. Most significantly, the new foundation would be empowered to employ a director to plan and execute the promotional work of the corporation which would be funded by a budget submitted to the General Assembly through the General Council.[57]

Commissioners to the 165th General Assembly meeting in Minneapolis enthusiastically endorsed the proposal for a Presbyterian Foundation, and incorporation procedures were completed on September 22, 1953. Wig was appointed chair of the Promotion Committee (later changed to the Development Committee) and secured the services of Frank M. Totton, recently retired vice president of New York's Chase National Bank, as the first director of the Foundation. For many years an elder in the Larchmont Avenue Presbyterian Church, Totton had extensive experience as a fund raiser for such organizations as the New York State YMCA, the United Negro College Fund, the New York State U.S. Savings Bond Advisory Committee, and was chairman of the national Presbyterian laymen's committee for the Restoration Fund and chairman of the Budget and Finance Committee of the General Council from 1945-48. Confirmed as director in April 1954, Totton opened an office in the Presbyterian Center at 156 Fifth Avenue in New York City and began to introduce the denomination to the services of the Presbyterian Foundation.[58]

Totton initiated a publicity campaign that included a mailing to 6,500 pastors and another to 1,500 Presbyterian lawyers and trust officers throughout the country. He placed advertisements in Presbyterian publications such as *Presbyterian Life* and *Monday Morning Magazine*, arranged luncheons for clergy and laity, and had meetings with national staff personnel and synod and presbytery officials. Individuals attending these meetings who expressed an interest in promoting the Foundation were given the title "Foundation Associates" and were asked to make contacts in their local areas. Receiving inquiries regarding participation in the Foundation, Totton planned increased outreach in 1955. Seven months into his tenure as director, however, Totton suffered a heart attack and died on November 1, 1954. His administrative assistant, Charles W. Earle, carried on Totton's program under the supervision of Wig until a new director was appointed. During calendar year 1954, responses to these efforts produced $9,150 in gifts, and seven churches completed trust agreements for an amount of $150,215.[59]

The Foundation trustees selected Hugh Ivan Evans, a clergyman known throughout the denomination for his communication skills and fund-raising abilities, to succeed Totton. In addition to a pastorate of thirty-two years at the Westminster Presbyterian Church in Dayton, Ohio, Evans had served as president of the Board of National Missions and as co-chairman of a successful $12 million denominational building fund. He served as moderator of the 162nd General Assembly in 1950. Evans assumed office as the foundation director in March 1955 and continued in that position until his sudden death in 1958.[60] Under the leadership of Pew and Evans, the Foundation began to establish itself as a major force in denominational financial operations.

Trustees completed working agreements with the Foundation of Southern California and three presbyteries of the North Coastal Area of the Synod of California, the Illinois Foundation, the Texas Foundation, and various other regional groups to administer funds or to cooperate on promotional activities. At the same time, in cooperation with the denominational boards, they established a joint committee to coordinate appeals for gifts from individuals and foundations through wills, bequests, and annuity contracts.[61] New programs included a "Department of Annuities," using the same rates as the boards and agencies and a "Tax-Free Life Income Plan," opened in September 1955, that offered an opportunity to those who wished to make outright gifts but needed income from their capital during their lifetime. Articles in *Presbyterian Life* promoted the Life Income Plan that demonstrated the versatility and practicality of the program.[62] Another new feature was the "Short Term Reserve Fund," restricted to cash and short-term bonds, that could be used for building funds and other projects of a limited duration that did not qualify for admission to the Combined Trust Fund.[63]

Aware that many Presbyterians died intestate, the Foundation emphasized the importance of making a will. Wig conducted a study that revealed that between 27,000 and 29,000 Presbyterians died annually with estates estimated in excess of $200,000,000, but that the total bequests received by all the boards of the church annually amounted to approximately $900,000, less than one-half of one percent. He cited one case in which a wealthy Presbyterian layman left an estate of fifteen million dollars. The man bequeathed $100,000 to a local church and the estate paid eight million dollars in taxes. Along with pamphlets and mailings, Evans wrote an article, "Will Your Will Speak For You?" for the July 23, 1955 issue of *Presbyterian Life*, which generated numerous responses from readers who informed the Foundation that they were remembering the church in their wills. In 1956, under the direction of the General Assembly, the Foundation cooperated with the National Council of Churches in an interdenominational "Wills Emphasis Program."[64]

With promotional activities and expanded programs, the trustees monitored expenses and modified their investment portfolio to adjust to fluctuating markets and economic trends. Initially the boards or Pew personally provided promotional expenses, but beginning in 1958 the promotion budget of approximately $100,000 was covered by General Assembly Funds.[65] Trustees tempered their zeal for profits with sensitivity to church-state relationships. Prior to 1954 almost any nonprofit organization could conduct a business which was not connected with its corporation and retain profits free of income tax. Section 511 of the 1954 Internal Revenue Code changed this so that income tax was imposed on unrelated businesses of all charitable organizations except a church or an association of churches. Because the Internal Revenue Service classified the Presbyterian Foundation as a church, the Foundation could invest in business enterprises and reap profits without any tax burden. While the trustees were of the opinion that there should be no such exemption for churches, they thought that as prudent trustees they were obligated to make the most profit possible. They requested the General Assembly to approve the policy but at same time to instruct the stated clerk to advise The Ways and Means Committee of the House of Representatives that the General Assembly opposed the exemption for churches on unrelated business income. At the direction of the General Assembly, Stated Clerk Eugene Carson Blake and Foundation Solicitor George McKeag testified in opposition to the exemption for churches which was subsequently removed.[66]

In 1956 a significant change in the Foundation's operations occurred when, for the first time since 1799, women were elected as trustees. Trustees first discussed the subject in 1954 when the denomination was debating the issue of ordaining women, a right ultimately granted by the General Assembly in 1955. In their annual report to the General Assembly in 1956, the trustees stated that "the distinction between men and women as responsible trustees of the Church's programs and investment no longer exists." In order to accommodate additional members, the bylaws were modified to increase membership from thirty to thirty-six. The women nominated were: Mrs. Thomas S. Watson, Sr., New York, N.Y., Mrs. Charles W. Bryan, Jr., Chicago, Illinois, Mrs. Arthur H. Compton, St. Louis, Missouri, Mrs. Robert C. Neff, Dayton, Ohio, and Mrs. Alfred G. Wilson, Detroit, Michigan.[67]

Although listed by their husbands' names, female board members had professional and voluntary career experiences that qualified them for service at the national level. Over the years, they brought a variety of expertise to the work of the Foundation.[68] To cite only a few examples, Dorothy Stone Neff, a long-time resident of Dayton, Ohio, lead a life filled with service to church and community. Her activities included local and national service to the YWCA, the USO, the United Fund, and the Ohio Citizens Council for Health and Welfare. Florence H. Archibald, an elder in the First Presbyterian Church of San Rafael, California, was a civic leader who served as a trustee on various local boards, including the Sunny Hills Children's Service, the Marin Music Chest, and the Marin Charity Foundation. Matilda Rausch Wilson, president of the Board of Directors of the Fidelity Bank and Trust Company of Detroit, served from 1932 to 1938 as a member of the State Board of Agriculture, the governing body of Michigan State University, and for a brief time as

Michigan's lieutenant governor. For many years president of the Salvation Army Auxiliary, she was also honorary president of the Detroit Federation of Women's Clubs and a leader in the Detroit Historical Society and the Friends of the Detroit Public Library. An elder and trustee in the First Presbyterian Church of Detroit, Wilson was active in the women's association and served as treasurer of the Michigan Synodical Society from 1921 to 1941.[69]

By the end of 1957, after only three years of promotional activity, the Presbyterian Foundation had generated denomination-wide interest in giving through wills and bequests and by increasing its financial assets. The trustees of the General Assembly had taken 154 years to accumulate a total of approximately two and a half million dollars. When the foundation development office opened in June 1954, the total market value of the Foundation's assets was $2,576,277. At the end of 1957, the assets totaled $5,266,394, an increase of $2,690,117. In addition, the trustees estimated that the Foundation had been named beneficiary in wills of more than $5 million.[70] With merger possible between the Presbyterian Church in the United States of America and the United Presbyterian Church of North America in 1958, the Foundation prepared for expanded service to the united denomination.

NOTES

1. *GAMPCUSA*, 1950, I:428-29 (beginning in 1923, the General Assembly Minutes were published in multiple volumes). See also Smylie, *A Brief History of the Presbyterians*, 137-56.

2. For a background of this period, see Fite and Reese, *An Economic History of the United States*, 528-50.

3. *GAMPCUSA*, 1923, I:189-91.

4. *GAMPCUSA*, 1924, I:140-41.

5. *GAMPCUSA*, 1924, I:143.

6. *GAMPCUSA*, 1924, I:147-49. The Finance Committee would consist of two members from the General Council, the treasurer of each of the four boards, a member of the finance committee of each of the four boards and of the trustees of the General Assembly, five members of the church at large, the comptroller of the General Assembly, and the Moderator and Stated Clerk of the General Assembly ex officio.

7. *GAMPCUSA*, 1925, I:36-37 and 1926, I:39-46. In 1928 the General Council approved a new plan for stewardship and promotion but continued to permit the boards to operate their own promotional programs. See Minutes of the General Council of the Presbyterian Church in the United States of America, May 23-30, 1928, PHL Archives. Hereafter General Council Minutes (PCUSA). Much of the debate between the Unified Budget Committee and the boards had to do with the issue of designated giving. For a description of this problem, see David G. Dawson, "Mission Philanthropy, Selected Giving and Presbyterians," *American Presbyterians: Journal of Presbyterian History* 68 (Summer 1990): 121-32 and 69 (Fall 1991): 203-25.

8. Trustee Minutes (PCUSA), May 1, 1924, and May 1, 1928.

9. Trustee Minutes (PCUSA), June 15, 1926.

10. Trustee Minutes (PCUSA), November 8, 1923, and May 1, 1924.

11. *The Philadelphia Enquirer*, 22 January 1936. See also *Encyclopedia of American Biography*, s.v. William Adger Law.

12. *GAMPCUSA*, 1923, I:412-13.

13. *GAMPCUSA*, 1927, I:328-29, 1928; I:358-59; and 1930, I:343-44.

14. *GAMPCUSA*, 1931, I:371; 1932, I:372.

15. Malcolm L. MacPhail, *A History of the First Presbyterian Church, Auburn, New York* (Auburn, 1936), 28-30. Some parishioners thought that Hubbard devoted too much of his time to social ministries and neglected pulpit and administrative duties. A group of members petitioned presbytery to dissolve the pastoral relationship, but the request was denied, and Hubbard continued in his ministry. See Minutes of Cayuga Presbytery (PCUSA), March 7 and 30, 1899, PHL Archives.

16. The duplex envelope contained compartments for local offerings and denominational benevolences. It simplified record-keeping and stimulated giving to denominational causes.

17. "One of the Best," *The Presbyterian Magazine* (July 1925): 348.

18. *GAMPCUSA*, 1913:201-03; "The Hubbard Memorial Press," *The Presbyterian Magazine* (August 1922): 496; and William Clubb, "A Man's Dream Come True," *The Presbyterian Magazine* (February 1928): 67.

19. *GAMPCUSA*, 1924:47-51; 1925, I:284-85. See also Trustee Minutes (PCUSA), January 12 and May 1, 1924. The trustees took legal title to forty-seven shares of capital stock belonging to the corporation.

20. Today the Hubbard Press continues to provide the denomination with stewardship materials under the aegis of the Corporate and Administrative Services (CAS) of the General Assembly. An interesting case of church-state relationships in regard to Hubbard Press occurred in 1946. The Press had not been making payment to the State of New York for unemployment compensation tax from 1936-46 on the assumption that the Press, operating without profit and for the benefit of the church at large, was exempt as a religious and charitable organization. Since its charter authorized the press to do a general job printing business, however, the referee held that the exemption did not apply, the test being not what the organization does but what it could do under its charter. Trustee Minutes (PCUSA), May 3, 1946.

21. For an analysis of the Presbyterian fundamentalist-modernist controversy, see Bradley J. Longfield, *The Presbyterian Controversy* (New York, 1991) and Lefferts A. Loetscher, *The Broadening Church* (Philadelphia, 1954), 90-155.

22. George Draper Dayton, *Autobiography* (Minneapolis, 1933), 77.

23. *Who Was Who In America* (Chicago, 1943), I:42.

24. Dayton, *Autobiography*, 294-95.

25. Ibid., 296-97.

26. Henry Barraclough, "Memo to the General Council," undated [c.1950], Record Group 121-14-26, PHL Archives; hereafter, RG, PHL Archives.

27. Dayton, *Autobiography*, 296-97. See also William P. Merrill to George D. Dayton, June 21, 1927; Henry S. Coffin to George D. Dayton, June 13, 1927; and Lewis S. Mudge to Charles R. Erdman, February 5, 1929, RG 125-1-18, PHL Archives.

28. Dayton, *Autobiography*, 73-75, and General Council Minutes (PCUSA), May 25, 1928, PHL Archives.

29. General Council Minutes (PCUSA), November 7, 1929.

30. General Council Minutes (PCUSA), March 5 and May 28, 1930.

31. *GAMPCUSA*, 1930, I:195-97.

32. Dayton, *Autobiography*, 74, and Charles R. Erdman, "The Presbyterian Foundation," *The Presbyterian Magazine* (November 1930): 648.

33. Lewis S. Mudge to Matthew C. Fleming, October 30, 1930, RG 125-1-18, PHL Archives. Duffield embraced the concept of an independent foundation because he thought that the General Assembly was too subject to theological pressures. "It might easily be if there should be a recurrence of the acute situation between extreme fundamentalism and extreme modernism that whichever faction controlled the General Assembly might devote the money for the advancement of the theological views which they concurred in. . . .I think these difficulties would be less likely to occur in a body of business men who would be apt to take less extreme views both on theological and public questions." Edward D. Duffield to Lewis S. Mudge, April 21, 1931, RG 125-1-19, PHL Archives.

34. Lewis Mudge to Edward D. Duffield, September 25, 1931 and Edward D. Duffield to Lewis S. Mudge, September 28, 1931, RG 125-1-19, PHL Archives.

35. General Council Minutes (PCUSA), November 18, 1931. The Council deemed it inadvisable "to prosecute actively the establishment of the Foundation until the present economic conditions shall be decidedly improved."

36. Andrew Achenbaum, *Shades of Gray: Old Age, American Values, and Federal Policies Since 1920* (Boston and Toronto, 1983), 29-30. For additional background, see Robert T. Handy, "The American Religious Depression 1925-35," *Church History* 29 (1960): 2-16.

37. Trustee Minutes (PCUSA), May 3, 1932; October 25, 1932; and May 2, 1933. In their annual reports to the General Assembly, the trustees listed only the book value of stocks and bonds rather than their actual market price. Not until 1939, when the worst of the Depression was over, did the trustees publish both book and market values. *GAMPCUSA*, 1939, I:293.

38. Trustee Minutes (PCUSA), October 31, 1933; May 3, 1938; and May 6, 1941.

39. Trustee (PCUSA) Minutes, June 12, 1934, and *GAMPCUSA*, 1934, I:185.

40. "In Memoriam Ruling Elder J. Howard Pew," *Annual Report of the United Presbyterian Foundation*, 1972, 118. Hereafter cited as *UPF Annual Report*. See also *New York Times* obituary, November 30, 1971.

41. Waldemar A. Nielsen, *The Golden Donors* (New York, 1985), 168-76. The story of the Pew family's rise to wealth and influence began on a farm in western Pennsylvania before the Civil War. The first American oil well was struck in 1859 at Titusville, Pennsylvania, just forty miles west of John Pew's farm and the subsequent oil and gas boom enabled his son, Joseph N. Pew, to become a millionaire. He was among the first to see the possibilities of natural gas for heating and lighting in private homes and in industrial processes. Pew died in 1912, leaving his wealth in a trust to be administered jointly by his wife and his five children. Within three weeks of his death, the family met and selected J. Howard Pew, then only thirty years old, to become president. Pew would hold office for thirty-five years and guide the growth of the company from three hundred employees to more than twenty-seven thousand by 1970. Pew and his wife Helen gave generously to a variety of religious and secular charities including schools, hospitals, and cultural institutions in the Philadelphia area, to the Presbyterian Church, and to conservative political organizations and publications. In addition to the Freedom Trust, the Pew family established the Pew Memorial Trust in memory of their father in 1948 and the J. Howard Pew Fund for Presbyterian Uses in 1958.

42. Trustee Minutes (PCUSA), May 2, 1944, and *GAMPCUSA*, 1944, I:434.

43. Trustee Minutes (PCUSA), May 4, 1943.

44. Trustee Minutes (PCUSA), June 14, 1945.

45. *GAMPCUSA*, 1948, I:410, and Trustee Minutes (PCUSA), November 25, 1947.

46. *GAMPCUSA*, 1948, I:410; *Minutes of the General Assembly of the United Presbyterian Church in the United States of America*, 1959, I:137-38. Hereafter, *GAMUPCUSA*. The investment portfolio in 1948 was: 33.37 percent common stocks, 11.45 percent preferred stocks, 29.15 percent U.S. government bonds, 3.2 percent state and municipal bonds, 17.65 percent railroad bonds, 1.79 percent public utility bonds, 2.49 percent mortgages, and the rest in "items of little or uncertain value and cash." In 1949 the trustees changed investment policies to allow for 50 percent of the funds in common stock and 15 percent in preferred stock. At the same time, the trustees employed Fidelity Trust of Philadelphia as investment counselors at a cost of $1,000 annually. *GAMPCUSA*, 1948, I:410, and PCUSA Trustee Minutes, November 22, 1949, and April 23, 1951.

47. R. Douglas Brackenridge, *Eugene Carson Blake: Prophet With Portfolio* (New York, 1978), 56-59.

48. *GAMPCUSA*, 1950, I:147-8.

49. General Council Minutes (PCUSA), January 30-February 2 and May 24, 1951.

50. *GAMPCUSA*, 1951, I:42.

51. Trustee Minutes (PCUSA), April 25, 1952, and *GAMPCUSA*, 1952, I:396-97. An illustration of the trustees' unwillingness to expand their operations is their response to a letter from Edward S. Miller, a member of the board of trustees of the First Presbyterian Church of Milville, New Jersey. Miller had read the trustees' 1951 report and was impressed with the income earned and the relatively low administrative costs. He asked if his church could deposit approximately $16,000 for investment and administration with the understanding that the net income would be paid to his church and principal could be withdrawn on request. The trustees responded, "It has not been the policy of the trustees of the General Assembly to administer funds of this kind under these conditions. The primary object of the trustees is to receive, hold, and administer funds for and on behalf of the General Assembly or the church as a whole, and not of a particular church. Trustee Minutes (PCUSA), November 27, 1951.

52. J. Howard Pew to Henry Barraclough, June 12, 1951, RG 121-14-25, PHL Archives.

53. Following the General Assembly, the Finance Committee of the Trustees of the General Assembly and the General Council's Committee on Bequests and Legacies met in Philadelphia to discuss a plan of action. Both groups agreed that the charter of the Trustees of the General Assembly could be reconfigured to accommodate the operation of a Presbyterian Foundation but they thought that the promotional aspects of fundraising "might well be within the General Council's present framework." Memorandum, September 17, 1953, RG 121-10-5, PHL Archives.

54. Clifford M. Drury, *Rudolf James Wig: Devoted Servant of Education and Religion* (Glendale, California, 1968), 185-276. According to Blake, Wig "was not the easiest man to work with, but a very good man, indeed, and basically an intellectual. No idea scares him, although his general position was always conservative, both in theology and politics," ibid., 196.

55. Drury, *Rudolf James Wig*, 279-80. These details were derived from letters written by Eugene Carson Blake and Glenn Moore.

56. General Council Minutes (PCUSA), March 3-4, 1953; Trustee Minutes (PCUSA), April 6, 1953.

57. *GAMPCUSA*, 1953, I:148-49; 1954, I:397-401.

58. *Presbyterian Life Magazine* (November 27, 1954): 13-14; Minutes of the Presbyterian Foundation of the Presbyterian Church in the United States of America, April 27, 1954, PHL Archives. Hereafter, Foundation Minutes (PCUSA).

59. *GAMPCUSA*, 1955, I:405-06; Foundation Minutes (PCUSA), March 29, 1955.

60. Foundation Minutes (PCUSA), March 29, 1955; *GAMPCUSA*, 1955, I:407.

61. *GAMPCUSA*, 1956, I:58-59; Foundation Minutes (PCUSA), September 28, 1955 and April 9, 1956.

62. *GAMPCUSA*, 1956, I:60-61.

63. Foundation Minutes (PCUSA), April 9 and September 25, 1956.

64. *GAMPCUSA*, 1956, I:59-60 and 1957:58-59.

65. General Council Minutes (PCUSA), September 25, 1956; *GAMPCUSA*, 1958, I:185-87. Pew paid expenses for the 1954-55 budget ($61,150) and later gave 1,000 shares of Sun Oil Company Stock for promotional purposes. Foundation Minutes (PCUSA), April 27, 1954 and September 28, 1955.

66. Foundation Minutes (PCUSA), March 26, 1957; *GAMPCUSA*, 1957, I:371-72.

67. Foundation Minutes (PCUSA), September 28, 1955; *GAMPCUSA*, 1956, I:62-63.

68. Women did not begin to be listed in Foundation records by their first name until late in the 1970s.

69. Minutes of the Trustees of the United Presbyterian Foundation, September 21, 1966, and September 29, 1971, PHL Archives. Hereafter, Foundation Minutes (UPCUSA). *Update* (September 1977): 4.

70. *GAMPCUSA*, 1958, I:179-82.

6

Time of Larger Service

The Foundation is entering a new era. In the future the Foundation will have to carry on its activities in closer cooperation with many more parts of the church than has been necessary in the past. Based on the experience the Foundation has had and the increasing use of its services by the church, it would seem that the Foundation may be approaching a time of larger service to the church.—Executive Director Donald A. Hall to Foundation Trustees, March 30, 1971

The quarter century between the formation of the United Presbyterian Church in the United States of America (UPCUSA) in 1958 and the reunion of southern and northern Presbyterian traditions in 1983 was one of the most tumultuous periods in American Presbyterian history. As did the country at large, the denomination debated issues relating to civil rights, civil disobedience, racial and gender equality, sexual orientation, poverty, and hunger in an atmosphere marked by protest marches and public demonstrations. Responding to calls for societal changes, General Assemblies in the 1960s and 1970s inaugurated various programs designed to promote social justice and to ameliorate the second-class status of minorities in the United States. The UPCUSA General Assembly elected its first African American moderator, Edler G. Hawkins, in 1964, and its first woman moderator, Lois Stair, in 1972, yet the social disorientation of the period debilitated church morale and led to a trend of declining membership and dwindling financial resources that triggered budget crises and programmatic retrenchment.[1]

During this period, the UPCUSA approved a major creedal revision and completed a restructuring process that significantly reconfigured the denomination's theological and institutional image. After almost a decade of discussion and debate, Presbyterians replaced their single doctrinal standard, *The Westminster Confession of Faith*, with a multiple *Book of Confessions* that contained *The Confession of 1967* and several historic creeds such as *The Scots Confession, The Heidelberg Catechism*, and *The Barmen Declaration. The Confession of 1967* emphasized the theme of reconciliation in family relations and in the areas of race, economics, and war, reflecting ancient as well as contemporary challenges. The reorganization, which became operational in 1973, dismantled the denomination's traditional program boards and decentralized decision-making processes by creating a system of regional synods and mandating diversified representation on national committees and agencies. For the Foundation, the reorganization enlarged its fiduciary responsibilities and necessitated deeper involvement in all aspects of denominational life. This precipitated tension among its trustees and staff and the denominational governing bodies and agencies regarding mission budgets, investment policies, and development activities.[2]

Presbyterians entered the sixties with a harmonious union of two Reformed bodies that had maintained separate existences since the eighteenth century. After six years of almost continuous negotiations, the General Assemblies of the United Presbyterian Church of North America (UPCNA) and the Presbyterian Church in the United States of America confirmed a Plan of Union in 1957. Commissioners from both General Assemblies consummated the merger in Pittsburgh on May 28, 1958, bringing into existence the United Presbyterian Church in the United States of America, a denomination of three million members.

The UPCNA traced its origins to Scotland where various groups had separated from the established church because of differing theological or political concepts. These dissenters, known as Covenanters and Seceders, came from Scotland and Northern Ireland, settled in New York, southeastern Pennsylvania, and South Carolina, and later moved to western Pennsylvania, their eventual center of strength. In 1753 the Seceders organized the Associate Presbytery of Pennsylvania, and in 1774 the Covenanters created the Reformed Presbytery of America. After several unions and divisions, the main body of dissenting Presbyterians united on May 26, 1858, in Pittsburgh, Pennsylvania, to form the United Presbyterian Church of North America. Most of the new denomination's adherents lived within a several-hundred-mile radius of western Pennsylvania, but by the mid-twentieth century the UPCNA had churches stretching from coast to coast and a membership of about 250,000.[3]

Following the pattern of other Presbyterian denominations, the UPCNA incorporated as the Trustees of the General Assembly under a charter approved by the Commonwealth of Pennsylvania on March 22,

1860, with a board of nine members.[4] The trustees administered The Aged and Infirm Ministers' Fund that had been created by the General Assembly in 1861. Initially supported only by annual contributions from local congregations, the Fund later established an endowment fund secured by voluntary contributions. After a slow start, the fund accumulated more than $100,000, most of which was invested in government bonds and Westinghouse Air Brake stocks. In order to elevate the status of ministerial relief, a group of laymen from Philadelphia Presbytery, led by businessman trustee treasurer James McCandless, petitioned the General Assembly in 1873 to create a Board of Ministerial Relief. Following General Assembly approval, the board was formally chartered in 1875 and assumed responsibility for the management and promotion of ministerial relief funds.[5]

Like their counterparts in the PCUSA and the PCUS, the UPCNA trustees presided over a small passive organization that operated in the shadow of pro-active mission boards and agencies. Frequently trustee reports to the General Assembly commenced with statements such as "There has not been any business of public importance attended to by them since your last meeting," or "Nothing of special importance has required our attention." One year the only good news from the trustees was that "the lives of all our members have been mercifully spared throughout the past year."[6] Bequests and gifts were small and infrequent and most donors directed the trustees to channel the funds to various boards and agencies for use in home and overseas missionary endeavors. Amounts ranged from $2.00 "from a dying Christian child," to $383 "to be used as much as possible in educating a native ministry in heathen lands," to $20,000 "for the support of a male (medical or ordained) missionary in the Indian Mission field."[7] In 1946 the trustees reported assets of $36,805.64, a third of which were invested in government saving bonds at 2½ percent interest and the remainder in mortgages. When union with the PCUSA took place in 1958, the UPCNA trustees brought a total of only $31,574 into the new denomination.[8]

The merger of the UPCNA and the PCUSA program agencies and corporations proceeded smoothly under the leadership of stated clerks Eugene Carson Blake (PCUSA) and Samuel W. Shane (UPCNA). To include immediate UPCNA representation on the Foundation's board of trustees, the General Assembly approved the addition of six new members, raising the number from thirty-six to forty-two.[9] The name for the new corporation required little discussion; all parties agreed that members in both former denominations would recognize and accept the title, The United Presbyterian Foundation.[10] J. Howard Pew continued as president, and Don Emerson Hall, a graduate of San Francisco

Theological Seminary and former pastor of the Menlo Presbyterian Church, Menlo Park, California, became director of development. Hall, who had served in various capacities on presbytery, synod, and national agencies, had ten years of business and investment experience before entering the ministry. Noted for his administrative skills and dynamic personality, Hall widened the Foundation's activities during his fifteen-year tenure as director of development and executive vice-president.[11]

At their initial meeting, UPF trustees adopted a policy statement that reaffirmed its commitment to cooperate with all denominational governing bodies and agencies on an equal basis and pledged to honor the wishes of donors rather than advocating special causes. In planning its expanded development programs, trustees agreed to promote a more extensive national profile and to seek increased staff and budget. Director Hall emphasized the importance of creating a team of well-trained regional field representatives who could cultivate prospective donors and counsel with governing bodies and local congregations. Within three years, the Foundation had three full-time regional representatives—one on the west coast, one in the midwest, and one on the east coast—and two special part-time representatives, Glenn W. Moore and Leonard Buschman in Florida.[12] Hall could not secure additional development staff because the General Assembly was not able to provide adequate funding. In fact, a denomination-wide budget crisis resulted in annual allocations for development purposes that never covered the actual expenses. The Foundation increased its development outreach only because each year Pew and other trustees contributed amounts in excess of $100,000.[13] This supplement allowed the Foundation to have seven field representatives by the end of the decade. Their effectiveness could be quantified by revenue produced and demonstrated by the church's heightened awareness of the Foundation's development program.[14]

Concurrent with expanding its development program, the Foundation sought closer working relationships with the development staffs of the Commission on Ecumenical Mission and Relations (COEMAR) and the Boards of Christian Education and National Missions. At Hall's initiative, Foundation trustees proposed in 1959 that the major boards and agencies create a joint committee chaired by the Foundation director to formulate cooperative development programs for major gifts and bequests.[15] Board secretaries rejected the proposal, viewing the Foundation's initiative as potentially threatening to their own money-raising activities, especially in deferred giving. A confidential staff memo to COEMAR trustees in November 1959 accused Foundation officials of dismissing the special gifts programs of the boards and agencies as "small and ineffective" and of asserting that the Foundation should be given a free hand to develop a unified stewardship program. Citing figures to refute these claims, the memo concluded, "Up to date the record of the Foundation has not been too impressive. On the basis of their returns, it is difficult to fathom their great confidence and insistence on unification."[16] Subsequently, the general secretary of COEMAR, John Coventry Smith, privately affirmed the solidarity of the three major mission boards in preserving the status quo rather than giving more authority to the Foundation. "We are all beginning to ask the same questions which we have asked, namely, why does not the Foundation go about its major business and not interfere with that of the other agencies?"[17]

In an effort to resolve tensions between the Foundation and the Mission boards, the Secretary of the General Council, Glenn Moore, invited representatives of the various organizations to meet at his home in December 1960 for an open discussion of issues. Mission board executives cited problems of competition for the same donors and urged the Foundation to provide leadership in developing new sources of revenue. They also expressed fears that turning over the responsibility for deferred giving entirely to the Foundation would result in a loss of funds for their particular organizations. Foundation representatives emphasized their desire to enhance the effectiveness of all program agencies and argued that their development strategies would ultimately benefit every denominational cause. Despite their differences, all participants agreed that steps should be taken to foster a cooperative spirit and to establish closer working relationships between the Foundation and the boards.[18]

At subsequent meetings both parties adopted operational guidelines to facilitate future relationships. They acknowledged solicitation of funds to be the work of all boards and agencies as well as the Foundation and that such efforts ought to be cooperative rather than competitive. Each agency agreed to be "reasonably sure" that it did not solicit the prospects or donors of another agency. They also endorsed a program of unified advertising with the understanding that exceptions for special projects would be worked out through consultations between the Foundation director and board development officers. Finally, they decided that the Foundation's annual report to the General Assembly should include a statement of the combined special gifts receipts of all boards and agencies so that church members could have a clearer picture of denominational fund-raising activities. Although residual tensions remained, the agreement opened up lines of communication between the respective parties and provided a means of conflict resolution.[19]

Field research indicated that many people in local congregations knew little about the Foundation and its services, so trustees increased its mass mailings and its advertisements in *Presbyterian Life Magazine* and other denominational publications. Immediate results to the promotions rarely were identified, but the staff estimated that approximately three-fifths of the donors through wills were unknown to the Foundation but had responded to some form of general solicitation.[20] Another development technique was to hold small group meetings with wealthy individuals who had connections to the United Presbyterian Church. Following a social period and dinner, Pew or a trustee officer would lead a discussion on the Foundation's opportunities for Christian stewardship. Such gatherings resulted in a number of substantial gifts and bequests for designated church programs as well as General Assembly discretionary spending.[21]

The semiannual trustee meetings adhered to a format that included a worship service, presentations by staff members of programmatic boards, committee reports, and an address by the director summarizing developments over the previous six months. The worship service was led by a regional clergyperson who delivered a sermon on some aspect of Christian stewardship such as "The Teaching of the New Testament Concerning the Solicitation of Funds." Following worship, trustees listened to presentations from representatives of such agencies as the General Council, COEMAR, the Board of National Missions, and the Board of Christian Education. Opportunities for questions and responses encouraged dialogue and increased understanding among the Foundation and the various committees and program agencies. Reports from Foundation committees—Finance, Development, Personnel—and a formal report by the director constituted the agenda during the remainder of the two-day meeting. Occasionally meetings included a training session to help trustees become more effective representatives of the Foundation in local churches and business-related contacts.[22]

Between meetings members of the Finance Committee monitored investment performances in order to respond to economic developments and market changes. Diversification by industry, territory, and by types of securities undergirded the Foundation's investment philosophy. During the 1960s, the Foundation held an investment portfolio of approximately 60 percent equities (common and preferred stocks) and 40 percent fixed securities. Public utility common stocks represented the largest holdings followed by oil, machinery, chemical and bank stocks.[23] To broaden its information base and secure better performance, the Foundation employed the independent investment counsel of Smith, Barney and Company Inc. of New York and the Fidelity Bank of Philadelphia.[24] As a result, distribution of income from invested funds topped $1 million for the first time in 1966 with a total of $1,104,465.[25]

The Foundation also introduced several new investment plans during the 1960s that attracted donors and produced funds for denominational programs. In addition to the previously established Pooled Income Gift Plan (formerly Combined Trust Fund), Tax-Free Life Income Plan, and the standard Annuity Gift Plan, the Foundation offered a Deferred Payment Gift Annuity, an Annuity Trust Gift Plan, a Unitrust Gift Plan, and a Revocable Life Income Plan. Each plan offered options designed to fit the donors particular financial circumstances. The Revocable Life Income Plan, for example, permitted them to withdraw part or all of the principal of the fund on any quarterly valuation date. Funds remaining at the death of the donor became an irrevocable gift to the denomination and provided appropriate tax benefits to the donor's estate. The Foundation also encouraged church members to name the Foundation as beneficiary on low-cost term life insurance policies that would qualify as religious contributions under existing income tax provisions.[26]

Despite a downturn in congregational financial support of General Assembly mission programs, gifts and bequests received by the Foundation during the years 1960-1970 increased annually at an average rate of twenty-two percent. New gifts, bequests, and trust interests for mission programs amounted to $25,565,733, and $11,052,576 was transferred to the Foundation for investment management, making a total of $36,618,309. Income earned and paid out from invested assets increased steadily and in 1970 was 12 percent greater than any previous year in the Foundation's history, amounting to $1,962,399. At the close of 1970, the total of all invested funds benefiting the denomination had a market value of $42,983,150.[27] Noting these achievements, a reporter for *Presbyterian Life Magazine* queried how this could be when general benevolence giving for current operations of the same causes continued to decline? His question went unanswered, yet it identified a trend that would continue throughout the remainder of the century.[28]

The Foundation received its first million-dollar contribution in 1963 from the estate of Frederick Lee, a retired IBM executive in Binghamton, New York. Lee left $1,023,000 and specified that the income derived from the bequest go to the West Presbyterian Church where he and his sister Viola were members. Lee had joined IBM in 1898 and remained in the Mechanical Engineering Department where his ability with computers led to the issuance of five patents in his name before his retirement in 1945. Lee became aware of the Foundation through conversations with his pastor, Samuel Colman, who had been impressed by the stability and success of the Foundation's investment program. Influenced by her brother's action, Viola Lee left the residue of her estate to the Board of National Missions. According to Hall, "They were quiet, humble people, but their works will follow them."[29]

Beyond development and investment responsibilities, trustees became increasingly involved in the denomination's rapidly expanding social witness agenda. Following the creation of the Commission (later Council) on Religion and Race (CORAR) in 1963, the UPCUSA instituted a variety of programs designed to promote racial equality and to address minority poverty. In 1965 five overtures to the General Assembly urged the denomination to invest funds in the construction of desegregated housing. The General Council encouraged boards and agencies, including the UPF, to invest a portion of their resources in certain Savings and Loan Associations in Chicago, Cleveland, Philadelphia, St. Louis, and San Francisco that were known to be providing nondiscriminatory mortgages. The Foundation reported that it had sizable investments ($275,000) in agencies related to the Federal government that made funds available for lending institutions that processed FHA or VA mortgages and assured the General Council that it would continue to seek investment opportunities that would be in accord with General Assembly policies.[30]

At the stormy 180th General Assembly in 1968 held in Minneapolis, commissioners responded to pleas from minority leaders to implement the denomination's racial equality pronouncements with specific program funding. The General Assembly mandated allocation of 30 percent of unrestricted funds held by national boards and agencies for loans to business and low-income housing enterprises owned and managed by minorities. Under the leadership of former General Assembly moderator Edler Hawkins, the Board of National Missions in cooperation with CORAR developed guidelines for the Presbyterian Economic Development Corporation, Inc. (PEDCO) to implement the General Assembly directive. While acknowledging that such loans were likely to be high-risk and low-yield investments, Hawkins and his committee members argued that the potential social and economic benefits for minorities far outweighed any monetary concerns.[31]

Trustees were reluctant initially to implement the General Assembly directive because of its apparent conflict with their fiduciary responsibilities. During several discussions about PEDCO in September 1968, many trustees expressed serious reservations about investing church funds in financially questionable operations. Before taking final action, the trustees directed solicitor George McKeag to examine all the particular funds classified as unrestricted and render a legal opinion if they could be responsibly invested in PEDCO. Following a favorable ruling from McKeag, the trustees empowered the executive committee to contribute 30 percent of undesignated Foundation funds with the understanding that the General Assembly would hold the Foundation and its trustees "harmless and without liability" for any losses incurred by such investments. Subsequently the Foundation transferred $622,420 of unrestricted income to PEDCO as directed by the General Assembly.[32]

In the midst of these social tensions, the UPCUSA finalized a reorganization process begun in 1963 with the appointment of a Committee on Regional Synods and Church Administration. Advocates of restructuring cited growing cynicism among church members toward centralized government and widespread dissatisfaction with inadequate local and regional representation in denominational decision-making processes. They also criticized the inefficiency of independent national program boards and agencies that competed with each other for human and financial resources. In a "Design For Mission" prepared in 1968, the committee supported the establishment of a network of regional synods and urged more "efficient lines of administrative responsibility." The new mission structure delegated authority to regional governing bodies to determine policy for their administrative agencies and proposed the creation of a nationally representative council of the General Assembly to set financial and other priorities for the entire church.[33]

About the same time, the General Assembly decided to limit service on national boards and agencies to nine years (three three-year terms) and to conduct the nominating process through a national Permanent Nominating Committee.[34] Previously Foundation trustees had been elected for six-year terms that could be renewed indefinitely if the Foundation so desired. Some trustees questioned the wisdom of such an action, citing the loss of continuity and valuable leadership that were so important to fund-raising organizations like the Foundation. The majority, however, cited the increased diversity and energy that would be generated as a result of the new operating policy. Trustee Gaylord Donnelley raised the issue of having African American members on the board, and by common consent trustees agreed to secure such representation.[35] Subsequently other trustees suggested that "some of the names submitted might be of younger persons."[36]

The extended reorganization process was completed in 1972 when the General Assembly approved the realignment of governing bodies into fifteen regional synods and the creation of a series of agencies to guide the work of the denomination at the national level. A new Program Agency combined the responsibilities of the former Board of National Missions, Board of Christian Education, and the Commission on Ecumenical Mission and Relations. A Vocation Agency assumed responsibility for serving the needs of ministers and laypeople who were engaged in professional services to the church, and a Support Agency provided integrated financial promotion, program interpretation, and stewardship development to the church at every level. Overseeing the work of these agencies, the General Assembly Mission Council (GAMC) was given authority, subject to the General Assembly's review and control, to propose priorities and budgets for the entire church.[37]

The new structure called for only two incorporated entities—the Board of Pensions and the United Presbyterian Foundation. The Board of Pensions functioned as a separate management body but was linked programmatically to the Vocation Agency. The Foundation would report directly to the General Assembly through the Standing Committee on Finance and retained its mandate to promulgate a broad educational and interpretative development program with a special emphasis on deferred giving. It also assumed the responsibility to manage, supervise, and administer all the assets of the former program boards and agencies, estimated at that time to be worth approximately $313 million and consisting of more than 500 different stocks and bonds.[38] Rather than merge and consolidate all the predecessor corporations, Foundation trustees chose to continue their corporate existences and establish identical trustees, committees, and officers for the twenty-seven constituent corporations, similar to the procedure followed in the 1923 reorganization. This facilitated the acceptance of testamentary and other gifts that utilized the previous names.[39]

In conjunction with reorganization, trustees discussed changing the Foundation's corporate name to more clearly express its function and relationship to the United Presbyterian Church. The Tax Reform Act of 1969 imposed numerous new restrictions on foundations that if applied to the UPF would have proved burdensome. In apprising trustees of potential legal problems, solicitor McKeag noted that the term foundation as generally employed referred to a charitable treasury that made grants for various public and philanthropic purposes. Because the UPF was not a fund-giving or fund-loaning agency but rather functioned as the corporate and civil counterpart of the General Assembly, McKeag deemed it advisable to make the legal name more descriptive of its actual function as a church entity. Accordingly, in 1973 trustees adopted the name "The United Presbyterian Church in the United States of America, a Corporation" for legal purposes, but it continued to use the UPF designation in promotional materials.[40]

Completion of the reorganization process also coincided with changes in Foundation leadership. For fifty years (thirty-six as president), J. Howard Pew had played a pivotal role in determining the policies and practices of the trustees of the General Assembly. His death on November 29, 1971, at age 89 marked the end of an era for the Foundation. Six-feet tall with a bushy-browed visage, Pew was a forceful speaker and distinctive presence at meetings of the General Assembly. One observer said, "He not only talks like an affidavit, he looks like one."[41] Pew's views on trade unions, government regulation of business, and other economic issues were marked by political and theological conservatism. Although he opposed church involvement in economic, social, and political arenas and promoted the establishment of the Presbyterian Lay Committee, Inc. and other conservative religious organizations, Pew never ceased his generous contributions to denominational causes.[42]

From this time forward, the position of chairperson (or president) of the board would be on a rotational basis, usually for a term of three years. The tradition of designating a layperson rather than a clergyperson to the position was continued. Between the death of Pew in 1971 and the UPCUSA-PCUS reunion in 1983, five laymen provided leadership for the Foundation: Glen A. Lloyd, attorney, Bell, Boyd, Marshall and Lloyd, Chicago, Illinois; Eugene N. Beesley, president of the Lilly Endowment Inc., Indianapolis, Indiana; Peter Kiewit, chief executive officer of Peter Kiewit Sons', Inc., Omaha, Nebraska; David A. Cort, vice-president and secretary of PPG Industries, Pittsburgh, Pennsylvania; Horace B. B. Robinson, partner, Dewey, Ballantine, Bushby, Palmer and Wood, New York, New York; and Riley H. Richards, economic consultant, Des Moines, Iowa. Each chairperson contributed time, talents, and financial resources to the ongoing work of the Foundation. Along with other volunteer board members, they provided the professional expertise to fulfill the Foundation's fiscal and programmatic responsibilities.[43]

Shortly after Pew's death, Foundation trustees began a search to replace director and executive vice president Don Hall who was scheduled to retire in 1973 after fifteen years of service to the Foundation. Job qualifications for the top staff position included knowledge of general business, finance, accounting, fund-raising, and public relations but also emphasized wide acquaintance with denominational laypeople, clergy, and governing body executives and specified prior membership on some national board or agency. Other requisite talents were ability to deal with interpersonal relationships, widespread experience in public speaking, and "resourcefulness in dealing with unusual circumstances."[44] The search ended with the selection of incumbent trustee, James E. Spivey, who came out of a background of pastoral ministries in Texas and Oklahoma and had served as an executive of St. Louis Presbytery and the Synod of Oregon. Described by one of his contemporaries as a man of "tenacious tact," Spivey possessed the personal traits and professional experience necessary to lead the Foundation during a period of change and turmoil.[45]

A veteran of denominational politics, Spivey recognized that in order to function effectively in the new denominational structure the Foundation would have to shed its ultra-conservative image created over the years under Pew's leadership. During the reorganization process, rumors circulated that the Foundation might disagree with some of the denomination's social programs and use its new power to delay or prevent the distribution of funds to the Program Agency. Spivey assured church leaders that the Foundation intended to cooperate fully with all denominational agencies, leaving decisions regarding the use of funds to the General Assembly and to the instructions of the donors. Although disagreements between the Foundation and various agencies arose from time to time, fears that the Foundation would be obstructionist in carrying out its fiduciary responsibilities gradually subsided as Spivey maintained communication with all denominational agencies.[46]

One of the first tasks facing the Foundation was to merge the financial records and assets of previous corporations into a unified accounting and management system. Personnel and policy changes brought about by restructuring had created an atmosphere of uncertainty and confusion that impeded the process of unification. According to several eyewitnesses, financial records were in disarray, and some board files arrived at Foundation headquarters in New York in a jumble of unmarked cardboard boxes. Although understaffed, Foundation personnel began the tedious process of sorting out the records, identifying endowment funds, and preparing an accurate list of monies available for General Assembly mission programs. The staff gradually brought order out of chaos while simultaneously keeping track of on-going gifts and bequests.[47]

The Foundation also worked closely with the GAMC through the chair of the Budget and Finance Committee, Richard H. Miller, to establish a budget process that would protect the denomination's assets and allow for continuing support of mission programs. As indicated earlier, the reorganization occurred during a period of financial exigency when boards and agencies transferred millions of dollars from undesignated reserves in order to cover budget deficits. The reorganization process itself cost $5 million, an expense that had not been budgeted by predecessor agencies, and could be met only by borrowing money from Foundation assets.[48] In 1975 Spivey informed trustees that the denomination's unrestricted reserves had dropped from $20 million to $7 million in fewer than two years and that contingent liabilities of over $11 million associated with minority schools and colleges sponsored by the former Board of National Missions hovered in the background. Affirming that the church had to cease drawing on reserves and bring operations into line with available resources, Spivey acknowledged that the Foundation was perceived by church members with ambivalence. "Some look to the Foundation as an inexhaustible money source. Others look upon it as a roadblock to programmatic goals."[49]

To address immediate concerns for funding mission programs and long-term necessities of increasing purchasing power to compensate for inflation, Foundation and GAMC staff utilized a spending formula devised by Carl Gerstaker, chair of the Foundation's Finance Committee, to enhance income to General assembly mission programs. The formula made available steadily increasing resources for church programs and provided the GAMC with a positive basis for calculating anticipated annual income. According to the formula, the Foundation would make available for program purposes funds totaling the prior year's distribution, plus an additional 3 percent and an amount equal to 5 percent of the principal of any new additions, based on the assumption that unrestricted reserves would no longer be used as contingency for regular budgetary operations.[50] The Foundation also expanded its investment advisory service to include managers specializing in fixed income portfolios, equity portfolios, and mixed or balanced portfolios, such as the Mellon Bank, Pittsburgh, David L. Babson & Company, Boston, and the United States Trust Company, New York City.[51]

With new responsibilities for the real and personal property of the entire denomination, the Foundation shifted abruptly from its marginal role in General Assembly activities to that of a major player in denominational fiscal decisions. In unprecedented numbers, Foundation representatives found their responsibilities intertwined with a variety of denominational agencies and governing bodies. In addition to a seat on the GAMC, Foundation trustees and key staff members were represented on two Church-wide Coordinating Cabinets, the Committee on Mission Responsibility Through Investment, and innumerable ad hoc conferences and special committees. Relationships with synods and presbyteries proliferated as governing bodies assumed more responsibility for benevolence budgets and fund-raising activities. On a day-to-day basis, however, the Foundation had more contact with the Support Agency through its Division of Financial Resources than any other denominational organization. According to reorganization design statements, the Support Agency had as part of its mission the responsibility to develop a unified program to solicit contributions from individuals over and above their local commitments "in coordination" with the United Presbyterian Foundation. The program included promoting capital campaigns and short-term projects, annual gifts, bequests, life-income contracts and annuities, and assisting program agencies in obtaining government and foundation grants.[52]

A Memorandum of Understanding between the Support Agency Design Team and the UPF, signed in 1972, specified that the Support Agency would pay bills and salaries, maintain payroll records, and purchase materials and supplies. Estates and trusts initiated by the Support Agency prior to December 31, 1973, would remain under their supervision but new estates would be referred to the Foundation. The Support Agency agreed not to take any actions through its Legal Services Department that would affect the Foundation and its constituted corporations without the approval of Foundation trustees. Each party promised to make joint periodic reviews of their respective operations in order to produce services "feasible, economical, and compatible with the responsibilities of both units." Because both agencies had authority to solicit funds from individuals, they agreed to establish a Bi-Lateral Staff Team to share relevant information, make policy decisions, and develop coordinated training programs.[53]

Minutes and correspondence indicate that relationships between the Support Agency and the Foundation required continuous refinement. Early in his tenure as director, Spivey informed trustees that procedures for such items as bank accounts, cash flow, and legal services had been worked out, but he noted that differences of opinion still existed in regard to development activities and that "tensions will be with us for some time."[54] The Support Agency wanted the Foundation field representatives to be more actively involved in special gifts campaigns and other restricted-term stewardship projects. While agreeing to assist in stewardship activities when possible, the Foundation was reluctant to commit field representatives to projects that would diminish their effectiveness as cultivators of deferred gifts and bequests. Another point of friction was having potential donors being solicited simultaneously by both Support Agency and Foundation staff, which sometimes resulted in donor withdrawal from both requests.[55]

Although the Bi-Lateral Staff team tried to reduce tensions between the Support Agency and the Foundation, it was unable to resolve problems of coordination of fund-raising activities in the regional synods. Support Agency and Foundation representatives met with GAMC officials in 1980 to identify and clarify issues of disagreement. With former Moderator of the General Assembly, William P. Lytle, serving as chair, the participants reached some basic conclusions: the Support Agency was the primary agency for annual fund raising and special gifts; the Foundation was the primary agency for deferred giving; and the Support Agency was responsible for leading both efforts, which included accountability for the development of comprehensive, church-wide strategies. The Support Agency was to initiate discussions with the Foundation and the synod executives in order to reach a consensus regarding staffing patterns on the basis of "professional judgment on behalf of the whole Church." Apparently the discussions were successful.

Chairperson Robinson reported in 1981 that relationships among the Support Agency, the synods, and the UPF "appeared to be in place." Although Support Agency and UPF staff continued to operate independently, they maintained close communications and referred potential donors and testators as appropriate. UPF field staff assisted the Support Agency in the area of special gifts although devoting limited time to such projects.[56]

At the General Assembly level, Foundation trustees felt the impact of new investment policy guidelines that transformed the denomination's investment functions from a largely passive to an active social role by endorsing such practices as divestment, shareholder resolutions, and boycotts, and by authorizing investments in socially responsible but fiscally marginal corporations. A policy statement adopted by the 1971 General Assembly described church investment as an instrument of mission and directed that it should be conducted in the context of theological, social, and ethical considerations. This commitment was followed by guidelines relating to the areas of peace, racial justice, economic and social justice, and protection of the environment. The General Assembly also directed the General Council to establish a committee to "identify and recommend opportunities for responsible use of investments." Following the reorganization of church agencies in 1972, the Mission Responsibility Through Investment (MRTI) Committee of the General Assembly Mission Council played an increasingly visible role in monitoring the investment policies of the Board of Pensions and the United Presbyterian Foundation.[57]

Foundation trustees immediately endorsed the concept of social responsibility and pledged to cooperate fully with General Assembly directives to the extent that they could do so and maintain fiduciary obligations. Investment policy guidelines called for "creative investment" strategies, a term used for the placement of the church's investment funds with the primary intent to implement the social policy and objectives of the General Assembly. The 1975 General Assembly approved policy and criteria for using up to 3 percent of unrestricted endowment funds in such ways, making approximately $1.25 million available.[58] Through this the Foundation supported such groups as Bread For The World, The Fund for an Open Society (Philadelphia), Watts Federal Credit Union, Los Angeles, Dwelling House Savings and Loan Association, Pittsburgh, United Woodcutters Federal Credit Union in Meridian, Mississippi, and Centro-Agro Industrial de Carite in Guayama, Puerto Rico.[59]

Under the new investment strategies, the MRTI Committee raised questions about the ethical conduct of some of the country's largest and most profitable corporations, such as General Motors and Control Data

Corporation (racial discrimination in South Africa), American Home Products (marketing infant formula in third-world countries), and U.S. Fidelity & Guarantee Company (insurance redlining).[60] Frequently the MRTI Committee requested that the Foundation and the Board of Pensions apply pressure on specific corporations by casting proxy votes, filing stockholder resolutions, or divesting themselves of all stocks in the targeted companies. Although the Foundation complied in most instances with the requests, trustees on several occasions questioned the wisdom of utilizing shareholder resolutions to change company policy without first establishing communications between MRTI representatives and transnational corporation executives. Members of the Foundation's executive committee offered their services as liaisons in order to avoid unnecessary conflict and adverse publicity.[61]

Tensions between the MRTI Committee and the Foundation heightened in 1981 when, in response to the General Assembly's call for peacemaking, the MRTI Committee drafted "Provisional Guidelines on Military Investment." The guidelines directed denominational boards and agencies to refrain from investing in the nation's ten leading military contractors, any of the 100 leading military contractors that were dependent on the military for more than 20 percent of their business, and companies that made key components for nuclear warheads. Although the guidelines permitted divestment decisions to be timed to avoid undue economic loss, Foundation trustees concluded that it would be impractical, unproductive, and costly to implement the directive. While agreeing not to invest in corporations whose production or sales were *principally* in military products to the extent that it was legally possible, they declined to endorse the guidelines as desirable or appropriate.[62]

Conversations between MRTI representatives and the Foundation regarding divestment of military-oriented securities continued throughout the following year. Foundation trustees adhered to their initial response and expressed their willingness to honor the intent of the guidelines without having to follow detailed percentages that might impact investment returns.[63] In an effort to reach accord with the Foundation and the Board of Pensions, MRTI officials made two modifications in the wording of the guidelines. A reference to "investment securities" was changed to "common stocks" in order to make the type of investment more specific, and the operative verb "direct" was changed to "urge" so that the guidelines would not be perceived as orders that abridged trustee authority and responsibility. Responding favorably, the Foundation informed the General Assembly in 1983 that it had withdrawn its holdings from four companies and had instructed its investment managers to sell the common stocks of other companies on the MRTI Committee list as soon as it was economically feasible to do so.[64] Subsequent annual reports by the Foundation to the General Assembly indicated adherence to MRTI Committee guidelines and noted that it had been achieved without detriment to fiduciary responsibilities.[65]

Although Foundation trustees and staff devoted considerable time to implementing General Assembly social policies and establishing relationships with other denominational agencies and governing bodies, they continued to generate revenue for denominational programs at the national, regional, and local levels. A review of gifts received by the Foundation between 1976 and 1982 showed that the average annual amount of gifts received over the seven-year period was $7,221,209 with a total of gifts received during the same time period of $50,649,468. Nearly 3,500 churches were participating in the Foundation's wills and deferred gifts program and 1,702 congregations reported additional receipts of $25,219,699 from endowments and memorial gifts in 1981. With funds available for investment totaling nearly $400,000,000, income distributed in 1982 to individuals and programs of the United Presbyterian Church amounted to $28,807,734. In 1982 a complete restructuring of the Foundation's investment operations resulted in all new investment management firms selected, most outside of New York City. Investment accounts, previously separately invested, were combined for efficient and cost effective management. From its modest beginnings in 1953, the Foundation had become a major component of the denomination's stewardship and development activities.[66]

Even with the extent of the Foundation's assets and the complexity of maintaining accurate and current records, the system functioned without benefit of computers until the early 1980s. The first indication of interest in technology occurred in 1978 when the executive director informed trustees that office efficiency could be dramatically improved by purchasing a word processor. Although the trustees agreed to "investigate the possible use of a computer," no reference to a purchase of such equipment appeared in the trustee minutes until 1981. At that time, interim president William P. Thompson installed a carpet in the office because employees were complaining about the noise factor of the new WANG computer. The Foundation had entered the modern age of information technology.[67]

Along with seeking new funds, the Foundation served as investment managers for resources inherited from former national boards and agencies. Two of the larger funds, the Jinishian Fund (COEMAR) and the Jarvie Commonweal Fund (Board of National Missions), illustrate the diverse programs underwritten by Foundation assets.[68] Established in 1925 by James Newbegin Jarvie, a New Jersey merchant and financier, with an initial capital of $1 million, the Commonweal Fund was designed specifically for the aid and assistance of "the genteel aged—persons of culture and education, within the Protestant faith, residing in the greater New York area" who were without sufficient means of support. Although greatly depleted by the stock market crash in 1929, the Fund survived the Depression and by 1950 had reached a market value of $17,500,000. In 1934, trustees of the Commonweal Fund transferred its assets to the administrative care of the Board of National Missions with a stipulation that up to 25 percent of any surplus annual income could be utilized for National Missions enterprises. Today the fund has assets in excess of $125 million and distributes about $5 million annually to needy older people in the New York Metropolitan Area and $1 million in unrestricted funds to the General Assembly mission budget.[69]

The Jinishian Memorial Fund was established in 1966 by Vartan H. Jinishian, a New York businessman of Armenian background, in memory of his parents, the Reverend and Mrs. Haroutune and Catherine Jinishian. Jinishian specified that the annual income from his $9 million estate should be spent exclusively for poor and disadvantaged Armenians residing outside of the United States. The task of recommending recipients was given to an Advisory Committee consisting of three Armenians and two representatives of the UPCUSA. The Advisory Committee presently reports to the World Wide Ministries Division in Louisville. Over the years the Jinishian Fund has provided food, clothing, and medical supplies for needy families in Turkey, Syria, Lebanon, and Israel and has supported child care centers for working mothers, employment and legal aid offices, community development programs, and small business revolving loans. Presently the Jinishian Program is working to establish a vocational and training center for the Republic of Armenia that will provide modern vocational and technical training for orphans. In recent years the fund has risen to $43 million and generates approximately $3 million in annual income.[70]

Following Spivey's retirement in 1977, the Foundation elected Charles Calvin Griffin, formerly pastor of the First Presbyterian Church of San Rafael, California, to become the Foundation's fifth director. Griffin resigned in 1980 to take a position on the Ghost Ranch Foundation Board in Santa Fe, New Mexico, and Stated Clerk William P. Thompson served as interim director while a national search was being conducted. In 1981 the Foundation again turned to an ordained clergyman for leadership, Aaron E. Gast, senior pastor of the First Presbyterian Church of Germantown, Pennsylvania. A graduate of Wheaton College and Princeton Theological Seminary, with a Ph.D. degree from the University of Edinburgh, Gast had served as dean and professor of theology at

Conwell School of Theology at Temple University. Participating in a variety of denominational committees including membership on the GAMC, Gast had considerable experience on foundation and stewardship organizations, such as the Philadelphia Presbyterian Foundation, the Charlotte Newcombe Foundation, and the National Committee of the Self-Development of People. For nearly a decade, Gast would employ his communication, interpersonal, and development skills to relate the Foundation theologically and programmatically to denominational life.[71]

As the Foundation marked the tenth anniversary (1983) of the reorganization that had projected it into the mainstream of denominational life, major changes loomed. For a number of years representatives of the PCUS and UPCUSA denominations had been exploring the possibilities of a reunion that would end a schism dating back to the Civil War. In 1977 the two General Assemblies agreed to meet concurrently in the same city in alternate years and to expand the range of their cooperative activities. The long road to reunion ended on June 10, 1983, in Atlanta, Georgia when the General Assemblies of each denomination confirmed the favorable vote of their respective presbyteries. During a communion service led by the moderators of the UPCUSA and the PCUS, James H. Costen, dean of Johnson C. Smith Seminary in Atlanta, and John F. Anderson, Jr., pastor of First Presbyterian Church in Dallas, the two men said together, "The Presbyterian Church (U.S.A.) is now constituted as a part of the one, holy, catholic and apostolic Church of our Lord and Savior Jesus Christ." The new denomination comprised more than three million members and 13,225 congregations.[72]

Reunion also would bring together the PCUS Foundation in Charlotte and the UPCUSA Foundation in New York. Shortly after the Atlanta General Assembly, former PCUS and UPCUSA executive staffs convened to discuss procedures for merging the two corporations. They exchanged charters and bylaws and agreed to rapidly implement the Plan For Reunion that called for the formation of a new corporate body.[73] As a new era in Foundation history was about to begin, G. Daniel Little reflected on the Foundation from his perspective as executive director of the GAMC during the turbulent decade following reorganization. Little concluded, "The Foundation has grown and matured over the eleven years since it took on the heavy assignment to manage all the assets of the General Assembly. We have together fashioned working relationships which are serving the whole church very well, and which offer useful models for the future."[74] Those relationships would be scrutinized, tested, and challenged in the years that lay ahead.

NOTES

1. For background on this time period, see Smylie, *A Brief History of the Presbyterians*, 122-31.

2. Ibid., 132-34.

3. Loetscher, *A Brief History of the Presbyterians*, 148-56. For the history of the United Presbyterian Church of North America, see Wallace Jamieson, *The United Presbyterian Story* (Pittsburgh, 1958).

4. The first officers of the UPCNA corporation were Robert Gracey, president; James McCandless, treasurer; W. M. Bell, corresponding secretary; and Graham Scott, recording secretary. *Minutes of the General Assembly of the United Presbyterian Church of North America*, 1861, II:97. Hereafter, *GAMUPCNA*.

5. The denomination added a modern pension component to its program in 1928. For background and development of UPCNA relief and pension programs, see Brackenridge and Boyd, *Presbyterians and Pensions*, 82-83.

6. *GAMUPCNA*, 1873, II:572; 1896, IX:50; and 1900, X:50.

7. *GAMUPCNA*, 1871, III:268; 1885, VI:248; and 1914, XIII:740. In addition to bequests and gifts, the trustees handled all legal matters for the General Assembly and other governing bodies and managed a denominational annuity program that was instituted early in the twentieth century. For examples of trustee activities, see *Minutes of the Trustees of the General Assembly of the United Presbyterian Church of North America*, 1860-1957, PHL Archives, as well as annual reports in *GAMUPCNA*, 1861-1957.

8. *GAMUPCNA*, 1946, XXXI:713; 1950, XXXII:781; and 1957, XXXIV:477.

9. *GAMPCUSA*, 1962, I:79. Trustees were elected for renewable six-year terms.

10. Hereafter referred to in the text as UPF or the Foundation.

11. Minutes of the Trustees of the United Presbyterian Foundation of the United Presbyterian Church in the United States of America, March 25, 1958, and September 19, 1973, PHL Archives. Hereafter, Foundation Minutes (UPCUSA).

12. Foundation Minutes (UPCUSA), September 28, 1960, March 28, 1961, and September 27, 1961. Through a special arrangement with the Southern California Foundation, the UPF established an area office in 1960 with Dan Myers as staff person. *GAMUPCUSA*, 1960, I:91.

13. Foundation Minutes (UPCUSA), September 25, 1968. Trustees argued that development costs were extremely low and merited additional staff. The cost per dollar of gifts and bequests was only $0.1091 in 1967. As late as 1976, the development budget of the Foundation was supported by past and present trustees to the amount of $193,388. Foundation Minutes (UPCUSA), September 22, 1976.

14. Minutes of the Executive Committee of the United Presbyterian Foundation of the United Presbyterian Church in the United States of America, September 25, 1968, and September 17, 1969. Hereafter referred to as Foundation Minutes (UPCUSA) (ex.com.). In 1967 the Foundation estimated that the cost per dollar of gifts and bequests was only $0.1091. Foundation Minutes (UPCUSA) (ex.com.), September 25, 1968.

15. "A Plan for Co-ordinating the Special Gifts Activities of the Four Program Agencies of the United Presbyterian Church with the Program of the United Presbyterian Foundation," (December 1959), RG 139-10-25, PHL Archives.

16. "Special Gifts," confidential memorandum, John Rosengrant to Executive Committee of COEMAR, 13 March 1959., RG 139-1-25, PHL Archives. Rosengrant stated that based on his examination of financial reports, the combined boards had averaged $2,102,995 annually during the previous five years while the Foundation had averaged only $98,049 during the same time period.

17. John Coventry Smith to Administrative Council, 10 November 1959, RG 139-10-25, PHL Archives. COEMAR staff member John Rosengrant also wrote, "It seems to me that the Foundation is far too much concerned with controlling what we do rather than leading us to get new funds. I don't feel that a substantial amount of money has been found to date. I am convinced that if we simply exchange the money from one pocket to another, we haven't added much to the grand total that we are hoping to raise. John Rosengrant to Daniel M. Pattison, 30 November 1959, RG 139-10-25, PHL Archives.

18. "Minutes of Meeting of Three General Secretaries and Representatives of Development Committee of the United Presbyterian Foundation," September 30, 1960, RG 139-10-25, PHL Archives.

19. Ibid., 16 December 1960, and "Statement Regarding Special Gifts Procedures," November 18, 1960, RG 139-10-25. The Foundation Annual Report in 1961 showed combined receipts of $22,845.39 from boards and agencies, which was in contrast to the Foundation figures of $778,932.19. The figures did not appear in subsequent years. GAMUPCUSA, 1961, I:195-96.

20. Foundation Minutes (UPCUSA), September 27, 1961.

21. Foundation Minutes (UPCUSA), March 31, 1970.

22. For typical meetings during this period, see Foundation Minutes (UPCUSA), September 28, 1960, September 27, 1961, and March 19, 1969.

23. Foundation Minutes (UPCUSA), September 24, 1958, March 24, 1959, March 22, 1966, September 27, 1967, and (ex.com.), September 25, 1968. By 1970 the Foundation's investment portfolio consisted of common stocks (50%), Government and Agency Bonds (4.0%), Canadian Bonds (3.4%), Industrial Bonds (16%), Finance Bonds (7.3%), Public Utility Bonds (13.6%), and Railroad Bonds (1.0%) for a total value of $28,090,528. Foundation Minutes (UPCUSA), March 31, 1970.

24. The board's investment policy statement affirmed: "Basically we are optimists convinced that America and private capitalism has unlimited possibilities for ever greater achievement. The longstanding policy of the committee is that none of its investment decisions will be influenced in any way by considerations of race, color, or creed." Trustee Minutes (UPCUSA), September 28, 1968, Appendix C.

25. *GAMUPCUSA*, 1967, I:115.

26. Detailed explanations of the various programs appeared in annual reports issued by the Foundation. See, for example, *Annual Report*, 1973, 2-17.

27. *GAMUPCUSA*, 1971, I:122-3-3. See also, "Outline of a Report to the Commission on Reorganization by the Special Committee on Organization of the United Presbyterian Foundation," November 11, 1971, RG 148-2-12, PHL Archives. Statistics for the decade can also be found in *Annual Reports* of the Foundation and in *GAMUPCUSA*, 1970, I:258-59.

28. "Fifty Million Fund Triumphs, General Mission Giving Puzzles," *Presbyterian Life Magazine*, June 1, 1967: 32-33.

29. Paul R. Carlson, "Family Portrait of a Million-dollar Gift," *Presbyterian Life*, August 15, 1963: 28-29.

30. *GAMUPCUSA*, 1966, I:500-01, and Foundation Minutes (UPCUSA), September 21-22, 1966.

31. *GAMUPCUSA*, 1968, I:545-46. For the philosophy and policies of PEDCO, refer to *GAMUPCUSA*, 1969, I:636-38, and "New Agency Lends First Million," *Presbyterian Life*, 1 December 1968: 26. The maximum permissible loan was $500,000 and interest rates were from 4½ to 7½ percent with repayment time from 1 to 15 years.

32. Foundation Minutes (UPCUSA) (ex.com.), September 25, 1968; March 19, 1969.

33. Loetscher, *A Brief History of Presbyterians*, 173-76. In 1969, the General Assembly sent down to the presbyteries a series of amendments to the *Form of Government* known as "Overture H" that defined the mission roles of sessions and presbyteries in relation to the priorities of the denomination as a whole. At the same time, the General Assembly created a Special Committee on Synod Boundaries and a Special Committee on General Assembly Agencies to work out the organizational details of the mission design. For a concise summary of the reorganization process written by Stated Clerk William P. Thompson, see Minutes of the Interim Personnel Committee, March 11, 1972, RG 146-2-11, PHL Archives. For the Foundation response to the mission design, see "Report to the Commission on Reorganization of General Assembly Agencies from the United Presbyterian Foundation," December 14, 1972, RG 179-4-17, PHL Archives.

34. Foundation Minutes (UPCUSA), March 19, 1969, and *GAMUPCUSA*, 1971, I:127.

35. Foundation Minutes (UPCUSA) (ex.com.), September 25, 1968, and March 19, 1969. The Foundation charter was amended in 1970 to conform to the new Assembly policy. Foundation Minutes (UPCUSA), September 23, 1970; March 30, 1971.

36. Foundation Minutes (UPCUSA), September 23, 1970.

37. Minutes of the Interim Personnel Committee, March 11, 1972, RG 146-2-11. The report is essentially that made by William P. Thompson.

38. *GAMUPCUSA*, 1971, I:498-99, and Foundation Minutes (UPCUSA), March 20, 1973. Varying estimates were given at the time due to the uncertainty of value of some funds. In addition, the denomination owned and used in its program nearly 1,000 pieces of property and 1,500 buildings in the United States and around the world. *GAMUPCUSA*, 1976, I:263.

39. George W. McKeag to Don E. Hall, 18 November 1971, RG 179-4-17, PHL Archives. For a complete list of the constituent corporations, see *GAMUPCUSA*, 1973, I:763-65.

40. *GAMUPCUSA*, 1973, I:734. See also Don E. Hall and George W. McKeag, Memorandum to Foundation Executive Committee, September 8, 1969; George W. McKeag to William P. Thompson, January 12, 1973, RG 148-2-2, and Foundation Minutes (UPCUSA), March 30, 1971 and March 20, 1973. McKeag cited the IRS Code of 1954 that provided that a donor could get an income tax deduction of 20 percent to charities and 30 percent to churches. The Foundation was required to prove to the IRS that it was a church within the meaning of the code. Only after several appeals did the Foundation receive a favorable ruling from the IRS. For a summary of the 1969 Tax Reform Law, see Arnold J. Zurcher, *The Management of American Foundations* (New York, 1972), 143-53.

41. Neilson, *The Golden Donors*, 168-70. Solicitor George McKeag related how Pew quietly gave large sums of money to various Presbyterian projects including the Presbyterian Historical Society. According to McKeag, when he consulted with Pew on Foundation business, "I listened and he talked." Interview, George McKeag with author, 17 July 1991.

42. "J. Howard Pew," *The Presbyterian Layman* (December, 1971): 1, 13; *GAMUPCUSA*, 1972, I:182-83; and Foundation Minutes (UPCUSA), March 29, 1972. In 1958 Pew established the J. Howard Pew Trust for Presbyterian Uses with assets of approximately $730,000, later supplemented by issues of Sun Oil Company Stock. The income was to be used for any special purposes at the discretion of the board of trustees.

43. For example, Peter Kiewit gave $1.5 million for development activities and another million for special projects. Foundation Minutes (UPCUSA) (ex.com.), May 1, 1980.

44. Foundation Minutes (UPCUSA), February 17, 1972, Appendix C2.

45. James E. Spivey, interview with author, 11 November 1991, and letter, S. Carson Wasson to W. Sherman Skinner, 21 September 1971, RG 179-4-17, PHL Archives.

46. James E. Spivey, interview with author, 11 November 1991.

47. James E. Spivey, interview with author, 11 November 1991, and Ernest Fogg, interview with author, 4 March 1997.

48. Foundation Minutes (UPCUSA), September 18, 1975. For an overview of the denomination's financial status at this time from the GAMC perspective by Richard H. Miller, see Memorandum, Otto K. Finkbeiner to Richard H. Miller, 28 September 1976, RG 148-2-11, PHL Archives.

49. Foundation Minutes (UPCUSA), March 20, 1974, Paper H, January 24, 1975 and "Report to Budgeting Section," 1975, RG 148-2-21, PHL Archives.

50. Foundation trustees periodically adjusted the formula as financial conditions permitted in order to generate additional income for mission programs without lessening the purchasing power of reserve funds. Foundation Minutes (UPCUSA), March 20, 1974, and September 18-19, 1979. With the approval of the General Assembly, the Foundation also retained all unrestricted bequests and gifts received during the years 1976-1979 for use as unrestricted reserves. *GAMUPCUSA*, 1976, I:96, and 1978, I:121.

51. *GAMUPCUSA*, 1974, I: 1010-01. In 1979 the Foundation created an Inter-agency Cash Management Fund so that sums held by the Office of the General Assembly and the Support Agency could earn higher interest rates than when they were deposited in low yield savings accounts in local banks. Foundation Minutes (UPCUSA) (ex.com.), January 10, 1980.

52. William P. Thompson, Memorandum to Special Committee on Organization, July 19, 1971, RG 148-2-12, PHL Archives. At the 1971 General Assembly during the report of the Council on Church Support (Support Agency), a motion was made from the floor to consolidate all fund-raising efforts by the two agencies under the direction of the Support Agency. That meant that the emphasis on wills and any other form of deferred giving promoted by the Foundation would be directed by the Support Agency. The motion was referred to the Commission on Reorganization and was rejected. See *GAMUPCUSA*, 1971, I:239. For a concise summary of the history of predecessor agencies and the responsibilities of the Support Agency, see *GAMUPCUSA*, 1974: I:973-1001.

53. "Memorandum of Understanding Between the Support Agency Design Teams and the United Presbyterian Foundation in Relation to Services to be Provided by the Support Agency, April 28, 1972," RG 179-4-17 and Foundation Minutes (UPCUSA), March 20 and May 17, 1973.

54. Foundation Minutes (UPCUSA), March 20, 1973.

55. Some field representatives were financed by the Foundation, some by the Support Agency, and some jointly by a synod and the Support Agency. See James E. Spivey, "Report of Director," September 19, 1973, RG 148-2-21, PHL Archives, and Foundation Minutes (UPCUSA) (ex.com.), November 1, 1979.

56. Memorandum, Horace B. B. Robinson and Donn Jann to Regional Representatives, January 30, 1980, Box Three, Foundation Letters, PHL Archives. See Foundation Minutes (UPCUSA) (ex.com.), May 1 and July 10, 1980; September 15, 1981; and Foundation Minutes, March 17-18, 1981. Foundation officials continued to insist, however, that they could not carry out their responsibilities effectively unless regional representatives were hired, trained, managed, and held accountable to Foundation headquarters.

57. For background on MRTI and the denomination's investment policies, see "The Church and Transnational Corporations," *Church and Society* (March/April, 1984):17-36.

58. Foundation Minutes (UPCUSA), March 23-24, 1976.

59. Foundation Minutes (UPCUSA) (ex.com.), July 9, 1981; March 18-19, 1980; and *GAMUPCUSA*, 1980, I:114. Occasionally, Foundation trustees rejected requests because they did not think the company met the requirements of the prudent-man rule. Such was the case of the Workers-Owned Sewing Company of Windsor, North Carolina. See Foundation Minutes (UPCUSA) (ex.com.), May 1 and July 10, 1980.

60. Foundation Minutes (UPCUSA), September 19-20, 1978.

61. Foundation Minutes (UPCUSA), March 29, 1972, September 20, 1976, and (ex.com.), September 20, 1977. Trustee chair Peter Kiewit arranged a consultation between UPF and MRTI committee representatives in 1977 in order to clarify church policies and relationships between the two bodies. Foundation Minutes (UPCUSA), September 20-21, 1977, Appendix I.

62. Foundation Minutes (UPCUSA) (ex.com.), January 8, March 17, and May 7, 1981, and September 15, 1981.

63. Foundation Minutes (UPCUSA) (ex.com.), September 15-16, 1981, March 21, 1982, and May 20, 1982.

64. Foundation Minutes (UPCUSA) (ex.com.), September 21, 1982, and *GAMPCUSA* 1983, I:208-36. For a summary of relationships between the Board of Pensions and the MRTI Committee during the same time period, see Brackenridge and Boyd, *Presbyterians and Pensions*, 136-42.

65. For a narrative account of Foundation policy in regard to social responsibility in investments, see "Authority and Responsibility For Our Mission Through Investment Practice," Foundation Minutes (UPCUSA), March 15, 1983.

66. *UPF Annual Report*, 1983, 4-5.

67. Foundation Minutes (UPCUSA) (ex.com.), September 19-20, 1978, and November 5, 1981.

68. The programs and service activities of these funds are directed by advisory committees as specified in the terms of the donors' bequests. See *GAMUPCUSA*, 1981, I:155.

69. William P. McCulloch, "The Jarvie Commonweal Fund" (Philadelphia, 1947), 5-25, "Jarvie Service Digest" (Philadelphia, 1943), 1-12, and "The Jarvie Commonweal Fund" (New York, 1970), 3-24. See also Foundation Minutes (UPCUSA), September 20-21, 1977, Appendix G. Statistics provided in 1943 indicate a total of 407 beneficiaries (326 women and 71 men). The average monthly grant for one person living alone was $89. Of the 407 beneficiaries, there were 109 Presbyterians, 101 Episcopalians, 34 Congregationalists, 30 Baptists, 40 Methodists, 13 Lutherans, 18 Dutch Reformed, 7 Unitarians, 6 Roman Catholics, 19 Christian Scientists, and 30 scattered among the other denominations. For recent figures, see *Update* (June 1997): 4.

70. "Jinishian Foundation, A Little-Known Charity," *The Armenian Reporter International*, 7 February 1998. See also Foundation Minutes (UPCUSA), September 20-21, 1980, Appendix H.

71. *GAMUPCUSA*, 1978, I:122, Foundation Minutes (UPCUSA) (ex.com.), March 18, 1980, and January 18, 1981. Gast's job description called for administrative skills, knowledge of the policy and organization of the denomination, skill in working with executives of governing bodies and church agencies, the ability to command the confidence of the broad constituency of the church and to provide inspired leadership for Foundation trustees and staff. The last sentence of the job profile reads, "He is expected to have knowledge and experience in the field of investment, fund development, and finance." Clearly this was a job description for a clergyperson rather than a layperson. Foundation Minutes (UPCUSA), September 15, 1981, Appendix A.

72. Loetscher, *A Brief History of the Presbyterians*, 184-86.

73. Foundation Minutes (UPCUSA), November 10, 1983.

74. G. Daniel Little to Riley H. Richards, 8 March, 1984, in Foundation Minutes (UPCUSA), March 20, 1984, Appendix A.

Expansion and Innovation

The funding of our national Presbyterian Church (U.S.A.)
mission budgets has reached a crisis level we can no longer
afford to ignore. This funding crisis is also real, although
experienced differently, for Presbyterian congregations. We
cannot reverse the situation by simply doing things better and
harder than we have always done them. New ideas and
solutions must be considered.—*Final Report of the
Comprehensive Strategy for Mission Funding Work Group,
September 1997*

Like most mainline Protestant denominations during the closing decades
of the century, the Presbyterian Church (U.S.A.) has been challenged to
rethink its institutional structures and mission priorities in the light of
declining membership and budget shortfalls. Recent studies indicate that
a national church with programs and policies formulated at a central
headquarters and disseminated to regional and local entities is no longer
a realistic model in the upcoming millennium. In its place is emerging a
more locally and regionally oriented structure with mission needs being
determined primarily by middle governing bodies and individual
congregations. Giving patterns clearly reflect this change. Between 1988
and 1996 unified resources for the General Assembly Mission Budget
shrunk from $33,298,290 to $22,692,763, while the total of all bequests
made to local Presbyterian congregations grew to nearly $169 million in
1995 compared to a little more than $20 million in 1980. Although it is
impossible to predict how the denomination will adapt to changing times,
one thing does appear certain: "The future shape of the denomination will
be different from what we now know."[1]

Responding to current changing cultural, financial, and theological environments, and anticipating future developments, the Foundation is preparing for the challenges of the next century. Following the merger of the PCUS and UPCUSA foundations in 1987, the Presbyterian Church (U.S.A.) Foundation took measures to professionalize operations in keeping with its fiduciary responsibilities as a denominational corporation. This included hiring experienced executive officers and specially trained staff to handle the increasingly complex tasks of a nonprofit foundation and the introduction of new programs and services to accommodate donor needs. Innovations include the creation of a trust company and several anticipated subsidiary organizations that allow the Foundation to widen its sources of mission funding. As a result, the Foundation has experienced a remarkable growth of assets, reaching $1.75 billion dollars in 1998. Although these developments have occurred in the context of ambivalent Foundation-General Assembly Council (GAC) relationships, recent agreements between the two have clarified some longstanding fiduciary issues and established a forum for ongoing conversations.

The 1983 reunion of the UPCUSA and the PCUS brought together two corporations with similar goals but different operational functions and philosophies. The PCUS Foundation relied almost exclusively on its small executive staff to direct advertising campaigns and conduct other development activities out of its Charlotte, North Carolina, office. The UPF employed a cadre of regional field representatives who cultivated donors and assisted governing bodies in stewardship activities. Housed in denominational headquarters in New York, the UPF established close working relationships with boards and agencies and was integrally involved with mission programs and policies in contrast to the Charlotte Foundation which functioned more as an autonomous entity removed from the General Assembly offices in Atlanta. Although the PCUS Foundation was a corporation established and sanctioned by the General Assembly, it was neither the sole corporation of the denomination nor the legal successor of previous boards and agencies. Moreover, while the PCUS trustees managed certain General Assembly funds, they also had the freedom to make some grants apart from General Assembly approval, a prerogative not awarded to the UPF. This contrast would be reflected in the discussions that led to a single denominational corporation.[2]

As background to reunion, the modern history of the Charlotte Foundation can be briefly recounted.[3] Prompted by the rapid growth of secular community foundations and the completion of successful denominational stewardship campaigns following World War I, the 1922 PCUS General Assembly endorsed an overture from the Presbytery of North Alabama calling for the creation of a Presbyterian Foundation.[4] Despite opposition from General Assembly trustees who argued that they lacked funding for promotional ventures and deemed it inappropriate to use donors' money for such expenses, the overture was finally implemented in 1925. The Assembly enlarged Board membership from nine to twenty-five in order to include one member from each synod and amended the charter to enable the trustees to sell annuity bonds and function fully as a denominational foundation.[5]

When the trustees failed to take the initiative, Marion E. Melvin, executive secretary of the General Assembly's Stewardship Committee, launched a promotional campaign for the Foundation that featured the establishment of synodical advisory committees and the employment of extensive advertising in denominational newspapers and magazines. Largely due to Melvin's efforts, corporation trustees reported their best year ever in 1927-28 with the sale of $23,000 in annuity bonds and the acquisition of new legacies totaling $44,000.[6] When Melvin resigned to accept a position as president of Westminster College in Fulton, Missouri, however, ties between the Foundation and the Stewardship Committee diminished, leaving the Foundation responsible for its own promotional efforts. Subsequent Foundation presidents Robert A. Dunn (1921-1939) and Thomas A. McPheeters, Jr. (1939-1956) guided the corporation through the Depression of the 1930s and World War Two but never attained the financial goals envisioned by Foundation advocates in the 1920s. Operating in the shadow of proactive executive committees, the PCUS Foundation in 1945 reported assets of only $294,921.[7]

After the end of World War II, the PCUS General Assembly undertook the first major denominational restructuring in its eighty-year history. Following several years of study, the General Assembly in 1949 approved the creation of the Boards of Annuities and Relief, Church Extension, Education, World Missions, and Women's Work to replace twenty-one committees and agencies. Noting that the Foundation was "relatively static," and had high administrative costs relative to the amount of income produced, the reorganization committee recommended that the Foundation be abolished and that its assets be transferred to the Office of the General Assembly in Atlanta, Georgia.[8]

Foundation trustees immediately launched a widely publicized protest campaign and succeeded in postponing implementation of the move and merger until additional studies could be conducted.[9] A committee chaired by John Cunningham, president of Davidson College, recommended in 1952 that the Foundation remain in Charlotte as the fiduciary corporation because of legal obstacles in securing a new charter but that the new General Council should assume full responsibility for promoting gifts, bequests, and annuities. The Council declined, citing a limited budget and commitments already made to other major projects. Subsequent efforts to link the Foundation with the Board of Annuities and Relief also proved futile. After nearly six years in ecclesiastical limbo, the Foundation seemed destined either to oblivion or extinction.[10]

While the future of the Foundation remained in doubt, Calvin T. Young, a prominent Florida businessman, died and left an estate to the Foundation estimated to be worth $1.2 million.[11] This bequest enabled the Foundation to obtain an autonomous status as a denominational agency along with an annual operating budget of $25,000 from the General Assembly. Cunningham resigned as president of Davidson College in 1956 to become the first salaried executive director of the Foundation. One of his first acts was to embark on a denomination-wide tour to raise development funds and familiarize congregants with giving opportunities available through the Foundation.[12] In successive terms, Cunningham (1956-1963) and Frank Caldwell (1964-1971) provided competent leadership to the Foundation in its dual function of administering endowment funds and soliciting resources for the denomination. Largely through their efforts, the Foundation refurbished its institutional image and substantially increased its assets. In 1971, the Foundation reported that it had distributed $311,845 to various boards, colleges, and agencies and that its funds had increased by more than a million dollars, reaching a total of $8,019,993.[13]

As a result of major restructuring in 1972, the Foundation assumed responsibility for the management and investment of endowment and trust funds, gift annuities, and bequests held by the General Assembly and its boards and agencies except for those of the Board of Annuities and Relief.[14] The Foundation continued to operate out of Charlotte, with a staff of four persons: executive director, associate director and treasurer, administrative assistant, and bookkeeper. Professional investment counselors from the Wachovia Bank and Trust Company of Charlotte under the supervision of the board's investment committee managed the Foundation's permanent funds. As previously, the PCUS Foundation employed no field representatives but relied on the executive directors, Warner T. Hall (1971-1981) and Frederick R. Stair (1981-1985), and individual trustees to cultivate donors from the various governing bodies. By the time of the UPCUSA-PCUS reunion in 1983, board chairman John F. Watlington, Jr. (1978-1987) reported that the Foundation held assets of approximately $41 million and that it had disbursed $2.7 million to 460 beneficiaries during the previous calendar year.[15]

In the interim following reunion and before consolidation, the UPF and the PCUS Foundations upgraded and expanded their respective programs. The UPF employed Cambridge Associates, one of the nation's foremost investment management consulting firms, and added diversified investment managers including John Templeton, a leading global investor. Between 1982 and 1986, having added seven regional representatives, it broke all existing records with a total of $150 million in new gifts, including two of the largest gifts in the history of the UPF, $7.75 million from Jane Newhall of San Francisco and $8.36 million from Foster McGaw, one of the founders of the American Hospital Supply Company.[16] During the same time period, the value of endowment funds increased from approximately $340 million to $560 million, and total returns on investments averaged in excess of 20 percent per year.[17] Meanwhile, the PCUS Foundation introduced a "Family of Funds" for quarterly disbursements and options to switch into funds in order to achieve investment objectives within the financial markets. The Family of Funds stimulated the influx of new money that resulted in a 46 percent increase in disbursements to the global mission of the church. At the end of 1985, the Charlotte Foundation reported total assets in excess of $52 million and distributions of $5.3 million compared to assets of $19 million and distributions of $1.7 million in 1980.[18]

Concurrently, the PCUS and UPCUSA Foundations initiated a series of cooperative efforts to prepare the way for linking their respective organizations. Prior to the formal merger in 1987, the two corporations were already doing business together as the Presbyterian Church (U.S.A.) Foundation, registering their name in Pennsylvania and North Carolina. They agreed to pool investments when feasible and approved a strategic plan, addressing budget, staff, programs, and service commitment for the three transition years, 1986, 1987, and 1988. The two groups held joint staff meetings, sent representatives to each of the board meetings, and prepared adjacent display booths and joint presentations for sessions of the General Assembly. They also took full-page combined advertisements in the *Presbyterian Survey* and cooperatively published a manual on wills and estate planning. At a joint meeting on October 8, 1986, the two foundations formally adopted the same resolutions and bylaws, elected officers to identical positions in both corporations, and functionally become one corporation pending final legal formalities.[19]

At the national level, the General Assembly Council appointed a Mission Design Committee and initiated a series of denomination-wide consultations to engage governing bodies and other groups in an examination of their mission needs and current activities. Out of this the Mission Design Committee produced *The Structural Design For Mission*, a document that received General Assembly approval in 1986. The mission design established nine Ministry Units to carry out most programmatic functions at the General Assembly level and provided for two corporations in addition to the Board of Pensions: the Central

Treasury Corporation (CTC), charged with the responsibility of holding title to operating assets utilized in mission activities, providing accounting and financial services to the General Assembly and its agencies, and functioning as a disbursing agent of income and principal derived from undesignated funds, and the Fiduciary Corporation (The Presbyterian Church (U.S.A.) Foundation), assigned the tasks of managing the denomination's endowment funds and directing a development program that emphasized deferred giving and bequests. Because of the close relationship between stewardship, mission funding, and deferred giving, *The Structural Design for Mission* specified trustee and staff linkage among the Foundation, the Stewardship and Communication Development Ministry Unit, and the General Assembly Council.[20]

In order to implement the new mission design, a Transition Planning Group chaired by Foundation trustee William M. E. Clarkson issued a report in 1986 that charted a new course for the Foundation in terms of staff leadership positions. Rather than following the precedent of having a single executive officer, Clarkson's committee proposed dual leadership positions, both of which would report directly to the chair of the Board of Trustees. The staff chairperson, Aaron Gast, would concentrate primarily on public relations and development and also function as a resource person for field representatives. The president and CEO would handle internal administrative duties and supervise the daily operations of the corporation. W. Terry Young, former associate director of the PCUS Foundation and an experienced corporate executive with Shoney's Restaurants, accepted this position on an interim basis. Although some trustees questioned the viability of having the chairperson and president co-equal, they ultimately adopted the proposal with the proviso that it be reviewed after one year to ascertain its effectiveness.[21]

Having prepared all the necessary legal papers and with the imprimatur of the General Assembly, PCUS and UPCUSA trustees and guests gathered on January 6, 1987, in the assembly room, Buttonwood Hall, of the First Presbyterian Church, Philadelphia, Pennsylvania, to create the unified corporation. Before the signing ceremony, participants worshipped in the First Presbyterian Church with General Assembly Moderator Benjamin M. Weir delivering the sermon. The chair of the Board of Trustees, Herbert B. Anderson, and Paul B. Bell, vice-chair, read the resolutions of the Board of Trustees adopting the bylaws of the new corporation. At a luncheon following the ceremony, scrolls of appreciation were presented to Riley H. Richards, Aaron E. Gast, Marvin C. Wilbur, and Robert B. Turner for their dedicated service to the United Presbyterian Foundation. In addition, George W. McKeag, legal counsel for the Presbyterian Church (U.S.A.) for forty-four years, was honored for his exceptional skills as a legal practitioner and for his role in shaping the Presbyterian Form of Government.[22]

In a short time the corporation commenced a national search for a new chief executive officer. Although the job description stressed the importance of a personal commitment to Jesus Christ and the mission of the Presbyterian Church, it also specified that applicants should have at least ten years of managerial experience, including a minimum of five years at a senior executive level of a major financial institution. In addition to understanding theological issues related to stewardship, the president would be expected to ensure that the corporation establish performance measurements, investment manager evaluations, and asset allocation reviews. Along with overseeing the day-to-day operations of the Foundation, the CEO would also develop long-term plans that would enable the Foundation to expand its services and increase its assets during the closing years of the twentieth century. By definition, this essentially excluded ministerial candidates from consideration, which would mean that the Foundation would take on a different character from the former PCUS or UPCUSA organizations, each of which had traditionally elected an ordained clergyman as the senior staff executive.[23]

Advertising in *New York Times* and *The Wall Street Journal*, the Foundation received approximately 150 letters of interest in the position, but serious inquiries diminished when the salary range, less than half of what the secular marketplace would offer such a candidate, became known. The sole nominee and unanimous choice for the presidency, Geoffrey R. Cross, brought extensive executive experience to the new position. After twelve years in the Sperry Corporation as Controller and Vice President and General Manager of Univac's Americas Division, Cross became the chief executive officer of International Computers Limited, which was then Britain's leading manufacturer of computers. From 1979 to 1982 Cross served as president and chief executive officer of the A.B. Dick Company, a subsidiary of Britain's General Electric Company. Prior to becoming president of the Foundation, Cross held the position of president and chief executive officer of Automated Microbiology Systems, Inc., a company he founded in California 1982. Ordained as an elder in Rancho Bernardo Community Presbyterian Church in San Diego, California, where he and his family had resided since 1978, he assumed his duties on February 1, 1988. The General Assembly confirmed his appointment in June of that year.[24]

According to the master plan for relocating General Assembly ministry units and agencies, the respective foundations were to close their New York and Charlotte offices and move to the Presbyterian Center in Louisville, Kentucky, in proximity to other ministry units and agencies.

Shortly after the merger, however, the trustees discovered significant tax consequences for the Foundation if it located in Kentucky. The state had an intangibles tax on assets that potentially could cost the Foundation several million dollars annually.[25] Following consultations with the executive committee of the GAC, the trustees decided that the prudent course for the Foundation was to move to southern Indiana, across the Ohio River from Louisville, and received permission from the General Assembly to relocate in that adjoining state.[26] Because no suitable facilities were available in the small town of Jeffersonville, the trustees broke ground for a two-story building to house its new headquarters on April 26, 1988. Under the supervision of acting President Young, the project was completed in 107 days from groundbreaking to occupancy.[27]

In late spring 1988, staff members in the New York and Charlotte offices finalized the move to the Indiana headquarters. Only ten of the forty staff members in New York and none of the Charlotte work force chose to transfer, so the move and the recruitment of some twenty-eight new employees put great pressure on the remaining staff to keep operations flowing smoothly. Veteran officers Dennis J. Murphy, Jack Stuart, Douglass Yeager, and newcomers Margaret Daniel and Julianne Singh, played key roles in making an efficient and effective transition into the new setting.[28] Other personnel changes about this time included the retirement of the associate director, Fred R. Stair, in 1988 and the resignation of staff chairperson Aaron Gast, who ended eight years of service in 1989 to accept a position with the Philadelphia Presbyterian Homes, Inc. The departure of Gast ended the dual president-chairperson leadership team and left Cross as the sole senior executive officer.[29] At the trustee level, Bell, vice-chair and an attorney from Charlotte, replaced Herbert B. Anderson in 1988, whose term of service had expired, as chair of the board of trustees. At the same time, Foundation trustees elected Helen Robson Walton as vice-chair, and two years later she succeeded Bell as chair. Her election marked the first time in the 190-year history of the Foundation that these offices were held by a woman.[30] Well-known for co-founding Wal-Mart Stores with her husband, Sam, Walton also was a volunteer leader in the First Presbyterian Church in Bentonville, Arkansas, the University of the Ozarks, Presbyterian Women, and seven years as a trustee of the Presbyterian Foundation. As trustee emerita, Walton continued her service to the Foundation as a member of the Development Committee by touring the country in 1993 at her own expense to promote the mission of the denomination.[31]

Under the leadership of Cross and his executive staff, Foundation trustees developed a series of long-term strategic plans to chart the course of the Foundation into the mid-1990s. Adopted by the Board of Trustees in October 1988, the initial plan established as major objectives the increase of new gifts from a 1987 level of $16.3 million to $50 million and of Foundation assets from a 1987 level of $680 million to $1,000 million. It also called for the increase of income provided for the denominational mission program and to annuitants from $35 million to $75 million and the expansion of the regional representative staff from seventeen to thirty-five.[32] Periodically updated to reflect new challenges, the strategic plan as implemented by the Foundation staff produced long-term results. By 1996 the goals had been reached and surpassed. Backed by a force of 35 development officers, distributions from assets amounted to $95.5 million, gifts increased to $51.4 million, and total assets reached a high of $1.4 billion.[33]

In quest of their goals, Foundation trustees and staff developed new programs to serve the denomination more effectively. The Foundation Volunteer in Development Program started with seventeen trained volunteers who assisted the regional representatives in presenting wills emphasis programs and other services of the Foundation to local churches and governing bodies. The Every Member Endowment Program was introduced to all churches in five presbyteries to encourage every church member to participate in endowing mission either in the present or in the future. The Foundation also established the Institutional Relations Program to assist and support Presbyterian-related colleges, agencies, and governing bodies in the area of planned giving. Special seminars led by Winton C. Smith, a nationally recognized planned giving specialist, and by Foundation staff were hosted for officers of the denomination's colleges, seminaries, retirement communities, hospitals, and children's programs. A Spirit of Stewardship Conference for pastors co-sponsored with the Stewardship and Communication Development Ministry Unit and the General Assembly Council in 1994 marked the beginning of a series of conferences well received by Presbyterian clergy.[34]

Under the direction of Senior Vice President Dennis Murphy, emphasis on Investment Management Services (IMS) featured prominently in the Foundation's overall strategy to expand its development outreach. By generating more income from the IMS, the Foundation was able to hire additional field representatives and to increase its contacts with middle governing bodies and local congregations. The Foundation offered four funds to IMS participants, each with a specifically designed investment objective. The Growth Fund sought long-term growth of capital by investing in common stocks with dividend income a secondary consideration. The Balanced Growth Fund was designed to optimize total rate of return performance in order to produce income that could provide support for mission. The objective of the Balanced Income Fund was to provide a growing stream of income and some capital growth by investing in all forms of securities, with a substantial portion in bonds. The Income fund sought to provide a high level of current income by investing entirely in bonds and short-term money market instruments along with conservation of the nominal principal as an additional objective.[35]

The introduction of new programs and the accumulation of rapidly mounting assets were achieved during a period of strained relationships between the Foundation and the General Assembly Council. Tensions between the GAC and the Foundation reflected differences between programmatic agencies and fiduciary corporations that had surfaced periodically in the denomination's history. On the basis of language in the *Articles of Agreement of Reunion* and in *The Structural Design For Mission*, the GAC carried responsibility for the denominational budgeting process and the overall coordination of the various ministry units and related bodies. Both documents, however, were imprecise regarding specific aspects of GAC control over related bodies such as the Foundation and the Board of Pensions. Most Council members and staff interpreted the documents as validating a relational model comparable to the former UPCUSA structure where the Foundation functioned as an integral part of a larger mission decision-making group. While acknowledging its linkage to the General Assembly through the GAC, Foundation trustees tended to view the corporation's fiduciary responsibilities under civil law as guaranteeing a substantial measure of autonomy from the GAC not afforded to other ministry units and agencies of the General Assembly. This interpretation indeed adhered more closely to the former PCUS Foundation that historically had experienced considerable freedom in its relationship with the General Assembly Mission Board. Beyond specific problems that arose from time to time, the GAC's role in the oversight of Foundation activities framed the context of most discussions between the two groups.[36]

At the first of their semi-annual board meetings in 1987, Foundation trustees devoted a major portion of their time discussing concerns over the "spending formula policy" (the guaranteed annual income paid by the Foundation to the GAC through the CTC) on the permanent endowment funds. Under the new structural design, setting the income level from general endowment funds was assigned to the CTC in conjunction with the GAC. Although the Foundation recommended a 4½ percent formula, the CTC initially adopted a 5 percent formula, which the GAC later raised to 6 percent in 1988 because of budget problems. The Foundation complied with the latter decision but adopted a resolution stating that continuation of a 6 percent spending rate would be an unwise policy due to high inflation rates and a loss of purchasing power. In response to the resolution, the 1988 General Assembly directed the Foundation and the GAC to develop a long-term spending policy. Working together, GAC and Foundation officials agreed on a formula by which the Foundation paid the CTC a fixed sum for five years, increasing from $7.0 million in 1989 to $7.8 million in 1992, calculated on the basis of 6 percent of the $113 million unrestricted endowment fund balance on December 31, 1987. Foundation and GAC representatives also agreed to meet annually to monitor the progress of the spending policy and to renegotiate the formula at the end of five years.[37]

Differences between the Foundation and the GAC also surfaced regarding the allocation of certain restricted endowment funds administered by the Foundation for General Assembly use. Record-keeping over the years had been inadequate and neither the Foundation nor the GAC could verify in detail the accuracy of their documentation. In 1988 the GAC initiated a comprehensive review of restricted endowments to identify donor restrictions, classify these gifts as "permanent" or "expendable," and assign use to appropriate mission program agencies. Panel members appointed jointly by the GAC and the Foundation scrutinized the documentation to ascertain the purposes of the donors and to match them with appropriate current Presbyterian work and opportunities. When identified, the donors' purposes were noted in Foundation and Council permanent records as a beginning point and guide for future generations.[38] Among other items, the GAC and the Foundation disagreed on the disposition of some $4.5 million in fifty-eight funds from the former PCUS Foundation, commonly referred to as "Z Funds." Based on its interpretation of the donors' intent, the Foundation argued that the funds had been raised primarily for development activities and should be utilized by the Foundation for the expansion of its deferred-giving program. The GAC asserted that the language of the donors indicated the funds were essentially unrestricted and should be utilized for general mission funding. Neither side gave any indication of willingness to modify their positions on the subject.[39]

Although the hurried review resolved some of the differences between the two groups, it failed to establish a mutually acceptable process for dealing with restricted funds where the instructions of donors were unclear or open to interpretation. Foundation-GAC consultations also failed to resolve broader disagreements relating to proposed changes in *The Structural Design For Mission* by the GAC affecting the regulation of staff salary policies, the appointment and evaluation of chief executive officers, the approval of changes in the bylaws, and the utilization of computer and legal support services. At the spring meeting of the

Foundation Trustees in 1989, Board Chair Bell reported that the GAC was moving forward unilaterally to request alterations in *The Structural Design For Mission*, a move that in his estimation would have an adverse impact on the duties and responsibilities of the Foundation. After consultation with the Stated Clerk, Foundation trustees voted to request that the upcoming General Assembly defer consideration of GAC mission design changes until a Committee on Review could be established by the 1991 General Assembly as provided in *The Structural Design For Mission*.[40] In light of the Foundation's opposition, the GAC agreed to defer submitting the proposed changes so that the two groups could negotiate a mutually acceptable resolution of their differences.[41]

After a series of conferences in 1989-90, GAC and Foundation representatives reached substantive agreements in four areas and pledged to maintain lines of communication between the two groups. According to trustee L. Neil Williams, Jr., who chaired the Foundation's team, the agreements affirmed the independence required by the Foundation to meet its fiduciary responsibilities and also articulated the Foundation's commitment to be an integral part of the church.[42] The disagreements over the interpretation of General Assembly salary policies lessened when the Foundation accepted the GAC personnel administration guidelines after agreed upon revisions in recognition of the Foundation's having flexibility in implementing annual salary increase programs. The right of the GAC to approve the Foundation's annual staff rationale was clarified when the Foundation agreed that the prerogative was a necessary check and balance. The Foundation also viewed the requirement in *The Structural Design for Mission* that changes in Foundation bylaws necessitated concurrence of the GAC prior to submission to the General Assembly as having the potential to impact its fiduciary responsibilities, citing the right of GAC to concur in Foundation's choice of President as an example. Although the Foundation accepted this constraint as a further check and balance, the GAC agreed that hiring initiatives and annual performance reviews were the primary responsibilities of the Foundation's Board of Trustees. To insure outside linkage, however, the Foundation accepted the stipulation that a member of the Stewardship and Communication Development Ministry Unit participate in such proceedings. Regarding the disputed "Z Funds," the parties reached a tentative compromise that allowed the GAC, for accounting purposes, to treat them as unrestricted funds but permitted their management and use by the Foundation for development purposes. Initially the agreement was for five years and could be renewed or renegotiated at that time.[43]

Having settled the immediate disagreements with the GAC, Foundation trustees and staff focused on improving internal operations of the corporation. In the area of development activities, the number of development officers grew from twelve (five of whom were part-time) in 1988 to thirty-eight in 1998, and the ratio between clergy and lay moved from about 50-50 to 75-25 laypersons. Attention was also given to a balance of gender and racial-ethnic representation among development officers. With the increasing complexities of financial planning, new development officers were required to have technical training and experience prior to service with the Foundation.[44] Statistics published by the Research Services Office in the Congregational Ministries Division among congregations in 1995 indicated that development officers were having an impact on congregational giving. Results from 2,500 congregations who reported an active endowment and wills emphasis program received bequests averaging more than $15,000 and those without $10,000. Churches using Foundation-supplied materials and support averaged 40 percent higher than those who did not. Those with IMS accounts and direct involvement of Foundation staff reported bequests 60 percent higher than the others.[45]

The Foundation increased its office efficiency in 1988 with the installation of state-of-the-art Unix computer systems from IBM. The systems were designed to grow with the expansion of the Foundation and to provide the necessary tools to meet the growing needs of donors and churches.[46] The accounting system was further computerized in 1991 to increase the promptness of financial statement preparation and the speed of access to all facets of donor funds, account balances and cash flow. Interlinked with the custodial bank (Wachovia Bank & Trust), the system detailed day-to-day transactions of the Foundation and maintained duplicate copies of all donor documents for safekeeping.[47] Subsequently the Foundation implemented direct deposit of payments to the individual bank accounts of annuity income recipients, a step that provided increased convenience and security and reduced administrative costs.[48] An Internet website, operational in 1997, afforded instant access to such topics as investment management service, gifts, resources and wills emphasis.[49]

Despite progress in enhancing the total effectiveness of Foundation operations, trustees received a setback in June 1992 when President Cross abruptly resigned, citing "personal problems" after having been recently elected for a second four-year term.[50] Following Cross's departure, the Foundation trustees appointed Robert F. Langwig, vice president for development, to serve as acting president while the corporation began the process of selecting a new chief executive. Langwig had joined the Foundation staff in 1983 as a regional representative in the Synod of Mid-America following a twenty-seven year career as pastor in Michigan, New York, and Pennsylvania and had been promoted in 1988 to vice president for development. A skillful facilitator and highly respected churchman, Langwig brought continuity and stability to the corporation during a crucial period of leadership transition.[51]

From a pool of some two hundred applicants, the search committee unanimously selected Larry D. Carr, a graduate of the University of Illinois with a Bachelor of Science degree in Finance, who came to the Foundation with more than twenty years of management and executive-level experience in both large and small profit and non-profit organizations. Most recently, Carr had been employed as the Executive Vice President and Director Chairman and CEO of the National General Insurance Company, the insurance arm of General Motors' GMAC financial services. Active in a variety of community service organizations, Carr was a member and trustee of several Presbyterian congregations in New Jersey and Michigan during his corporate career. In his statement of personal beliefs, Carr stressed the importance of seeking the guidance of the Holy Spirit in the midst of a complex and rapidly changing world. "While our faith is most certainly rooted in the past," Carr emphasized, "we must not allow it to be frozen there."[52]

As chief executive officer, the forty-six-year-old Carr brought energy and focus to the Foundation. One of his first tasks was to cultivate a sense of community and trust among trustees and staff who had experienced constant change since the move to Jeffersonville. Conducting meetings of all employees, bringing in outside consultants to discuss interpersonal dynamics, and having informal conversations with trustees and various components of the office staff, Carr and his leadership team have fostered a spirit of group commitment to the Foundation that has increased productivity and boosted morale.[53] He also addressed improving the effectiveness of existing programs and of leading the corporation into new areas of endeavor. Cognizant that the denomination was entering a period of tremendous change in charitable giving patterns, whereby nationally in the next twenty years some $10 to $20 trillion in wealth would be transferred between generations, in the spring of 1994 the board appointed a group of trustees to work with staff to examine a wide range of fundamental issues and to bring specific recommendations regarding the expansion of services to the denomination. Out of this study came a series of new programs including The Investment and Loan Program, Donor Advised Funds, the Guardian Fund, and the creation of a spending formula for restricted funds and new cost recovery procedures.[54]

Each of these new programs increased the potential for funding mission activities at every governing body level. A Foundation trustee-staff team in cooperation with the GAC and middle governing bodies developed the Presbyterian Church (U.S.A.) Investment & Loan Program, approved by the General Assembly in 1995.[55] Through certificates available to all Presbyterians for purchase including tax-advantaged accounts such as IRAs, the Investment & Loan Program gathers funds to provide loans for capital projects throughout the denomination. At the Foundation's request and approved by the General Assembly, the new corporation is autonomous and has its own board of directors.[56]

To optimize endowment distribution, the Foundation implemented a spending policy for restricted endowments to increase and stabilize income distribution while recognizing the current state-of-the-art in total return investing. This decision increased funding to mission across the denomination by more than $5 million annually. The Foundation adopted a fundamental change in the approach to cost recovery by segregating all investment and custody charges out of the fee and charging these expenses directly to the assets managed at cost. Under a new three-tiered fee structure, IMS, endowment accounts, and life income plans were assessed according to the actual costs of providing the service.[57] The Foundation also has expanded its range of prospective gifts by creating The Steward Fund which made it possible for donors to make an immediate contribution but to delay their decision regarding the specific recipients of the distribution. An endowment campaign among present and former trustees, led by Terry Young, Helen Walton, and Bob Cuthill, has established the Guardian Fund to ensure that the Foundation will always have sufficient resources to carry on its development program.[58]

A second round of strategic studies, begun in the fall of 1995, examined the changing legal and regulatory environment in which the Foundation was operating. As a result, the Foundation filed a request for a Private Letter Ruling in 1995 from the Internal Revenue Service to enable the Foundation to operate beyond the traditional definition of a church in the tax code. Approval from the IRS the following year made it possible for the Foundation to serve Presbyterian-related and ecumenical organizations in which the PC(U.S.A.) had significant involvement, such as the National or World Councils of Churches, interdenominational entities, or partner denominations that shared the PC(U.S.A.)'s mission of promoting Christianity. To insure that the Foundation retained its primary focus, the IRS specified that activities in these ancillary areas be limited to no more than 30 percent of the Foundation's total assets and clients.[59]

With this ruling and the endorsement of the General Assembly, Foundation staff and trustees began implementation, and on January 2, 1998, opened the New Covenant Trust Company, N.A., the nation's first charity-owned, federally chartered trust company, a taxable entity venture designed to administer charitable trusts for churches and other religious bodies. The New Covenant Trust Company contemplates starting an investment subsidiary that will offer clients a family of mutual funds regulated by the Securities and Exchange Commission and allow them to make daily deposits and withdrawals in contrast to a monthly timetable under trust laws governing the Foundation's present system. An insurance company planned for late 1998 or early 1999 will permit the Foundation to offer charitable gift annuities in every state. The Foundation previously had refrained from promoting gift annuities in certain states because of regulatory limits.[60]

Although Carr affirmed that "Our objective is not to take over the world," he admitted that the Foundation's plan could eventually provide competition for established companies that have historically managed charitable assets such as Fidelity and Merrill Lynch. In an interview with a reporter from *The Chronicle of Philanthropy*, Carr emphasized that the main thrust of the restructuring was to insulate the Foundation from new restrictions in charities, such as limits on the types of trust and annuity activity permitted and to facilitate compliance with charity laws that vary from state to state. Under the restructuring, the Foundation is able to avoid a recent federal ruling that limits the options charities have for investing money from revocable trusts and to be exempted from technical rules that some states impose on trust agreements.[61]

Recent figures released by the Foundation reflect the continued confidence of the denomination in the corporation's money-management policies and its wide range of programs and services. For the first time in the history of the Foundation, gifts and deposits exceeded $100 million in a single year—totaling $127.8 million in 1996. Between 1992 and 1997 annual gifts and bequests almost doubled from $26.5 million to $53.2 million, and IMS deposits in the same time period grew from $62.6 million to $86.8 million. Distribution from assets rose from $55.6 million in 1994 to $130.3 million in 1997. Beneficiaries of income from permanent funds in 1997 included the General Assembly (38 percent), congregations (37 percent), presbyteries, synods and others (14 percent), education, retirement and children's homes (8 percent), and the Foundation (3 percent). The Foundation's investment managers continued to utilize their research techniques and investment strategies in the stock portfolio to produce a 19.3 percent net return for 1997 which resulted in a 22.3 percent average annual total return over the previous three years and more than 15 percent for both the last ten- and fifteen-year periods. At the end of 1997, the total assets of the Foundation were approximately 1.6 billion dollars.[62]

These dramatic changes in Foundation programs and structures have taken place in a context of extended and sometimes heated disagreements with the General Assembly Council. Although wider issues of autonomy and control loomed in the background, specific incidents relating to fiduciary responsibility and disbursement of funds surfaced periodically to exacerbate relationships between the two groups. In 1992 Foundation trustees expressed serious concerns about the Social Justice and Peacemaking Ministry Unit's handling of Jarvie Commonweal Fund income and effected a restructuring of the administration and governance of the fund that gave more authority to the Foundation.[63]

Differences in regard to the use of designated or restricted endowment funds and the accumulation of unused or underutilized restricted General Assembly funds also generated friction. In 1994 the Foundation reported that its staff had been unable to determine whether donor instructions were being carried out on seventy-four designated memorial funds valued at $1.3 million and directed the controller to cease payment to the CTC until verification had been received.[64] One case in particular became a flashpoint. Income from the Jennie Wimer Fund, designated for work among Navajo Native Americans at the Ganado Mission in Ganado, Arizona, had been used in part to repair a roof and pay faculty salaries at Cook College and Theological School in Tempe, Arizona. Because the Ganado school no longer existed and Cook College served some Navajo people, the GAC reasoned that this alternate use of funds was within the framework of the Wimer bequest. Foundation officials thought otherwise. From their perspective, the expenditures at Cook College were inconsistent with the intent of the original donor, and they threatened to place in escrow $136,018.69 from unrestricted funds to cover the amount of disputed GAC disbursements from the Wimer Fund.[65]

Efforts to resolve these difficulties eventually proved fruitless and reached a breaking point in February 1996 when GAC and Foundation officials clashed over the decision by the GAC to conduct an internal audit of disbursements of restricted endowment earnings. Foundation representatives, who objected strenuously, wanted to reach an agreement on joint auditing activity between the GAC and the Foundation.[66] At their plenary meeting in April 1996 Foundation trustees approved a report to the General Assembly that called for definitive clarification of Foundation responsibilities and relationships with the General Assembly Council. The report requested the General Assembly to affirm that the Foundation is not required to forward funds to the CTC if the use of such funds was deemed inconsistent with donor's instructions and that the Foundation should not permit unused or underutilized restricted General Assembly funds to accumulate. It also requested permission to make funds that accumulated more than one year of income available to

General Assembly synods and presbyteries for uses consistent with donor directions. Finally, the Foundation asked the General Assembly to decide if the GAC either directly or through the Corporate and Administrative Services had the right "to dictate, to control, the actions of the Trustees of the Foundation."[67]

With both disputants holding firm to their convictions and communications between the GAC and the Foundation severely impaired, it appeared that the issues would have to be publicly debated and resolved at the forthcoming General Assembly in Albuquerque, New Mexico. A final meeting between Foundation and GAC representatives scheduled in Chicago on May 16 before the General Assembly convened appeared to offer little hope of resolving differences. Confrontation on the floor of the General Assembly was avoided only by a last-minute agreement between GAC executive director James M. Brown and Foundation president Larry Carr just two days before the Chicago meeting. Two key principles emerged from the Brown-Carr agreement. First, the GAC was recognized to be the body with the responsibility for General Assembly mission allocation decisions. Second, the Foundation was acknowledged as the final authority regarding compliance with donor instructions. Both organizations agreed to complete a jointly conducted analysis of restricted funds and to require a confirmation by the end user of the actual uses of the funds. Foundation and GAC executive committees met by teleconference on May 20 to ratify the agreement and adopt a joint report communicating their new understanding and agreements. The Albuquerque Assembly confirmed the agreement and authorized the GAC and the Foundation to begin a process of implementation.[68]

During the course of the extended GAC-Foundation disagreements, Foundation staff under the leadership of Thomas R. Drake were developing two new programs with the acronyms CARE and PRECIS for preventing disagreements over the use of restricted funds. In November 1996 the two programs were endorsed by the Foundation Board and ratified the following spring by the General Assembly Council. The CARE program (Comprehensive Analysis of Restricted Endowments) researches, scrutinizes, and preserves the original instruction of every endowment received and held by the Foundation since its inception in 1799. Using optical imaging scanners, staff members are entering into the CARE database the terms of wills and trust documents that state the donor's instructions. Information will be indexed in several categories to facilitate easy retrieval. A joint staff entity of the GAC and the Foundation, the Designations Review Committee, provides overall policy guidance on matters involving the scope, use, or nature of restrictions for donor designated funds.[69]

The second program, PRECIS (Presbyterian Restricted Endowment Compliance Information System), currently in development, is designed to facilitate the use of Mission Partnership Funds, a program approved by the General Assembly in 1997. By means of Internet access to donor instructions, PRECIS allows Presbyterian governing bodies at every level to apply for the use of funds listed in the CARE database. In 1997-98 approximately 550 governing bodies applied for the new partnership funds with requests totaling $9.5 million. Proceeds from forty funds were available for the first round of allocations and netted to 178 recipients more than $729,000. Subsequently a list of more than 800 restricted funds has been sent to each session, presbytery, and synod for their examination and possible utilization in 1998-99.[70]

Along broader lines, the General Assembly Council in 1995 approved the formation of a Work Group on a Comprehensive Strategy for Mission Funding composed of members of the GAC, middle governing bodies, the Funding Development and Stewardship Network, and local pastors. After a careful examination of existing structures, the Work Group concluded that the denomination had no consistent church-wide plan to challenge church members to make more of their accumulated wealth available to the church. The Work Group agreed that the Foundation must be included as an integral part of a comprehensive mission funding strategy and cited the success of a three-year experimental process in South Carolina involving lay volunteers who are trained and equipped by the Presbyterian Foundation. The volunteers are making one-on-one calls to Presbyterians and friends to enlist additional funds to support and strengthen mission programs.[71]

Concerns regarding relationships among the GAC, program agencies, and other related bodies led the 1986 General Assembly to retain a consultant to evaluate the denomination's organizational structure. Conducted by the Arthur Andersen Company and completed in 1997, the report referred to the national entities as "six tarantulas in a bottle" and concluded that the current organizational structure had led to conflict among individuals and authority clashes among related entities. Because the General Assembly was the only common authority recognized by each entity, relationships inevitably tended to fray and fracture. In regard to the issue of fundraising and development, the report predicted recurring disputes until the denomination was able to centralize responsibility in one defined organizational unit and urged the church to address this issue at an early date. As an illustration of organizational tensions, the Andersen report cited the recent GAC-Foundation dispute that resulted in considerable financial expense as well as emotional and physical burdens on the participants.[72]

As the Presbyterian Church (U.S.A.) seeks to create an organizational structure that will provide the unity and flexibility required to sustain and expand its mission programs, the Foundation stands poised on the threshold of its 200th anniversary to face the challenges of a new century. If Elias Boudinot and Ashbel Green were alive today, they would see some striking parallels between the situation facing the corporation trustees in 1799 and 1999. Then, the denomination faced a financial crisis that threatened to imperil the implementation of much-needed mission programs. It also was grappling with the problem of creating an organizational structure that would effectively carry out the General Assembly's vision of a national church. The role of the corporation trustees in funding mission projects was another issue under debate. Traditionalists like Ashbel Green resisted efforts to make the trustees more proactive in the areas of stewardship promotion and cultivation of deferred giving and looked to the General Assembly for leadership in these areas. Activists like Elias Boudinot envisaged a wider field of responsibilities for the trustees, including the management of fund-raising tours, the recruitment of missionaries, and the development of specialized ministries to Native Americans and African Americans. Boudinot saw no conflict between these activities and General Assembly programs so long as the corporation's projects were sanctioned by the national body.

The contrasting perspectives of Green and Boudinot are reflected in the attitudes of contemporary observers. Some Presbyterians view with alarm the growing professionalism and power of the Foundation and regard its distinctive headquarters and emphasis on fiduciary responsibility as a means of securing more autonomy in denominational life. Many would like to institute more checks and balances on Foundation operations, especially linkages with the General Assembly Council. Other commentators acknowledge that the Foundation provides services for the church that no other entity is prepared to offer and that it can address funding issues at all levels—national, regional, and local. Because of its expertise, experience, and unsullied reputation as a fiduciary corporation, they believe that the Foundation can be trusted to serve the church in all aspects of its mission programming.[73]

While Presbyterians may differ on their views of the Foundation, virtually all agree that the Foundation will be a major component in shaping the denomination's future effectiveness as a Christian enterprise. The original mission of the Foundation, to receive and manage donations and bequests for "benevolent and pious purposes," has remained unchanged since the General Assembly incorporated in 1799. Although the scope and complexity of fulfilling that mandate has been greatly magnified in modern times, the Foundation exists only to enable the denomination to "do mission" in the fullest sense of that term. How that process translates into structure and substance in the coming century will be for future historians to describe.

NOTES

1. "Comprehensive Strategy for Mission Funding Work Group, Final Report to the General Assembly Council," September 22-27, 1997:15. (Presented to the General Assembly in June 1998.) Although distributions to General Assembly causes by the Foundation continued to increase quantitatively, over the past forty years the pattern of giving has moved the Foundation away from its exclusive role in serving as Trustees of the General Assembly. The beneficial interest in the assets held by the Foundation has changed significantly and at an accelerated pace, with the percentage of General Assembly funds decreasing and the percentage of funds benefiting non-General Assembly uses showing a corresponding increase. In 1991, for example, 55.6 percent of the distributed assets went to General Assembly causes and 44.4 per cent to non-General Assembly uses. In 1993 the figures were reversed, with 55.1 percent going to non-General Assembly uses and 44.9 percent to General Assembly causes. Foundation *Annual Report,* 1993:4.

2. Foundation Minutes (UPCUSA) (ex.com.), May 9, 1984, and September 18-19, 1984. The relationship of the PCUS Foundation with various denominational entities is summarized in *Minutes of the General Assembly of the Presbyterian Church (U.S.A.),* 1984, I:317. Hereafter *GAMPC(U.S.A.)*

3. For the early history of the PCUS General Assembly trustees, see pp. 46-48.

4. *GAMPCUS,* 1922:27, and *The Christian Observer,* 31 May 1922:27 and 7 June 1922:6. The overture was referred to a committee of three laymen and two clergymen who reported to the following General Assembly. A majority report stated that the creation of a Foundation was "unwise and impracticable" because the trustees of the General Assembly already possessed sufficient powers to accomplish what the overture proposed. A minority report signed by one person, Eugene L. Hill, pastor of the First Presbyterian Church of Athens, Georgia, argued that an enlarged Foundation with broader powers was necessary in order to cultivate wealthy donors and promote the general welfare of all denominational agencies. Hill's rhetoric influenced a majority of commissioners to support the creation of a denominational foundation. *GAMPCUS,* 1923:47, 73, and 108-10.

5. *GAMPCUS,* 1924:146-51; 1925:11-12; and 98-100. The official title of the new organization was The Trustees of the General Assembly and the Presbyterian Foundation, Incorporated.

6. *GAMPCUS,* 1928:94-99. See also "The Presbyterian Foundation," *The Christian Observer,* 9 June 1926: 2. A biography of Melvin is in *The Christian Observer,* 17 November 1954: 12. Melvin was the author of a widely used stewardship promotion book endorsed by the national United Stewardship Council. See M. E. Melvin, *Royal Partnership* (New York and Chicago, 1926).

7. *GAMPCUS,* 1950:104, in which comparative figures for the period 1925-1950 are given. For a biography of Dunn, see *The Christian Observer,* 4 April 1945: 4.

8. *GAMPCUS,* 1949, 130-35. See also "The Reorganization," *Presbyterian Outlook,* 17 and 24 October 1949: 8, and 3 July 1950: 9. For historical context, refer to Thompson, *Presbyterians in the South,* 3:366-83. An analysis of the Foundation by an independent consultant for the reorganization committee criticized the trustees for having no plans "except to continue the status quo" and for failing to coordinate their activities with other

denominational agencies. The report can be found in General Assembly Trustees Correspondence, Box 2, Archives of the Historical Foundation, Montreat, North Carolina.

9. Foundation Minutes (PCUS), May 2, 1951. In defense of the Foundation, trustees pointed out that the percentage of earning of the Foundation was consistently the highest of any denominational agency, averaging just under 4 percent from 1940-49.

10. For a summary of these developments, see *GAMPCUS*, 1980, I:370-71. For specific actions, see *GAMPCUS*, 1952:137-8;, 1954, I:94-5; and 1955, I:56.

11. Foundation Minutes (PCUS), May 4, 1955.

12. *GAMPCUS*, 1956, I:56, Foundation Minutes (PCUS), May 2 and August 29, 1956, and "Presbyterian Foundation," *The Christian Observer*, 7 November 1956: 2. Serving as presidents of the board of trustees during this time period were Frank L. Jackson (1957-59), Philip F. Howerton (1960-64), Paul E. Manners (1965), William F. Mullis (1966-68 and 1971), Paul M. Edris (1969-70), and Frederick V. Poag (1972).

13. The total value of thirty-nine legacies received by the PCUS corporation trustees between 1866-1955 was $819,094. Not counting the Young bequest, between 1955-1960 the Foundation received twenty legacies valued at $2,337,117. Foundation Minutes (PCUS), March 14, 1961. For the 1971 figures, see *GAMPCUS*, 1971, I:297.

14. *GAMPCUS*, 1972, I:94, 179. In addition to the Board of Annuities and Relief and the Foundation, the PCUS General Assembly maintained corporate entities at the level of the General Assembly Mission Board and the Publishing House. From a legal perspective, the General Assembly Mission Board was considered to be the fiduciary successor of the former executive committees and boards and agencies of the denomination.

15. *GAMPCUS*, 1983, I:317. Relationships between the Foundation and the General Executive Committee, later the General Assembly Mission Board, and the Council on Church and Society, parallel those of the UPCUSA Foundation with the GAMC and the MRTI Committee during the same time period. General Assembly Minutes and Foundation Minutes for the period 1973-1983 describe the particulars of these issues. A valuable summary document, "Study team/Presbyterian Foundation, Inc. (U.S.) Report to the Office of Review and Evaluation, Presbyterian Church in the United States," can be found in *GAMPCUS*, 1980, I:370-75.

16. "McGaw Gives $8 Million to Foundation," *Presbyterian Outlook* (August 1985): 4, and Marvin C. Wilbur, "Giving Is His Business," *Presbyterian Life Magazine* (December 1, 1967): 12-14, 35. For background on Newall, see *Cornerstone* (Summer 1996): 4.

17. Foundation Minutes (UPCUSA) (ex.com.), September 18, 1984. Other changes included the modification of the formula for distributing funds to General Assembly agencies and the establishment of a management fee on endowment funds for development income. After more than a year of work with Cambridge Associates, the Vice President for Finance, Dennis Murphy, and the Finance Committee devised a formula wider in scope and more stable than the previous "Gerstaker Formula," based on the concept of total return. It was applicable for the first time in the budget year 1985. Prior to 1985, the development budget had not been charged against endowment funds but was raised from support from the GAMC, trustees, and some synods. The fee scale was set at 1 percent, but by use of a formula devised to ascertain the actual cost, the figure for 1985 was .82 percent. See Foundation Minutes (UPCUSA), March 20, 1984, and (ex.com.), November 8, 1984.

18. *GAMPC(U.S.A.)*, 1984, I:318; 1985, I:508. See also Foundation Minutes (PCUS), October 6-8, 1986.

19. Foundation Minutes (UPCUSA) (ex.com.), May 9, 1984, Appendix A, and *GAMPC(U.S.A.)*, 1986, I:592; 1987, I:699.

20. *GAMPC(U.S.A.)*, 1986, I:388-91. For a full description of Mission Design, see pp. 365-417. The Mission Design also provided that the Foundation report directly to the General Assembly with a definitive copy to the General Assembly Council, which had the right to comment on the report.

21. Foundation Minutes (UPCUSA), March 17-18, 1986, and (ex.com.), October 6 and 7, 1986. Subsequently, the corporate officers were elected: Dennis J. Murphy, Senior Vice President, Chief Financial Officer, and Treasurer; Fred R. Stair, Executive Director (Charlotte Office); Donn Jann, Vice President, Regional Representatives and Funds Development; John D. Stuart, Controller and Assistant Secretary; Norman R. Lotz, Assistant Vice President, Gift Administration and Assistant Secretary; Barbara B. Wright, Assistant Vice President, Gift Administration and Assistant Secretary; Douglas E. Matthias, Assistant Treasurer and Assistant Secretary; James E. Andrews [Stated Clerk], Secretary; and Otto K. Finkbeiner, Assistant Secretary. Minutes of the Trustees of the Presbyterian Church (U.S.A.), September 16-18, 1987 (hereafter Foundation Minutes, PC[U.S.A.]), and, *GAMPC(U.S.A.)*, 1988, I:430.

22. Foundation Minutes, PC(U.S.A.), January 7, 1987. See also *Presbyterian Church (U.S.A.) Forum* (Winter, 1987): 1-2.

23. Foundation Minutes, PC(U.S.A.), June 14-15, 1987, Appendix A. Search committee chair William Clarkson indicated that it was preferred that the new president be Presbyterian but was not mandatory. Foundation Minutes, PC(U.S.A.), September 16-18, 1987.

24. *GAMPC(U.S.A.)*, 1988, I:431. See also *Presbyterian Church (U.S.A.) Forum* (Summer 1988): 3.

25. Foundation Minutes, PC(U.S.A.) (ex.com.), September 18 and October 27, 1988.

26. *The Presbyterian Church (U.S.A.) Forum* (Spring 1988):2. See also *GAMPC(U.S.A.)*, 1988, I:432, and Foundation Minutes PC(U.S.A.) (ex.com.) September 17-18; October 27, 1987; January 30, 1988; and February 9, 1988. The CTC applied for and received an exemption on the tax from the Kentucky Attorney General, but Foundation counsel advised against such a procedure because the Attorney General's opinion was not binding on the state legislature.

27. Foundation Minutes PC(U.S.A.) (ex.com.), September 12, 1988, and W. Terry Young, interview with author, 25 April 1992.

28. *GAMPC(U.S.A.)*, 1989, I:569.

29. *GAMPC(U.S.A.)*, 1990, I:723.

30. Foundation *Annual Report*, 1988:2; 1990:5.

31. Foundation *Annual Report*, 1990:3 and Foundation Minutes, PC(U.S.A), April 24, 1993. Editor Robert H. Bullock, Jr. of the *Presbyterian Outlook* said that the most interesting thing about Walton was not her star quality as a retailer par excellence but her "deeply held faith in Jesus Christ, her gentle way, her positive outlook on life in general and the PCUSA in particular." According to Robert Langwig, vice president of development, the Foundation received $12 million in gifts and invested funds following one of Walton's trips to Florida. Travels included appearances in San Francisco, San Jose, Denver, Chicago, Des Moines, Philadelphia, and several cities in New York State. "Helen Walton Touring in Support of Presbyterian Foundation," *The Presbyterian Outlook* (15 November 1993): 1, 5.

32. *GAMPC(U.S.A.)*, 1989, I:570.

33. Foundation *Annual Report*, 1996:6-8. For the first time in the Foundation's history, gifts and deposits exceeded $100 million in a single year, totaling $127.8 million in 1996.

34. Foundation *Annual Report*, 1991:12, Foundation Minutes, PC(U.S.A.), April 22, 1994, and David McCreath, interview with author, 5 March 1998.

35. Foundation *Annual Report*, 1996:13-15.

36. The suggestion that there were two different concepts of Foundation-GAC relationships stemming from the two denominational streams emerged from conversations with program and foundation officials on several occasions.

37. Foundation *Annual Report*, 1988:3 and Foundation Minutes PC(U.S.A.), April 29-30 and October 21-22, 1988, and *GAMPC(U.S.A.)*, 1989, I:569-71. To produce the guaranteed amount, the Foundation agreed to use realized capital gains when necessary. If there was an income in excess of the guaranteed dollar in any given year, the Foundation would establish a restricted expendable account for the GAC that would be invested as the GAC instructed. When the balance in this account exceeded 50 percent of the guaranteed dollar amount, it was to be retained for the purpose of assisting the Foundation to pay development costs. When there was no balance in the account and income did not equal the guaranteed delivery amount, the Foundation agreed to pay from realized capital gains.

38. Foundation *Annual Report*, 1988:3, and *GAMPC(U.S.A.)*, 1989, I:249. The investigation into restricted funds also revealed that $14.8 million of principal was not being used and that funds designated for certain colleges had been disbursed to other institutions by the CTC without informing the affected institutions. Foundation Minutes (PC(U.S.A.) (ex.com.), December 19, 1990.

39. Foundation Minutes PC(U.S.A.), September 11, 1989.

40. Foundation Minutes, PC(U.S.A.), May 6, 1989.

41. *GAMPC(USA)*, 1990, I:337.

42. Foundation Minutes, PC(U.S.A.), April 22-24, 1990. In a letter to Geoffrey Cross, Williams expressed his confidence in the basic concepts of the mission design and recommended that the Foundation not become more independent than it already was unless structures presented a genuine risk of adverse tax consequences. L. Neil Williams, Jr. to Geoffrey R. Cross, 26 March 1991.

43. Foundation Minutes PC(USA) (ex.com.), July 17, 1989 and April 22-24, 1991, Appendix A, "Report on the Joint Consultations between General Assembly Council and Presbyterian Church (U.S.A.) Foundation. At this time the Foundation also secured the right to retain its own legal counsel and maintain its own payroll system. A Shape and Form Committee in 1992 recommended a downsized and simplified administrative structure. Nine ministry units and four related bodies were reduced to three divisions and one support unit under the General Assembly Council through its executive director. Changes in the language of the new mission design based on recommendations of the General Assembly Committee on Review, which also reported in 1992, caused the relationship of the Foundation to the GAC to be less specific. Regarding linkage to the GAC, the mission design stated that the Foundation reports to the General Assembly with a definitive copy to the GAC which may comment on the report. See *GAMPC(U.S.A.)*, 1992, I:271 and 1994, I:253-65. The statement was modified in 1995 to add a concluding sentence, "The Foundation reports directly to the General Assembly." *GAMPC(U.S.A.)*, 1995, I:313.

44. Foundation Minutes PC(U.S.A.), April 20, 1996, and Robert W. Langwig, interview with author, 9 March 1998. The specialized interpreters—African American, Hispanic, Asian, and Native American—were already at work in 1996.

45. *Update* (October 1994): 2. Other figures were less encouraging. In response to a Presbyterian Panel question in 1994, "Are you familiar with the Presbyterian Church (U.S.A.) Foundation?," 40 percent responded "no, not really," and 31 percent responded "no, not at all." *Monday Morning Magazine*, 20 May 1996: 13. When asked if their congregations had programs for planned giving, endowment funds, or wills emphasis, the majority of respondents said that they did not. When asked if their congregations had used any of the services of the Foundation in the last three years, most respondents answered in the negative. *Monday Morning Magazine*, 22 April 1996: 19.

46. *GAMPC(U.S.A.)*, 1992, I:816.

47. Foundation *Annual Report*, 1990:8 and Foundation Minutes PC(U.S.A.) (ex.com.), October 24, 1991.

48. Foundation *Annual Report*, 1993:7. Prior to computerization, the preparation of trust agreement forms could take as long as two to three months. With technology, most agreements can be drawn up and transmitted in fifteen minutes. Douglass Yeager, interview with author, 9 March 1998.

49. *The Cornerstone* (Spring 1997): 5.

50. Foundation Minutes, PC(U.S.A.) (ex.com.), July 12-13, 1992. Vice President and Controller Terri Molter resigned at the same time. For details, see *"In Brief,"* *Presbyterian Survey* (July/August 1992): 31, and *The News of the Presbyterian Church (U.S.A.)* (July 1992): 1, 8.

51. Foundation Annual Report, 1992:4, and *GAMPC(U.S.A.)*, 1993, I:829.

52. "Presenting Larry D. Carr as President and Chief Executive Officer of the Presbyterian Church (U.S.A.) Foundation," [1997], n.p.

53. *Update* (May 1997): 1-2, and Thomas R. Drake, interview with author, 10 March 1996.

54. Larry D. Carr, "Report to Trustees" (October 1997): 5.

55. Impetus for the Investment and Loan Program came from a Task Force on Church Membership and Growth that reported to the General Assembly in 1991 and recommended that the Evangelism and Church Development Ministry Unit with the Stewardship and Communication Development Ministry Unit and the Foundation be directed to explore new and creative ways of funding new church developments, redevelopments, and loans to support an expected increase in the number of new church developments and redevelopments. See *GAMPC(U.S.A.)*, 1991, I:461.

56. *GAMPC(U.S.A.)*, 1995, I:364-68, and Foundation *Annual Report*, 1995:9.

57. Direct funding from the General Assembly for the Foundation's marketing, development, and gift administration costs had decreased from 100 percent in the mid-1980s to less than 5 percent in the mid-1990s. In order to compensate for this loss of funding, the Foundation increased its cost recovery rate from a level of .4 to .6 percent to just under 1 percent, a fee that covered all foundation expenses: development, investment, processing, and administration. Because various services provided by the Foundation had different cost structures, it determined that the creation of differentiated fees to more equitably recover the costs of operations would be fairer to donors and to the denomination in 1994. Foundation Minutes, PC(U.S.A.), October 27-28, 1995.

58. Foundation *Annual Report*, 1995:11. Other improvements included the monthly availability of funds for participants in the Investment Management Service and the renegotiation of the spending formula for unrestricted endowment funds. The Boudinot Covenant Society, launched in 1994 to recognize the generosity of Presbyterians at the local level, honored individuals who planned to give to the church or any church-related organization though a will or other estate plan. See Foundation *Annual Report*, 1996:26.

59. *Update* (November 1996): 2-3. Background of the litigation that prompted the move is described in *Update* (April 1997): 1, 3.

60. As a result of this conversion, it is estimated that record-keeping costs will drop approximately 20 percent producing a savings of more than $300,000 annually. See Thomas Billitteri, "Putting Faith in a Trust Company, *The Chronicle of Philanthropy*, January 15, 1986, 29-36, and Gerald A. Fitzgerald, "Presbyterians Form Commercial Bank," *In Trust* (New Year, 1998): 22.

61. Billitteri, "Putting Faith in a Trust Company," 35-36. Because the Foundation is chartered in Pennsylvania, for example, donors must have their agreement crafted according to Pennsylvania commonwealth law.

62. Foundation *Annual Report*, 1996:7 and 1997:3-10. Numbers of such proportions need to be viewed alongside other figures made available by the Foundation. Only 4.3 percent of the gifts received in 1997 exceeded $100,000 in value. Almost 75 percent of all contributions for the denomination received by the Foundation were less than $5,000. Presbyterians with limited resources coming from diverse backgrounds with varied interests collectively contribute much to the ongoing mission of the church.

63. Foundation Minutes, PC(U.S.A.), April 26 and October 24, 1992. Questions regarding use of Jarvie Fund income had previously been raised by Cross and his staff. Foundation Minutes, PC(U.S.A.) (ex.com.), January 18-19, 1988. See also "Foundation Tightens Controls on Jarvie Fund,' *The Presbyterian Layman* (May/June 1993): 12-13; "PCUSA Foundation Remains Faithful To Jarvie's Vision" (January/February 1996): 5.

64. Foundation Minutes, PC(U.S.A.), October 24, 1994. An estimated $60 million in unused or underutilized restricted funds was available at a time when the denomination was experiencing a short-fall in mission giving.

65. Foundation Minutes, PC(U.S.A.), April 19-20, 1996. Examples of disagreements over the use of restricted funds are given in a report produced for the Foundation in 1996. Gujranwala Theological Seminary reported uses of a bequest for aid to theological students in India for scholarships and academic expenses of students, programs to build up theological awareness among pastors and church leaders, and for outreach, i.e., evangelization. The Foundation examiner said that evangelization was not in accord with donor instructions. Another grant to the Board of National Missions "for medical missions where personal evangelism is emphasized," uses of funds in 1995 included assistance with face-to-face and conference call meetings of the Presbyterian Health Network and attendance at the annual meeting of the American Public Health Association. The Foundation reviewer ruled that the emphasis on personal evangelism was not carried out through the activities reported. Finally, funds from a grant "to assist deserving students attending the theological seminaries approved by the Board of Christian Education," were disbursed to students attending non-Presbyterian seminaries. The Office of Higher Education justified disbursements by saying that it asked the Committees on Preparation for Ministry of the Presbyteries if the students were in good standing with their CPMs and that they were approved to attend a particular school. The reviewer said that the intent of the donor was to give assistance to students attending theological seminaries related to the General Assembly of the Presbyterian Church. See "Report of Storthman & Company, P.S.C.," in Foundation Minutes, PC(U.S.A.), October 20, 1996.

66. *Update*, (March 1996):3 and Foundation Minutes PC(U.S.A.), April 19-20, 1996, Attachment A.

67. Foundation Minutes, PC(U.S.A.), April 19-20, Attachment A.

68. *Update* (May 1996): 1-3, and "GAC Backs Down From Dispute With PCUSA Foundation," *The Presbyterian Layman* (May/June 1996): 7, 17. The formal agreement is reproduced in *GAMPC(U.S.A.)*, 1996, I:377-78.

69. Foundation Minutes, PC(U.S.A.), November 1-2, 1996.

70. *Presbyterians Being Faithful to Jesus Christ* (Spring 1998): 3.

71. Report of the Comprehensive Strategy for Mission Funding Work Group to the General Assembly Council, September 22-27, 1997: 8.

72. "Presbyterian Church (U.S.A.): An Organizational and Management Assessment," Arthur Andersen, March 31, 1997: 73-83.

73. These observations are based on the author's interviews and conversations with many Presbyterian officials and laypeople during the course of his research from 1992-98. Virtually no one seems to question the effectiveness of the Foundation in securing funding for mission programs. The only questions come from the perspective of ecclesiology and the precise function of the Foundation within the larger framework of denominational supervision and interaction.

Appendix

The names of trustees of the various foundations have been gathered from *Minutes of the General Assembly* of the PCUSA, PCUS, UPCUSA, and PC(U.S.A.) denominations and from the minutes of the Trustees of the General Assembly [Foundation] of the respective denominations. The dates represent the year in which they were first elected as trustees. Not included are ex officio trustees, although, because they were not always so identified, some such names may appear in these lists. In a few instances records are inconsistent and incomplete, thus making it difficult to verify the precise spelling and dates of the entries. When women became trustees in the 1950s, their first names were not given. Later that practice was changed. The names shown here are as they appeared in the official records. The list of trustees for the Presbyterian Church (U.S.A.) Foundation begins in 1987 with the names of people who were also trustees in the former PCUS and UPCUSA Foundations. In the initial list, we have indicated their denomination of origin. After 1987, however, no reference is made to former denominational affiliations.

Trustees of the General Assembly/Foundation PCUSA/UPCUSA
1799-1986

1799
    John Rodgers
    Alexander McWhorter
    Samuel Stanhope Smith
    Ashbel Green
    William M. Tennent
    Patrick Alison
    Nathaniel Irvin
    Joseph Clark
    Andrew Hunter
    Jared Ingersoll
    Robert Ralston
    Jonathan B. Smith
    Andrew Bayard
    Elias Boudinot IV
    John Neilson
    Ebenezer Hazard
    David Jackson
    Robert Smith

1801
    John McKnight
    William Hazlet
    Jonathan Smith
    John Blair Linn
    Robert McMullin

1802
    David Jackson

1803
    Samuel Blair
    Henry Rutgers

1804
    John Woodhull

1806
    Alexander Fullerton

1809
    Francis Markoe

1811
    Archibald Alexander
    George S. Woodhull

1812
    John W. Doak

1817
    James P. Wilson
    William Neill
    William Latta

1817 (continued)
    George C. Potts
    Thomas Latimer
    Alexander Henry

1821
    John W. Thompson
    Era Stiles Ely

1822
    Thomas Bradford, Jr.

1823
    Charles Chauncey

1829
    John Stile

1833
    Matthew Newkirk
    James Bayard
    Matthew L. Bevan
    Solomon Allen
    Ambrose White
    John McDowell

1835
    Cornelius C. Cuyler

1837
    Henry A. Boardman
    William Brown
    John K. Kane

1838
    Alexander Symington
    James N. Dickson

1842
    Stephen Colwell

1843
    Joel Jones

1846
    Cortlandt Van Rensselaer
    John M. Krebs
    Alexander W. Mitchell
    James Dunlap

1849
    Thomas L. Janeway
    Robert Steel

1853
Joseph H. Jones
Kinsey Johns
Francis N. Buck
Singleton A. Mercer

1861
Henry Steele Clarke
Oswald Thompson
Charles Macalester
Morris Patterson
George Junkin, Jr.
George Sharswood

1865
Alexander Reed
Villeroy D. Reed
William E. Schenck
Samuel Hood

1869
George Hale
D. A. Cunningham
John K. Findlay
Archibald McIntyre
James T. Young
Robert Cornelius
H. Lenox Hodge

1870
William Strong
Joseph Allison
Alexander Whilldin
Herrick Johnson
William G. Crowell
John C. Farr

1878
Thomas J. Shepherd
William T. Eva
Samuel C. Perkins
William E. Tenbrook
James T. Young
H. Lenox Hodge

1886
Arthur T. Pierson
Joseph Beggs
John Elliot Wright
William B. Noble
J. Howard Dixon
John Dixon
Barker Gummere
Charles M. Lukens
Enoch Taylor
Andrew Blair

1887
B. B. Comegys
R. Dale Benson

1888
Benjamin L. Agnew
T. Charlton Henry

1889
Edward B. Hodge

1891
John J. McCook

1892
John H. Converse
William M. Paxton

1893
George T. Harris

1895
Edward T. Green

1896
J. Addison Henry
Henry N. Paul

1897
William M. Lanning

1898
H. C. McCook
George E. Sterry
James A. Beaver

1899
George Stevenson

1900
Francis B. Reeves

1901
William A. Patton

1902
Charles H. Matthews

1904
William H. Miller
George W. Bailey

1905
William H. Scott
William H. Roberts

1907
Mervin J. Eckels
Joseph W. Cochran
Edward Yates Hill
John H. Dingee

1908
William P. Potter
Warner Van Norden

1910
J. Milton Colton

1912
John Harvey Lee
George V. Massey

1913
H. Alford Boggs
William L. Austin

1914
William Hiram Foulkes
Walter F. Hagar
W. Austin Obdyke
John C. McKinney

1916
William A. Law

1917
Cheesman A. Herrick

1918
William C. Ferguson
Craig N. Ligget
Alexander Henry

1920
J. Renwick Hogg

1921
Lewis S. Mudge

1922
Alexander MacColl
J. Howard Pew
Clarence A. Warden

1924
Raymond H. Gage

1926
Richard L. Austin
C. Waldo Cherry
Edward D. Duffield

1927
Harden L. Crawford

1931
Edwin M. Bulkley

1932
Jesse E. B. Cunningham

1933
Arthur W. Jones
Van Horn Ely
George H. Stuart
George E. Gillespie

1935
Frank Benjamin

1936
William T. Hanzsche
William G. Moore

1937
William Barrow Pugh
Robert E. Lamberton

1940
George W. McKeag

1942
Earl L. Douglass
Howard Biddulph
J. William Hardt
T. Edward Ross

1943
David G. Hunter

1945
Henry B. Strock
Frank C. Roberts, Jr.
W. Logan MacCoy

1946
Howard J. Bell

1947
Willard G. Purdy
S. Carson Wasson

1948
Arthur Littleton

1949
Frederick S. Vogenitz
Orus J. Matthews

1950
P. John Galbraith

1951
S. Blackwell Jones
Boyd T. Barnard
Sumner B. Emerson

1952
Thomas B. McCabe
Eugene Carson Blake

1953
R. J. Wig
Mark E. Lefever
Rex S. Clements
Charles H. Albers
Paul Gerot
Melvin H. Baker
Robert L. Kirkpatrick
Ben R. Marsh
Glenn W. Moore
Benjamin Strong
Richard Pacini
Mark E. Putnam
Foster G. McGaw
William T. Payne
Guy C. Saunders

1955
Robert H. Heinze
John L. Bates

1956
William O. Master
Mrs. Thomas J. Watson, Sr.
Mrs. Charles W. Bryan, Jr.
Mrs. Arthur H. Compton
Mrs. Robert C. Neff
Mrs. Samuel D. Archibald
Mrs. Alfred G. Wilson

1958
David A. Cort
Martin Tollefson
Paul M. Gillis
Arthur B. McBride
F. Lloyd Smith
Ray G. Woodburn
David W. Proffit

1959
S. Bayard Colgate

1961
Arthur B. Langlie

1962
Mrs. Walter B. Driscoll
Roger Hull
Theophilus M. Taylor

1963
Gaylord Donnelley
Glen A. Lloyd

1964
Glenn C. McGee
Kelly Y. Siddall

1965
Walter K. Bailey
John M. Black
Carl A. Gerstacker
David A. Hamil
John W. Humphrey

1966
S. Davidson Herron, Jr.
William P. Thompson
Robert Young

1967
Eugene N. Beesley
Peter Kiewit
L. William Lane, Jr.
F. Ritter Shumway

1968
John G. Buchanan, Jr.
Richard O. Kearns
Mrs. Ogden R. Reid

1969
James A. Colston
Ruben J. Dailey
Charles P. Neidig
Mrs. Reuel D. Harmon

1970
James E. Spivey
Henry E. Stalcup
Edmund R. Swanberg

1971
Edward M. Green
Mrs. William H. Hudnut, Jr.
W. James Westhafer
Stanton L. Young

1972
Mrs. James P. Buchanan
James H. Doss
Theodore R. Lilley

1972 (continued)
R. Bruce McBratney
Forrest L. Parr
Mrs. J. S. Stocker
Osborne K. Taylor

1973
Robert E. Daniel
Raymond R. Day
Hugh Holmes
Merle S. Irwin
James C. Piper
Horace B. B. Robinson

1974
Mrs. Merrill P. Anderson
Edward B. Eisenhart
Arthur R. Hall
Charles E. Morris
Albert J. O'Brien
Alfred W. Spriggs
Foster B. Whitlock
Alfred W. Wishart, Jr.

1975
Harrison Ray Anderson, Jr.
Paul Justus
Robert J. Lamont
Sharon Clay Risk
Donald N. Soldwedel
James Sperber
Jean Triplett
Thomas F. Creamer

1976
Helen W. Buckner
Otto P. Butterly
Eugene S. Callender
William G. Jenkins
Thomas H. Lake
Robert R. Lavelle
G. Daniel Little
Richard H. Miller

1977
Fletcher L. Byrom
Charles S. Northern, III
Clarence C. Wood
Frank H. E. Wood

1978
Carl C. Dietrich
Irene Nunemaker
Jonathan Michael McGee
William C. Schram
John H. Ware, III

1979
W. Grant Annable
William J. Hage
Howard Jacob
Holly M. Lockhart
Charles O. Peyton
Riley H. Richards
Samuel C. Rue
Eugene C. Yehle
Margaret L. Brown

1980
George A. Butler
Thomas J. McCausland, Jr.
William M. E. Clarkson
James H. Costen
Julia Piper
Michael F. Ryan
Lois H. Stair
Wallace R. Weitz
Wanda L. Sawyers

1981
Gary R. Bower
Wiley A. Bucey
Harry James Collins
Janet W. Doak
Lucille Garber Ford
Norman N. Honeycutt
Charles Gerald Monroe
Jay Vawter

1982
William B. Clemmens
Bruce C. Clinesmith
Robert Lee
Charles E. McCloskey
Stewart G. Neel

1983
Emily V. Gibbes
Anne Bateman Noss
Deborah London Wright
James S. Little
Robert Louis Lowry

1984
Herbert B. Anderson
Gilberto Cardona
Myra B. Robinson
Ann M. Van Den Berg
Helen R. Walton

1985
George Edward Herbert
Trisha C. Pitts
Donald B. Register

1985 (continued)
Sun K. Shin
Shelton B. Waters
Elmore A. Willets

1986
Claire L. Armentrout
Charles R. Ehrhardt
James C. Harrison
John I. Lee
Robert H. Meneilly

Trustees of the General Assembly/Foundation PCUS
1866-1986

1866
Thomas C. Perrin
B. M. Palmer
Samuel McCorkle
Joseph H. Wilson
Jesse H. Lindsay
Robert Adger
J. A. Ansley
J. A. Crawford
James B. Walker
J. A. Inglis
John Whiting
R. M. Patton
George Howe
J. L. Kirkpatrick
William L. Mitchell

1868
James Hemphill
Harmon Brown
D. A. Kennedy
John Handy
Samuel McKinney

1870
E. Nye Hutchison
J. A. Young
James M. Hutchison

1871
John Douglas
John L. Brown
John E. Brown

1879
J. J. Gresham

1880
R. D. Johnston
R. E. Harding

1881
R. I. McDowell

1883
N. M. Woods

1885
George E. Wilson
J. C. Burroughs

1886
John E. Oates

1887
George F. Bason
J. Y. Fair

1889
Rufus Barringer
James P. Irwin
J. B. Shearer

1894
A. G. Brenizer

1896
D. W. Oates
John R. Pharr

1897
Peter M. Brown

1898
J. W. Stagg
J. R. Howerton

1904
M. D. Harden

1906
J. H. Wearn

1907
Alexander Martin

1908
Robert A. Dunn
A. R. Shaw

1912
John B. Ross

1914
P. S. Gilchrist
A. A. McGeachy

1918
George M. Rose, Jr.

1922
John R. Ross

1924
H. N. Pharr

1925
James H. Kennedy

1926
R. D. Johnston, Jr.
J. P. McCallie
A. B. Banks
F. C. Groover
C. A. Rowland
David M. Sweets
V. D. Mooney
A. A. Little
C. R. Nisbet
Chris Matheson
Allen J. Graham
J. W. Orr
J. F. Hardie
Herbert W. Jackson
E. W. Minter

1927
Marion E. Melvin
John A. Law
J. Layton Mauze
J. R. Hampton

1929
W. F. Stevenson
C. T. Caldwell
F. C. Brown

1932
T. S. McPheeters

1933
C. M. Richards
Charles A. Cannon
W. H. Hopper
T. S. Smylie
C. M. Boyd

1935
F. L. Jackson

1936
A. L. Currie
E. G. Gammon

1938
W. F. O'Kelley
Roland Sims
Charles E. Diehl

1939
Neal Y. Pharr
C. Gratton Price

1940
W. Calvin Wells
Walter L. Bellingrath

1942
Donald L. McLaurin

1943
C. Groshon Gunn

1944
J. A. Christian
Harvey H. Orr

1945
W. Payne Brown
W. Ivey Stewart

1946
A. C. Holt
C. M. Richards
John W. Melton, Jr.

1947
A. R. Shaw, Jr.
R. McFerran Crowe

1948
H. T. Tumilty
William H. Barnhardt

1949
R. T. Fewell
C. T. Caldwell

1950
R. S. Robinson
R. R. Craig

1951
James F. Hardie
D. W. Robinson
Walton Litz

1952
J. Chester Frist
Carl Pritchett

1953
Louis L. Rose, Sr.

1954
John S. Cansler

1955
J. Cecil Lawrence

1958
William H. Kadel
William R. Perkins, Jr.
Kenneth S. Keyes
Halbert M. Jones
A. Van Prichartt
J. P. Hobson
Mrs. A. R. Craig
Mrs. Charles S. Ragland

1959
Paul B. Manners
Philip F. Howerton
Halbert M. Jones
H. Dale Holderness
George Mauze
Homer Gebhardt

1960
William B. Neely
Jack L. Oliver
C. Newman Faulconer
Grayson L. Tucker, Jr.
Charles C. Wise

1961
Linton E. Allen
Orrick Metcalfe

1962
J. Martin Singleton
Angus Powell
Paul M. Edris
Edward H. Sutter
George K. Cavenaugh

1962 (continued)
Harry L. Dalton
Steele Hayes
John McMillan

1963
William F. Mulliss
R. S. Reynolds, Jr.

1964
A. C. Bryan
Harry L. Dalton
Walker B. Healy
Harry M. Moffet, Jr.
A. V. Prichartt

1966
John W. Sterchi
J. Mason Wallace, Jr.
Mrs. Hal. H. McHaney
W. Stell Huie
John A. Tate, Jr.

1967
William H. Grier
A. W. McCain
Mrs. B. S. Howell

1969
Frank M. Hubbard
Frederick V. Poag
Hayes Picklesimer
D. J. Walker, Jr.

1970
W. Graham Duncan
R. Brawley Tracy
W. S. Lee, III
William E. Nodine
Parks B. Pedrick, Jr.
W. A. L. Sibley, Jr.
William F. Winter

1971
G. D. McCall
John A. Caddell
James G. Cannon
Thomas E. Downie
William C. Wilkinson, II

1972
Floyd Read
Louis L. Rose, Jr.
Allen M. Steele
Robert S. Stroud
Mrs. Thomas H. Magness, Jr.

1973
   Eben L. Reid
   James C. Robinson
   Joseph W. Grier, Jr.
   Tom Brown
   Martha Guy
   James H. Wetter

1974
   Robert P. Corbett
   Ida Hicks
   Hulett Smith

1975
   Jeannette Cutler [Brinkman]

1977
   Elmer H. Dodson
   Edward F. Johnston, Jr.
   Arthur C. Morales

1978
   Lewis C. Harrison
   Alex E. Booth, Jr.
   John F. Watlington, Jr.
1979
   John P. Wright
   Paul B. Bell
   Francis F. Lewis
   Toddie Lee Wynne, Jr.

1980
   Sidney Anderson
   Patricia McClurg
   Henry Hills
   Charles C. Cowsert
   William A. Adams
   Catherine M. Shipley

1981
   Lamont Brown
   Ethel Darden
   Donald Peck
   James M. Smith
   Maria Elena Garza
   Morrell Trimble
   Ben T. Vernon, Jr.
   J. Howard Woodward
   John P. Wright

1982
   Jean McArthur Davis

1983
   Jeanine N. Arnold

1985
   Elizabeth K. Hicks
   Wayne McCoy
   William Wilde
   L. Neill Williams, Jr.
   Irvin Elligan, Jr.

1986
   Evelyn W. Fulton

Trustees of the Presbyterian Church (U.S.A.) Foundation
1987-1998

1992
Gail Duree
Deborah Gambrel-Chambers
Ronald W. Roe
George Walker Smith
Stephanie Wimmer
Wilton Vincenty

1993
Bruce E. Franklin
Sheila C. Gustafson
W. Frank Harrington
Robert V. Martz
Dorothy I. MacConkey
Clarence S. Ross, III
Sam Robinson Sloan

1994
Anne E. Clifton
Areta Crowell
John R. Evans
Harry H. Kim

1995
Kenneth Bateman
Eugene C. Bay
Peter Glanville
R. James Henderson
Janice Kreamer
Opal G. Smith

1996
Dwight K. Bartlett III
Carl Bosteels
Stuart Broberg
Stewart Clifford
Peggy Klingeman
William Lauderbach
N. Gerald LeVan
Patricia A. McClurg
Ray Tanner

1997
Laura G. Dunham
Bryant George
Cynthia S. Gooch
Edwin T. Johnson
Aubrey B. Patterson
Merrell M. Peters
Judith G. Stephens
Bette Tranbarger
Phillip H. Young

1998
Karen C. Anderson
James K. Babcock
Carl A. Carpenter

1998 (continued)
Robert O. Hickman
Alison King
John F. Kraushaar
J. Roger Lee
Burton Dix Williams

1999
Lynwood Battle
Avis Devine
D. Fort Flowers
Carol Giltz
Robert McNeely
Richard Ray

Bibliography

Archival Materials
*The following archival records are located in the Department of History (PHL),
Philadelphia, Pennsylvania, or at the Department of History (Montreat),
Montreat, North Carolina.*

Record Group 121: Philadelphia, Pennsylvania—Mariners' Church/Seamen's and
 Landsmen's Aid Society Records, 1841-1972 (PHL)
Record Group 124: Eugene Carson Blake Papers (PHL)
Record Group 125: Lewis Seymour Mudge, Stated Clerk's Correspondence,
 1921-1938 (PHL)
Record Group 139: John Coventry Smith, Office of the General
 Assembly—General Secretary's Files, 1959- 1970 (PHL)
Record Group 146: Office of the General Assembly (UPCUSA) Correspondence
 Files, 1963-1977 (PHL)
Record Group 148: Office of the General Assembly (UPCUSA) Correspondence
 Files, 1961-1973 (PHL)
Record Group 179: Commission on the Reorganization of General Assembly
 Agencies Records, 1971-1973 (PHL)
Minutes of the Trustees of the General Assembly [Foundation] of the
 Presbyterian Church in the United States, 1868-1986 (Montreat)
Minutes of the Trustees of the General Assembly [Foundation] of the
 Presbyterian Church in the United States of America, 1799-1957 (PHL)
Minutes of the Trustees of the General Assembly [Foundation] of the
 Presbyterian Church (U.S.A.), 1987-98 (PHL)
Minutes of the Trustees of the General Assembly [Foundation] of the United
 Presbyterian Church in the United States of America, 1958-86 (PHL)
Minutes of the Trustees of the General Assembly of the United Presbyterian
 Church of North America, 1858-1957 (PHL)
General Assembly Trustees (PCUS) Correspondence, Boxes 1-2 (Montreat).

Denominational Records and Publications

Minutes of the General Assembly of the Cumberland Presbyterian Church, 1840-1906

Minutes of the General Assembly of the Presbyterian Church in the United States, 1866-1982

Minutes of the General Assembly of the Presbyterian Church in the United States of America, 1789-1957

Minutes of the General Assembly of the Presbyterian Church (U.S.A.), 1983-97

Minutes of the General Assembly of Presbyterian Church in the United States of America [New School], 1837-69

Minutes of the General Assembly of the United Presbyterian Church in the United States of America, 1958-82

Minutes of the General Assembly of the United Presbyterian Church of North America, 1858-1957

Minutes of the Presbyterian Church in America 1706-1788, Guy S. Klett, editor. Philadelphia, 1976

Annual Reports

The Presbyterian Church (U.S.A.) Foundation, 1987-97
The United Presbyterian Church Foundation, 1966-86

Newspapers and Periodicals

A.D. Magazine, 1972-95
The Christian Century, 1990-97
The Christian Observer, 1890-1930
Cornerstone [Foundation], 1989-98
Monday Morning Magazine, 1990-97
The Presbyterian, 1840-50
Presbyterian Life Magazine, 1948-72
Presbyterian Outlook, 1949-96
Update [Foundation], 1994-98

Books

Baird, John. *Horn of Plenty: The Story of the Presbyterian Ministers' Fund*. Wheaton, Illinois, 1982.

Balmer, Randall, and John R. Fitzmier. *The Presbyterians*. Westport, Connecticut, 1993.

Barrus, Ben M., Milton L. Baughn, and Thomas H. Campbell. *A People Called Cumberland Presbyterians*. Memphis, Tennessee, 1972.

Boyd, George Adams. *Elias Boudinot: Patriot and Statesman*. Princeton, 1952.

Brackenridge, R. Douglas, and Lois A. Boyd. *Presbyterians and Pensions 1717-1988*. Atlanta, 1988.

Bremner, Robert H. *American Philanthropy*. 2d ed. Chicago and London, 1988.

Bruchy, Stuart. *Enterprise: The Dynamic Economy of a Free People*. Cambridge, Massachusetts, 1990.

Clark, Barbara. *Elias Boudinot: The Story of Elias Boudinot IV, His Family, His Friends, and His Country*. Philadelphia, 1977.

Coalter, Milton J., John M. Mulder, and Louis B. Weeks. *Vital Signs: The Promise of Mainstream Protestantism*. Grand Rapids, Michigan, 1996.

———. *The Organizational Revolution: Presbyterians and American Denominationalism*. Louisville, Kentucky, 1992.

———. *The Re-Forming Tradition: Presbyterians and Mainstream Protestantism*. Louisville, Kentucky, 1992.

Hoge, Dean R., Benton Johnson, and Donald A. Luidens. *Vanishing Boundaries: The Religion of Mainline Protestant Baby Boomers*. Louisville, Kentucky, 1994.

Drury, Clifford. *Presbyterian Panorama*. Philadelphia, 1952.

Fite, Gilbert C., and Jim E. Reese. *An Economic History of the United States*. 2d ed. Boston, New York, and Atlanta, 1965.

Hall, Joseph Frazier. *Andrew Carnegie*. New York, 1970.

Hoge, Dean R., ed. *Money Matters: Personal Giving in American Churches*. Louisville, Kentucky, 1996.

Jamieson, Wallace N. *The United Presbyterian Story*. Pittsburgh, 1958.

Jenkins, Edward C. *Philanthropy in America: An Introduction to the Practices and Prospects of Organizations Supported by Gifts and Endowments 1924-1948*. New York, 1950.

Johnson, Douglas W., and George W. Cornell. *Punctured Preconceptions: What North American Christians Think About the Church*. New York, 1972.

Kepple, Frederick P. *The Foundation: Its Place in American Life*. New York, 1930.

Klett, Guy S. *Presbyterians in Colonial America*. Philadelphia, 1937,

Loetscher, Lefferts A. *A Brief History of the Presbyterians*. 4th ed. Philadelphia, 1983.

Longfield, Bradley J. *The Presbyterian Controversy: Fundamentalists, Modernists, and Moderates*. New York, 1991.

Mackie, Alexander. *Facile Princeps: The Story of the Beginning of Life Insurance in America*. Philadelphia, n.d.

Magat, Richard. *Philanthropic Giving: Studies in Varieties and Goals*. New York and Oxford, 1989.

Marsden, George. *The Evangelical Mind and the New School Presbyterian Experience*. New Haven, 1970.

Myers, Margaret. *A Financial History of the United States*. New York, 1970.

Nielsen, Waldemar A. *The Golden Donors: A New Anatomy of the Great Foundations*. New York, 1985.

Olson, Jeannine E. *Calvin and Social Welfare: Deacons and the Bourse Française*. London and Toronto, 1989.

Roof, Wade Clark, and William McKinney. *American Mainline Religion: Its Changing Shape and Future*. New Brunswick, New Jersey, 1987.

Slosser, Gaius Jackson. *They Seek A Country: The American Presbyterians*. New York, 1955.

Smylie, James H. *A Brief History of the Presbyterians*. Louisville, Kentucky, 1996.

Stivers, Robert L. *Reformed Faith and Economics*. New York and London, 1989.

Sweet, William W. *Religion on the Frontier: The Presbyterians*. 2 vols. New York and London, 1936.

Thompson, Ernest Trice. *Presbyterians in the South*. 3 vols. Richmond, 1963, 1963, and 1973.

Trinterud, Leonard J. *The Forming of an American Tradition: A Re-examination of Colonial Presbyterianism*. Philadelphia, 1949.
Vallet, Ronald, and Zech, Charles E. *The Mainline Church's Funding Crisis: Issues and Possibilities*. Grand Rapids, Michigan, 1995.
Wuthnow, Robert. *The Crisis in the Church: Spiritual Malaise and Fiscal Woe*. New York, 1996.
Wuthnow, Robert, and Hodgkinson, Virginia. *Faith and Philanthropy in America*. San Francisco, 1990.
Zurcher, Arnold J. *The Management of American Foundations: Administration, Policies, and Social Role*. New York, 1972.

Articles
Amerson, Philip, Stephenson, Edward J., and Shipps, Jan. "Decline or transformation? Another view of mainline finances." *The Christian Century* 114 (February 5-12, 1997): 144-51.
Baker, Wesley C. "Mission Funding Policies: An Historical Overview." *Journal of Presbyterian History* 57 (Fall 1979): 404-23.
Dawson, David G. "Mission Philanthropy, Selected Giving, and Presbyterians. Parts 1, 2." *Journal of Presbyterian History* 68 (Summer 1990, Fall 1991): 121-32, 203-25.
Luidens, Donald A. "Cash and Character: Talking About Money in the Church," *The Christian Century* 114 (December 3, 1997): 1127-30.
Ronsvalle, John, and Sylvia Ronsvalle. "The end of benevolence? Alarming trends in church giving." *The Christian Century* 113 (October 23, 1996): 1010-14.
Wuthnow, Robert. "Pious Materialism: How Americans View Faith and Money." *The Christian Century* 110 (March 3, 1993): 238-42.

Interviews With Author
Tape recordings of the following interviews are located in the Archives of the Presbyterian Church (U.S.A.) Foundation, Jeffersonville, Indiana.

Andrews, James E. April 20, 1996.
Bell, Paul B. May 29, 1998.
Berry, Bruce W. October 9, 1996.
Brown, Herbert. September 30, 1996.
Brown, James M. April 3, 1998.
Diaz, Frank. April 2, 1998.
Drake, Thomas R. March 9, 1998.
Finkbeiner, Otto. July 8, 1997.
Firth, Richard. July 23, 1990.
Gast, Aaron E. June 27, 1990.
Hall, C. Kenneth. April 20, 1996.
Langwig, Robert F. March 9, 1998.
Little, G. Daniel. February 9, 1998.
McCreath, David. March 5, 1998.
Miller, Richard H. March 18, 1998.
Murphy, Dennis. October 4, 1991 and March 11, 1998.
Spivey, James E. November 11, 1991.

Stair, Frederick R. September 30, 1996.
Stuart, John D. October 4, 1991.
Thompson, William P. March 16, 1998.
Walton, Helen R. April 25, 1992.
Yeager, Douglass J.. October 4, 1991 and March 10, 1998.
Young, W. Terry. April 25, 1992 and October 30, 1996.

Index